BLACK TOMMIES

British Soldiers of African Descent
in the First World War

BLACK TOMMIES

British Soldiers of African Descent in the First World War

RAY COSTELLO

LIVERPOOL UNIVERSITY PRESS

First published in 2015 by
Liverpool University Press
4 Cambridge Street
Liverpool
L69 7ZU

Copyright © 2015 Ray Costello

The right of Ray Costello to be identified as the author of this book has been asserted by him in accordance with the Copyright, Designs and Patents Act 1988.

All rights reserved. No part of this book may be reproduced, stored in a retrieval system, or transmitted, in any form or by any means, electronic, mechanical, photocopying, recording, or otherwise, without the prior written permission of the publisher.

British Library Cataloguing-in-Publication data
A British Library CIP record is available

ISBN 978-1-78138-018-5 hb

ISBN 978-1-78138-019-2 pbk

Typeset by Carnegie Book Production, Lancaster
Printed and bound in Poland by BooksFactory.co.uk

This book is dedicated to my mother, Edith Mary Costello, as always, and also to the memory of a lovely elegant lady who survived both world wars and lived for more than a hundred years: Evelyn Vera Knowles, known to those whose lives she brightened as Auntie Vera.

CONTENTS

	Acknowledgements	ix
	Abbreviations	xi
	List of Illustrations	xiii
	Introduction	1
1	Whose War?	17
2	The Invisible Army – The Search	45
3	Black Volunteers – The Empire and Beyond	67
4	Black Officers, White Soldiers	91
5	The Black Empire Arrives – Conscription	113
6	The Return of the Heroes	133
7	Epilogue	163
	Notes and References	175
	Bibliography	197
	Index	211

ACKNOWLEDGEMENTS

I owe much to those people who have shown great interest in this book and have generously given me their time, advice, assistance and encouragement. I will never be able to thank them enough. In no particular order, they include: Karen O'Rourke, Curator of the Liverpool Kings Regiment Museum, Museum of Liverpool, who inspired me to reappraise a long-abandoned study; Diane Frost of the School of Sociology and Social Policy, University of Liverpool; Joan von Linstow and her husband Kurt, of Denmark; Leslie Braine-Ikomi, Peter Brydon, Peter Betts, Lilian Bader, Audrey and Hussein Dewjee, Jeffrey Green, David Killingray and Charles Kay, who all provided valuable practical assistance and ideas, often without being asked.

This book could never have been completed without the extraordinary help of my long-suffering friends Dave Corker and Mike Cheeney during the proofreading stage, who also supplied me with additional useful information on more than one occasion.

A number of black British families have been particularly kind and supportive: Lilian Bader and family, the Brew family, the Cole family, especially Suzanne Morris and Barbara Tasker, the Quarless family and the Guy/Gibson family descendants.

I would also like to thank the staffs of the libraries and archives I have visited and contacted, including those of Merseyside Maritime

ACKNOWLEDGEMENTS

Museum Archives, the National Archive, the Queen Square Library, Archive and Museum, the Imperial War Museum, the British Library and Liverpool Record Office. I am also grateful to the Master and Governors of Dulwich College, London, and Mrs C.M. Lucy, Keeper of Dulwich College Archives. The help of Mrs. P. Justad of the Walter Tull Archive was invaluable in the production of this book.

Last, but certainly not least, my publisher, Liverpool University Press, particularly Alison Welsby, the Editorial Director, who believed in me and gave me endless encouragement, all the staff, my reviewers, the team at Carnegie Book Production and the many others who helped to make this book a reality.

If I have failed to mention anyone who has been so kind as to provide assistance in any way, I offer my sincere apology.

ABBREVIATIONS

ANC	African National Congress
ASC	Army Service Corps
AWM	Australian War Memorial
BCRGA	Bermuda Contingents of the Royal Garrison Artillery
BEEF	British Egyptian Expeditionary Force
BEF	British Expeditionary Force
BL	British Library
BVRC	Bermuda Volunteer Rifle Corps
BWIR	British West Indies Regiment
C	Chancery papers
CEF	Canadian Expeditionary Force
CO	Colonial Office
CWGC	Commonwealth War Graves Commission
DCM	Distinguished Conduct Medal
IWM	Imperial War Museum
JP	Justice of the Peace
KAR	the Kings African Rifles
KOSB	King's Own Scottish Borderers
LRBDM	Liverpool Register of Births, Deaths and Marriages
MMM	Merseyside Maritime Museum Archives

ABBREVIATIONS

NARA	National Archives and Records Administration, Washington, D.C., United States of America
NCF	No-Conscription Fellowship
OTC	Officer Training Corps
RAMC	Royal Army Medical Corps
RDP	Registration District Poplar
RFC	Royal Flying Corps
RWAFF	Royal West African Frontier Force
SALC	South African Labour Corps
SAMR	South African Mounted Rifles
SANLC	South African Native Labour Contingent
SANNC	South African Native National Congress
SIW	self-inflicted wounds
T	Treasury papers
TNA	The National Archives
UNIA	Universal Negro Improvement Association
UNIA-ACL	Universal Negro Improvement Association and African Communities (Imperial) League
VC	Victoria Cross
WAFF	West African Frontier Force
WIR	West India Regiment

LIST OF ILLUSTRATIONS

1 'The Recruitment Officer c.1815' showing a black trumpeter rallying locals. (Reproduced by permission of Leslie Braine-Ikomi)   9
2 Marcus Bailey, a First World War sailor in the Royal Navy, with an unknown black soldier. (Reproduced by permission of Marcus Bailey's daughter, Lilian Bader)   48
3 An unknown Black British soldier posing in front of his unit. (Reproduced by permission of Jeffrey Green)   55
4 Liverpudlian Gunner Albert James with his wife, Ethel. (From the author's private collection)   57
5 A group of men of the King's (Liverpool) Regiment and an unknown Black British soldier and woman. (Reproduced by permission of Peter Brydon)   63
6 This photograph of men of the British West Indies Regiment at work, stripped of their formal dress uniform, shows the reality of their wartime service. (Reproduced by permission of Crown Copyright IWM)   77
7 Second Lieutenant Walter Tull, often erroneously credited with being the only Black British officer in the First World War. (With kind permission of the Walter Tull Archive, part of the Finlayson Family Archive)   93

LIST OF ILLUSTRATIONS

8 George Edward Kingsley Bemand, second lieutenant in the Royal Field Artillery. (With kind permission of the Governors of Dulwich College) 99
9 Dr Risien Russell, who was commissioned with the rank of captain in the Royal Army Medical Corps during the war. (Image courtesy of the Queen Square Library, Archive and Museum. Copyright National Hospital for Neurology and Neurosurgery) 108
10 John Williams 'The man whom white soldiers call "the black V.C."' (Reproduced by permission of ©The British Library Board. All Rights Reserved, c12343-01) 137
11 'A West African soldier "walking out" in London'. A soldier of the British Army who served during the First World War. (Reproduced by permission of ©The British Library Board. All Rights Reserved, c12343-02) 148
12 Joseph Gibson is seated at the end of the first row in football strip. (Reproduced by permission of Anne Audley, representing the Guy/Gibson family descendants) 151

INTRODUCTION

The first shot of the Great War by a British serviceman on the Western Front was reportedly fired by Corporal Edward Thomas, a bandsman of the 4th Royal Irish Dragoon Guards, in an engagement with German cavalrymen outside Mons, Belgium, at 7 am on 22 August 1914.[1] There was, however, another contender many miles away on the African continent. When the United Kingdom declared war on Germany on 4 August 1914, the British Gold Coast Authorities sent African troops into the small German colony of Togoland. Advancing on the Togoland capital, Lomé, from the British Gold Coast, a patrol of the Gold Coast Regiment encountered the German-led police force, a quasi-military unit, on 7 August 1914.[2] When the Germans opened fire on the British patrol near a factory in Nuatja, the Gold Coast trooper Alhaji Grunshi returned fire,[3] technically earning himself the distinction of being the first soldier in British service to fire a shot in the war.[4]

Although this almost forgotten incident might seem a minor item of historical military trivia, it serves as a reminder that the Western Front was not the only theatre in a conflict that would encompass the planet and embrace most races. The First World War involved all the world's great powers, divided into two opposing alliances: the Allies (the United Kingdom, France, Russia and Italy) and the Central Powers (Germany,

Austria-Hungary and the Ottoman Empire from October 1914). Of the 70 million military personnel mobilised by the end of the war, some 9 million combatants would lose their lives.⁵ As well as including the initially neutral United States of America, this global conflict would also draw in all the colonial possessions of those powers, involving most races on the planet, some against neighbours of the same ethnic and cultural group whose divided countries happened to be under the jurisdiction of their colonial masters' enemy.

Before embarking upon any scrutiny of the role and experiences of British-born and domiciled black soldiers in the regular army, it is helpful to have an overview of the general background of the scale of the global conflict and of the part played by troops of the wider Black British Diaspora. It is perhaps appropriate that the mother continent of all black soldiers should be the place where the opening shot of the First World War was fired, by a black serviceman. Although sandwiched between the British Gold Coast, now Ghana, and then French Dahomey, the West African colony of Togoland was of strategic importance to Germany's overseas empire for it was home to powerful radio transmitters near Atakpamé, which served not only as a communications link between Germany and shipping in the South Atlantic, but between its South-West African colony and German East Africa.⁶

Since the end of the Franco-Prussian war in 1871, the newly unified Germany had aspired to join the other European powers in possessing its own empire, as proclaimed by the treaty signed in the Hall of Mirrors at Versailles in January of that year. By 1914, commercial enclaves had been established in Cameroon, Togo and South-West Africa (Namibia) on the west coast, and what is now Tanzania on the east coast, along with islands in the south and central Pacific and a coastal region of China, including the port of Tsingtao.⁷ British West African military forces in 1914 numbered approximately 7,550 at the outbreak of the First World War, the total figure for military and police forces available to the British colonial authorities in the Gold Coast numbering nearly 3,000 from a population of approximately 1.6 million.⁸ The Gold Coast Regiment numbered some 1,500 men, supplemented by paramilitary forces such as the 320 troopers of the Northern Territories Constabulary, mainly ex-servicemen, 330 volunteers and 790 police.[9]

Originally formed in 1900 to garrison Britain's West African colonies, the West African Frontier Force (WAFF) was a multi-battalion field force that would become the Royal West African Frontier Force (RWAFF) in 1928. Fears of French colonial expansion in territories adjacent to Northern Nigeria had led to the decision in 1897 to raise a new locally recruited force. All existing British colonial military forces in West Africa were amalgamated soon after, the force comprising the Gold Coast Regiment, Northern Nigeria Regiment, Southern Nigeria Regiment, the Sierra Leone Battalion and the Gambia Company, administered by an Inspector General.[10] Distinguished by khaki drill shorts with red fezzes, West African soldiers were legendary for marching barefoot day and night, if necessary, with rifle, bandolier ammunition, blanket and machete or native axe. Their marching song 'Rule Britannia' was also heard in German East Africa in 1916, both East and West African troops remaining active in this theatre until 1918.[11]

At the outbreak of war, the British and French attacked Germany's colonies while their Japanese allies moved against Tsingtao and the central Pacific islands the Marianas, Marshalls and Carolines. By 27 August, Togoland had been quickly overrun by the West African Rifles and the French *tirailleurs sénégalais*, but the conquest of Kamerun (now Cameroon), a much larger territory, proved more difficult. About 1,000 Europeans and 3,000 Africans of Germany's colonial forces faced British troops of the Nigeria, Gold Coast and Sierra Leone regiments supported by French African infantry and a contingent brought up from the Belgian Congo. Supported by tens of thousands of carriers, the army swelled to a strength of 25,000, striking across the Nigerian border by the end of August. Three separate British columns advanced towards the towns of Mora, Yarua and a third destination nearer the coast, all three encountering strong resistance and initially turned back with heavy losses. A coastal bridgehead was seized by the French, who managed to defeat the Germans south of Lake Chad, the British and French capturing Douala, the colonial capital and wireless station, and securing the coast on

27 September.¹² While the Allied advance was delayed by the torrential rainy season and skilful German resistance, the African soldiers cultivated gardens to supplement their intermittent rations supply until November, when the weather changed. The Allies forced most of the Germans into the neutral enclave of Spanish Guinea and the last German outpost of Mora finally surrendered in February 1916.

The German South-West African colony was an enormous territory inhabited by only 180,000 Africans, mostly Herero, one of whose first Imperial Commissioners was no less than the father of Hitler's future Reichsmarschall, Hermann Ernst Goering (1885–90). In 1904, the German governor faced a rebellion which he subdued with a particular ruthlessness. As the German population of South-West Africa comprised only a garrison of 3,000 plus 7,000 German settlers, Berlin had hoped that a mutual pre-war commitment between the colonial powers to neutrality in Africa would endure, however vague. They were to be disappointed, however. The British withdrew their garrison from the neighbouring Union of South Africa at the beginning of war, leaving them dependent on a defence force consisting largely of Britain's former opponents from the Boer War of 1899–1902. The South African Defence Force launched an attack upon the German South-West African colony with troops including Anglo South African regulars loyal to Britain during the Boer War, including white Rhodesians, and former South African enemies, such as General Smuts and General Louis Botha, now in British service. Some of the Boer generals openly rebelled, including the commander Christiaan Beyers, forcing Britain to deal with both a Boer rebellion and a colonial campaign against the Germans. The rebellion quashed, the British were able to advance upon German centres of resistance from the coast, the Orange River and Bechuanaland, converging upon Windhoek, the German colonial capital, which fell on 12 May 1915. The Germans eventually surrendered unconditionally on 9 July 1915.¹³

Of all the German colonies, German East Africa (present-day Tanzania) was the most important. Togoland was insignificant compared to the geographically large and sparsely populated Cameroon, whilst South-West Africa was a beautiful but empty desert. German East Africa, bound by the great lakes of Tanganyika, Nyasa and Victoria, possessed the greatest potential as the most productive part of the continent. The real struggle between German and Allied forces in the continent was therefore in German East Africa, a theatre that would remain active beyond the European armistice of November 1918. This strange state of affairs was due to the outstanding leadership of a particular German officer and his African army. Colonel Paul Emil von Lettow-Vorbeck, commander of the colony's *Schutztruppe*, the African colonial armed force of Imperial Germany, roughly translated as 'protection force', was to be the bane of the Allied forces in East and Central Africa. The tacit pre-war understanding between the powers to keep black Africa out of hostilities might have prevailed, had the Governor of German East Africa had his way, as he had forbidden offensive operations, and his British counterpart, the Governor of British Kenya, had made a similar declaration that his colony had no 'interest in the present war', partly because of a lack of suitable forces on both sides.[14] At the beginning of the twentieth century, the Kings African Rifles (KAR) had been used by the British colonial government in expeditions against rebels opposing British rule. After moving the headquarters of the KAR from Mombasa to Nairobi by 1902, the British felt they had contained resistance to their rule by 1904 and the 5th Battalion of KAR, mostly made up of Indian troops, was disbanded chiefly because of maintenance costs. The unit was reconstituted in 1916, however, to face the continuing German threat, and was stationed in Meru.[15]

Both the British 'hawks' and Colonel von Lettow-Vorbeck ignored their governors and girded their loins for the imminent battle for Africa. Formally, German hostilities with the British and French forces in German East Africa ceased following the bombardment of the port of Dar es Salaam by the British in 1916. This apparent ceasefire soon lapsed owing to the remarkable Lettow-Vorbeck, a veteran of the Boxer Rising in China and the German South West campaign.[16]

The war in East Africa had begun with a brief naval engagement off the East African coast, the British driving the battered hulk of the German cruiser the *Königsberg* into the swampy depth of the Rufiji River, later inspiring the popular film *Shout at the Devil*. She had harassed the British for some time, despite her poor condition. Using some of the *Königsberg*'s guns as artillery, a number of her crew would later join Lettow-Vorbeck's initial force of approximately 2,500 *askari*s (local soldiers) and 200 white officers. Though very much creatures of their time in an era when the eugenics movement, with its doctrine of a racial hierarchy, was very active in most European countries, the German High Command found it necessary to follow the British lead in allowing African troops to bear arms and take part in active combat against the enemy, at least in Africa, despite the discomfort of the home government at the idea of black colonials bearing arms at all. The key factor seems to have been that German colonial troops were not fighting a European enemy, a recurring fear amongst all the European powers. Lettow-Vorbeck thought nothing of crossing into the territory of other European colonial powers with his African army, at one point even raising the German flag on British territory under Mount Kilimanjaro in Kenya and raiding into Uganda.

The Allies waged a full-scale military expedition against Lettow-Vorbeck's African army as it engaged in inland naval operations on the Great Lakes. Two brigades of British regulars and Indian troops landed at Tanga on 2 November 1914, only to face humiliation when the Indian regiments ran away and the British got lost. The British and their colonial Indian force were forced to retreat to the beaches, re-embarking on 5 November, despite outnumbering Lettow-Vorbeck's force by eight to one, leaving behind sixteen machine guns, hundreds of rifles and 600,000 rounds of ammunition. Lettow-Vorbeck's troops were living off the land. Ammunition and supplies did not come easily, as he was made aware when his askaris had fired off 200,000 rounds at his minor victory at Jassin. In order to last out a long, protracted campaign, he would need to economise his resources, resorting to guerrilla warfare rather than set engagements with the enemy.

With the conquest of South-West Africa, forces under Jan Smuts began to arrive from South Africa; a planned offensive aided by the forces of other powers whose boundaries Lettow-Vorbeck had violated resulted in a convergent attack from Kenya, Nyasaland, the Belgian Congo and Portuguese Mozambique, Germany having declared war on Portugal in March 1916. Lettow-Vorbeck's askaris responded with a series of ambushes, slipping away before superior reinforcements arrived.[17] The British Nyasaland forces under Colonel Northey fought off the Germans, who were never allowed to get very far across the border in several determined attempts to invade the country. Nyasaland troops themselves were far inside German territory, and had done a good deal in subduing it.[18] A war of attrition followed, the German African troops living off the land, destroying anything useful to the enemy. The vastness of the African bush meant that capture and defeat by the Allies was almost impossible and this conflict in the East African theatre of war was to continue unresolved until hostilities ceased and the First World War finally came to a close.[19]

In addition to black soldiers serving in the African theatres of war, there were others of the Black Diaspora serving in other capacities than combat on the Western Front. In the period leading up to hostilities, men and women of the British West Indian islands and mainland possessions on the South American mainland, such as British Honduras and Guiana, would also play their part in the coming conflict. At the outbreak of the First World War, the British public would find black soldiers a lot closer to home than the colonies however.

If Black British colonial troops have been long neglected by historians, the existence of any narrative around Black British soldiers enlisting in the United Kingdom during the First World War is even less well known. The aim of this book is to establish the little-known existence of Black British, born and domiciled, United Kingdom-based soldiers in the First World War, rather than dealing with that other historical deficiency, overseas colonial black soldiers, who are themselves only now receiving attention. While demographic evidence may be difficult to quantify, an important part of that aim is the collecting, collating and recording of as wide a range as possible of available evidence, in order to disseminate and popularise the story of Black British soldiers before it is lost. In the course of writing this book it has been necessary to use a wide variety of

INTRODUCTION

tools at the disposal of the historian, from primary documentary sources in archives to private material kept in the metaphorical (and actual) shoe boxes of the descendants of black Tommies. Secondary sources have tended to deal only with individuals or specific phases or aspects of colonial history, necessitating all means of enquiry in the reclamation of this group narrative. This being the case, the collation of existing evidence is as important as the original research in this book. It remains an extremely difficult task to piece together a seamless, contiguous narrative of British-born or domiciled black soldiers in the First World War, as the racist and sociopolitical ethos in which they lived, and the fact that they have largely been forgotten, has made their history hard to retrieve a century later. At the present time, information about individuals often seems disproportionate, little information surviving for some, while others enjoy a lengthier biography due to factors such as celebrity status, press coverage and others examined in this book. Nevertheless, the disparate group of participants and events chronicled in this study provides irrefutable evidence of the part played in this global conflict by British soldiers of African descent.

Black soldiers based in the United Kingdom would seem to have been a component of the British Army for a very long time. The military historian John Ellis found that black men were recruited from all over Britain for more than a century before the outbreak of the First World War and there is some evidence to suggest that the British Army actively sought black soldiers during the late eighteenth and early nineteenth centuries. William Fletcher of the 69th South Lincolnshire Regiment of Foot was on enlistment at twenty-four years old; born in Montreal and a labourer by trade, he was five feet nine inches, of 'Tawny' complexion with dark hazel eyes, black hair and a round face. William's enlistment is interesting. He was recruited at the Tower of London on 28 September 1827 by Private Mumford of the 69th, 'A man of colour enlisted by special authority from the Commander in Chief, Horse Guards' on 26 September 1827, a British-born Black, from Dumfries, Scotland. Robert Mumford had previously served with the 31st Huntingdonshire Regiment of Foot (August 1817–November 1819) and the 5th Dragoon Guards (March

INTRODUCTION

1. 'The Recruitment Officer c.1815' showing a black trumpeter rallying locals. (Reproduced by permission of Leslie Braine-Ikomi)

1820–January 1825). Mumford likewise had been recruited by another black soldier, Leo Simons of the 69th, once again 'A man of colour enlisted by the Commander in Chief' on 24 August 1827.[20] It would seem, at least in some cases, that not only were black soldiers used to identify other able-bodied members of their race for recruitment, men perhaps known to them, but the army of the time considered black recruits a useful source of manpower.

The term 'Tommy' was a popular nickname for the British infantryman and is derived from *Thomas Atkins*, a name randomly chosen to be used in specimens of official recruitment forms completed during the nineteenth and early twentieth centuries. It is comparable to the name 'doughboys' given to soldiers of the United States Army or Marine Corps, especially members of the American Expeditionary Forces, dating back to the Mexican-American War of 1846–48. In this book I have taken the perhaps forgivable liberty of applying the term 'Black Tommy' more widely, not just to the infantry, but including officers, British artillerymen and cavalrymen of African descent and at least two airmen serving in a unit of the British Army yet to be designated as a separate air force at that time.

Who, then, were Black Tommies? Where did they serve and what happened to them at the conclusion of hostilities? Although the numbers of British-born or domiciled Black Tommies may have been relatively small among the hundreds of thousands of Britons who fought and died in the First World War, in order to place them in context it is necessary to know something of other black soldiers in the colonies, particularly the West Indies, as troops arriving from this part of the British Empire would have a bearing upon how Black Tommies were perceived and recruited into British units. It is not necessary to search as far as Africa or the West Indies to find black soldiers in the First World War however. Black settlements such as in Bristol and London had existed in Britain for centuries. Many black Liverpudlian families have lived in the port for generations and Cardiff, another port, has had a British-born Black population since at least the late nineteenth century.[21] Vibrant black communities developed in several of Britain's ports during the nineteenth century as sailors added to established settlers and other immigrants. As

INTRODUCTION

Liverpool and Cardiff were a ready source of British-born and domiciled black soldiers at the time, it is no surprise that the majority of recruits found in this book were from these ports. During wartime, these populations increased more than any other and with the outbreak of war in 1914, such was the pull of 'King and country' that many men of the British colonies did not wait for their imperial homeland forces to be mobilised, but left their own distant shores to travel to Britain to join up in regular army units, thus helping to boost the small numbers of British-born black Tommies already to be seen in uniform on the streets of the United Kingdom and the battlefields of the Western Front and the Middle East, without forgetting the tremendous work done in the African theatre by those other black soldiers of the Empire who were not. Colonial troops were therefore not only to be found in their own designated national units; some had already settled as new Black Britons.

At the time of writing this book, there are no others that feature British-born soldiers of African descent besides Stephen Bourne's recent *Black Poppies* (History Press, 2014), which, while devoting some space to the experiences of black soldiers, devotes more attention to black civilians' contributions to the war effort in such capacities as workers and entertainers. The nearest, and possibly the only, publication is David Killingray's chapter, 'All the King's Men? Blacks in the British Army in the First World War, 1914–1918', in Rainer Lotz and Ian Pegg's *Under the Imperial Carpet: Essays in Black History 1780–1950* (Rabbit Press, 1986), which provides an excellent summary of some of the experiences of Black British soldiers. *Black Tommies* is more comprehensive and detailed in its scope, but builds upon Killingray's pioneering work in the hope of continuing further research in this area and contributing to the reclamation of the group narrative of the present-day Black British population's ancestors.

Black Tommies has been written to help prevent a number of people who played a significant part in the First World War being consigned to the dustbin of history by employing a personalised, biographical account of British soldiers of African descent who took part in the First World War, rather than recounting the various African theatres of war in which Black British colonial peoples took part, certainly another historical deficiency. Simply rehashing the statistics would be to repeat the work of other historians of colonial conflict during that period. Instead, black soldiers are named individuals with families, hopes and aspirations, the goal being the reclamation of a lost human narrative rather than stark figures and descriptions of large movements of men. This prosopographical approach aims to give soldiers of African descent a face and draw attention to the interest and importance of a previously under-researched history.

The notion of the 'Black Tommy' may still seem something of an anomaly to some, but it would seem that they were almost commonplace as early as the late eighteenth century. Lack of knowledge of the very notion of British-born Black soldiers has rendered almost invisible these representatives of their race in the First World War, perhaps perversely given their distinctive colour. Issues of identification serve only to add to this 'invisibility'; common English-sounding names and the way the British census is recorded also play a part in making life difficult for the researcher of an interesting aspect of the Great War.

Although many Black British soldiers, born or domiciled, were recruited in British ports in poor 'sailortown' districts, as a group they were no more likely to be of the same social class than white troops. There were initially differences in recruitment between those enlisted overseas and those at home. At the beginning of the war, a British-born Black soldier could be recruited as an individual and assigned to a regular army unit with few others of his race, while black soldiers in Britain's African or Caribbean possessions would be recruited to serve together in homogeneous units of men from their own homeland. This situation would not endure, however, as later there are examples of British-born Black recruits being placed in racially homogeneous units of West Indian troops and there is at least one case of a 'coloured' unit raised in the United Kingdom. Similarly, examples of black officers leading white troops are to be found in this study, against the rules laid down in King's Regulations that only officers of pure European ancestry could receive a commission. These latter findings correct the current widespread belief that Second Lieutenant Walter Tull was the first black officer in the British Army.

Although it was inevitable that the war between the major powers of Europe became a struggle that required all the manpower they could get, there were issues around the use of black troops, particularly in combat situations. African colonial troops were deployed by the British in a combat capacity in African theatres, where they would be fighting black colonial troops, but on European battlefields, where they would be fighting a white enemy, they were restricted to labour battalions. The need for manpower being so great, this situation would be contested throughout the war by a group of very eminent campaigners, but would prove difficult to resolve. Black troops raised in the United Kingdom were something of an enigma to the authorities, as in some cases they were 'home grown', often isolated individuals, and did not pose the same potential threat of colonial rebellion or pressure for independence that trained soldiers of a black colonial army might, in time, should they be so inclined. Black troops raised in the United Kingdom would find themselves in an unusual position; fighting and dying on the Western Front alongside their white comrades in some cases and at other times transferred without choice to labour duties in the British West Indies Regiment (BWIR). The issue of British-born and domiciled blacks being placed in the BWIR would mean a special relationship beyond that of other black units of the Empire arriving in the United Kingdom. The Canadian 'Black Battalion', the Bermudians and the South African Native Labour Contingent would all serve on the Western Front, but the significance of the arrival of the BWIR and its impact upon the status of some Black Tommies already enlisted is reflected in the following chapters as the fates of British-born soldiers and West Indians became intertwined.

The question of black participation, and what form it might take, was also asked when the United States declared war against Germany on 6 April 1917. The term 'The White Man's War', examined in Chapter One, cropped up in the contemporary chronicle of the war by African American author E.J. Scott, who commented in jingoistic style that the

INTRODUCTION

black population in the United States believed 'that it was not to be a white man's war, nor a black man's war, but a war of all the people living under the "Stars and Stripes" for the preservation of human liberty throughout the world'.[22] There was certainly a considerable amount of trepidation on the part of the American Army authorities about using black troops. On 7 August 1918, secret information concerning African American troops was sent from General Pershing's headquarters, through the military mission stationed with the American army, saying that they were 'not to eat with them, not to shake hands or seek to talk or meet with them outside of the requirements of military service.' They were asked also not to commend too highly the black American troops in the presence of white Americans.[23] This contrasted markedly with the official face of High Command. General Pershing would later be fulsome in his praise of African American troops, declaring:

> The only regret expressed by colored troops is that they are not given more dangerous work to do. I cannot commend too highly the spirit shown among the colored combat troops, who exhibit fine capacity for quick training and eagerness for the most dangerous work.[24]

Pershing was referring to a compromise by which African American troops were taken into French service to expedite their being used in combat against Europeans, initially forbidden while in American service. Under French command, such units as the famous 369th 'Harlem Hellfighters' Regiment received many accolades. General Pershing was originally for the idea of deploying black troops, but appears to have vacillated, in the end bowing to political expediency and allowing black soldiers to take part in the fighting, ostensibly as part of the French army.[25]

In our time the phrase 'The White Man's War' is still heard in discussions on the First World War and sometimes the Second World War. This book will show that Britain's part in the First World War was anything but a white man's war and the part played by people of African descent was significant in the ultimate success of the Allies.

In the case of all Britain's black allies, when hostilities ceased, troops returning to the United Kingdom were, like their white comrades, disappointed by their reception back home, as is discussed at length in Chapter Six. At the end of the war, many returning British-born and domiciled black soldiers faced competition for jobs with poor whites, who now viewed them as aliens after years of fighting alongside them and, in some cases, previously living and working with them as part of the same working class. Severe riots broke out in 1919 in which many British-born Black ex-servicemen were attacked, their homes and lodgings burned. The plight of black soldiers and seafarers was taken up by early black journalists and politicians amongst other sympathisers in the major ports and cities. Black British people, born or resident in the ports, differed from black 'aliens' (although many of the so-called aliens were from British colonial countries, in fact, and not strictly foreigners) in that they were paid the same rates as white employees. As they were often confused with foreign black workers, they were nevertheless considered cheap labour by poor white workers and therefore a threat. Some of the legislation passed after the war also had a bearing upon the lives of former black soldiers. Increased agitation by the unions was to lead to the Aliens Order of 1920 and the Special Restriction (Coloured Seamen) Order of 1925, which resulted in many British-born Black men of several generations from older black communities being required to carry documentary proof of identity alongside seamen from Britain's colonies. These measures were directed primarily at black seamen, but in practice all black men, whether seafarers or not, were often treated by the police as aliens, including returning soldiers, mistakes in identification of status or nationality, made by the police, being received by British-born Black ex-servicemen as a source of annoyance.

Many black troops from the colonies had entered the war in a spirit of optimism, looking forward to an end to racial inequality and the expectation of taking part in future councils of Empire on a par with the white dominions. Although British fair play and legality was sought before and during the war, rather than a break with the Empire, state retrenchment led to their hopes receding in the post-war years. The notion of a compact was not found to be forthcoming as the Mother Country herself had to adjust to a diminished status in the new world

INTRODUCTION

economy and politics of this new era. Many modern British schools are still struggling to get to grips with issues of inclusion and the preservation of the memory of those who fought in the First World War. The British National Curriculum does deal with the period covered by this study under 'History key stage 3: European and world history':

> The changing nature of conflict and cooperation between countries and peoples and its lasting impact on national, ethnic, racial, cultural or religious issues, including the nature and impact of the two world wars and the Holocaust, and the role of European and international institutions in resolving conflicts.[26]

The difficulty for teachers lies in the fact that while the role played by soldiers of African descent can be found in many libraries in our country in a very fragmentary form, all too often it may be necessary for the zealous teacher committed to stretching pupils' minds to resort to researching primary material, searching for appropriate material that may not be easy to find. This situation has created a vicious circle in education that *Black Tommies* may help to remedy by offering an overview, at least the beginnings of a collated study, of the role played by Black British soldiers in the First World War. There is still a long way to go in rectifying an omission that the modern progressive mind would not dignify by maintaining. Hopefully, this exploratory study of black soldiers in the First World War will provide a basis that is currently missing for future scholars to build upon, and others will take up the issue and add to the material found in this book.

CHAPTER ONE

WHOSE WAR?

It was against the backdrop of the European powers' imperial aspirations and large movements of men over vast geographical areas that Black Tommy would take his place in the broad panorama of the First World War in a variety of roles, ranging like comrades of other races from heroes, victims, liberators and officers, to the ordinary foot-sloggers and survivors that typify the majority of those who took part.

Governmental attitudes towards black colonial troops

In order to understand the experience of Black British soldiers in the regular army, those born or domiciled in the United Kingdom, it is necessary to know something of British attitudes of the time towards black troops in the colonies. It was by no means taken for granted that black soldiers were, in fact, wanted in the forthcoming struggle, despite the Allies' mounting need for manpower as the war progressed. The term 'The White Man's War' was first used at the beginning of the Boer War, when the question of whether to use armed African allies brought complaints from the Boers about the British use of African forces to support their own cause.[1] At the beginning of the First World War, there was a good deal of trepidation about the use of colonial troops to fight against white troops, especially on European soil, due in part to the prevalent belief in a racial hierarchy, with white Europeans at the top and black Africans at the bottom, and any encouragement of 'lesser breeds' to fight Europeans was difficult to countenance. It was felt that colonial troops gaining experience in a modern war, killing Europeans, could lead to rebellion against their colonial masters, not only in Europe, but on the North American continent, where there was reluctance in both the United States and Canada to use black troops in a combat capacity. In areas outside Europe, such as Africa and the Middle East, black troops were certainly used by the European colonial powers from the beginning of the war, but the question of whether troops of African descent would be allowed to bear arms or serve in labour corps on the Western Front would be a point of debate throughout the war. Prior to the war, expressing a view similar to that of the American general Pershing when the United States entered the war, Brigadier-General Sir James Willcocks commented:

> It is always judicious [...] never to give the black man an idea that you seek his assistance against other white men [...] [W]ith our soldiers [...] we always spoke as if all they would have to do would be to fight other black soldiers and avoid reference to their white commanders [...] First must come the white man to whatever race he may belong.[2]

In British parliamentary circles, there were also issues around whether black troops should be allowed to engage in combat. Although reliant upon African colonial troops in continental Africa, no African troops were deployed in a combat capacity on European battlefields by the British despite the existence of a group of officers, journalists and politicians in Britain, among them men like Sir Harry Johnston, Josiah Wedgwood and Winston Churchill, who campaigned for a large African army for use in Europe along the lines of the French model.[3] There were those who opposed the use of black soldiers on the grounds that they considered blacks to be inferior in every capacity, a view held by both the Colonial Office and the War Office at the beginning of the war. Although the manpower available on the African continent justified their use at a time of shortage of white soldiers, and despite the economic considerations of employing the cheaper African soldiers and carriers, the idea was flatly rejected by the War Office.[4]

In a House of Commons speech in May 1916, Winston Churchill insisted that not only ten to twelve Indian divisions should be trained for deployment in Europe but also African units:

> Let us [...] think what historians of the future would write if they were writing a history of the present time and had to record that Great Britain was forced to make an inconclusive peace because she forgot Africa; that at a time when every man counted [...] the Government of Great Britain was unable to make any use of a mighty continent [...]. It would be incredible; but it is taking place [...]. What is going on while we sit here, while we go away to dinner, or home to bed? Nearly 1,000 men – Englishmen, Britishers, men of our own race – are knocked into bundles of bloody rags every twenty-four hours [...]. Every measure must be considered, and none put aside while there is hope of obtaining something from it.[5]

The debate about whether black troops from British colonial territories should be deployed in a combat role continued in Parliament until the end of the war. In a House of Commons debate as late as 30 July 1918, Sir Robert Houston asked the Under-Secretary of State for War, Sir James Macpherson:

> whether he was aware that in the recent French advance a large proportion of General Mangin's victorious army was composed of native Africans recruited from Senegal, Morocco, and Algeria; whether a great French coloured army is now being created; whether he is aware that Great Britain has reservoirs of coloured subjects anxious to take their places in the fighting line; and whether, in view of the success which France has achieved with coloured soldiers, he will recommend to the War Office that we should follow the French example of employing coloured fighting men in the firing line and thereby relieve in a large measure the shortage of skilled and other white labour in this country, and avoid the necessity of calling up elderly men from

business and trade occupations who in many instances are producers and taxpayers and substantial contributors to the Revenue?[6]

The colonial 'Scramble for Africa' during the late nineteenth century had meant that the French could call upon their own overseas manpower in their hour of need. Houston was referring to the fact that France had taken a different route from other European powers, or those with a European hegemony such as Canada or the United States, in that she had deployed large numbers of African troops on the Western Front as combat troops, rather than confining them to the African theatre.[7]

Replying to Houston, Macpherson protested that the proportion of 'native' Africans in Mangin's army was somewhat exaggerated, and that every endeavour was being made to utilise 'coloured' men in British spheres of influence. He said that he had been informed that the number employed by the British Government was far greater than that employed by the French, and would hopefully be further increased. Houston then asked a critical question as to whether these soldiers were employed fighting in the front line rather than merely in labour battalions behind the line, to which the Secretary of State for War disingenuously assured him that they were employed in both capacities.

Colonel Josiah Wedgwood then complained that no effort at all had been made to recruit black troops in British Sudan, and Macpherson admitted that he did not know much about Sudan, but, as far as he knew, the recruiting figures in other protectorates were remarkable. Colonel Wedgwood retorted that it was well known that 'Soudanese are the best fighting men',[8] a reminder of the contemporary British belief in the theory of 'martial races', perhaps unsurprisingly in view of the fact that the legendary 'breaking of the British square' by Sudanese 'Fuzzy Wuzzies' at the Battle of Tamai on 13 March 1884[9] was still relatively fresh in the national memory, having been immortalised in Rudyard Kipling's lines:

> So 'ere's to you, Fuzzy-Wuzzy, at your 'ome in the Soudan;
> You're a pore benighted 'eathen but a first-class fightin' man;
> An' 'ere's to you, Fuzzy-Wuzzy, with your 'ayrick 'ead of 'air---
> You big black boundin' beggar---for you broke a British square![10]

Some Frenchmen saw the deployment of African soldiers as shock troops not simply a case of using their black forces as cannon fodder, but as offering them 'the privilege' to occupy the most dangerous posts, which permitted them to enrich their book of traditions and past glory. This French view seems crass, and, rather than worry about any danger of being used as cannon-fodder, it was precisely the complaint of Black British colonial forces and African Americans that they were not being allowed to serve in combat roles. It is possible that the French were only too aware of these complaints and were cynically using them for their own political purposes. Colonel Petitdemange, the officer in charge of West Africans' training in the camp of Fréjus in southern France, clearly stated in a letter that they were indeed 'cannon fodder, who should, in order to save whites' lives, be made use of much more intensively', a view supported by Prime Minister Georges Clemenceau, who said, expressing a sentiment remarkably like that of Winston Churchill, that if we

> are going to offer civilisation to the Blacks. They will have to pay for That [...] I would prefer that ten Blacks are killed rather than one Frenchman – although I immensely respect those brave Blacks –, for I think that enough Frenchmen are killed anyway and that we should sacrifice as few as possible![11]

There were, of course, logistical problems in bringing African troops to the Western Front, as evidenced by the fate of the *Mendi*, described in Chapter Five, but racism also played its part in British attitudes towards black recruitment and when the Americans entered the war, the British Army chose to reject the training of African American soldiers for the front, an option shown to have been taken up by the French. Despite the continuing controversy in Parliament over whether colonial forces should be deployed on the Western Front in a combat role, British colonial African troops certainly fought in the Middle East and in Africa in the British service.[12] Graham Smith's comment that the government's reaction to the Second World War was to prevaricate and 'never squarely fac[ing] up to the problem until its hand was forced, and equivocat[ing] throughout the war', could well be applied to the Great War.[13]

Caribbean troops

Black troops could not only be found fighting for the British on the African continent. Other British colonial soldiers of African descent were also mobilising on the other side of the Atlantic Ocean. Although many Caribbean men had volunteered as individuals to serve in the British Army at the outbreak of war, leaving the colonies to join their British-based black 'cousins' in enlisting in regular British regiments in the United Kingdom, it was not until late 1915 that a new corps utilising the true potential of the islands was formed, the British West Indies Regiment (BWIR).

In the months following the outbreak of hostilities, public anger in the colonies had risen over the procrastination of British officials over the creation of a West Indian contingent. The liberal newspapers fulminated against the War Office's suggestion that black West Indians were of limited military value, the *Federalist* citing the humiliating defeat suffered the British at the hands of African groups like the Zulus as a refutation. Noting that French West Indians were being recruited from their colonies, the *Federalist* blasted the British authorities' failure to use blacks as 'the nasty cowardly skin prejudice characteristic of the empire'.[14] Individuals in England with interests in the West Indies, such as the Earl of Dundonald, were concerned for the safety of property within the region and were worried that harm would be done if officials persistently refused the black population's wish to participate.[15] He suggested that a possible solution might be for a West Indian battalion to be formed for service in a temperate climate, rather than on the Western Front, allaying any fears of black soldiers fighting a white enemy whilst removing any danger to property in the West Indies by satisfying an angry populace.

As the Colonial Office and the War Office failed to agree once more, King George intervened in the discussions, instructing his emissary Lord Stamfordham on 17 April 1915 to write to the Colonial Office conveying his thoughts on the matter. He was in favour of a West Indian contingent, believing it to be very politic to gratify the wish of the West Indies to send a regiment to the front, possibly to be put to good use in

Egypt. Surprisingly, in view of the direct intercession of the king, Lewis Harcourt, Secretary of State for the Colonies, replied on 20 April that he believed that West Indian participation was impossible because of the War Office's intransigence.

King George's response was to approach the War Office through Lord Kitchener, who replied somewhat disingenuously that he would gladly accept a West Indian contingent, but managed to avoid the issue of where they would serve, as his own concern was to keep them away from the Western Front, a theatre seen as a European war. Pressed by the king,[16] Harcourt at the Colonial Office resented the idea of being cast as the block to West Indian military participation and suggested raising another battalion of the existing West India Regiment entirely under War Office control, their duties when they arrived overseas being kept vague. The decision to begin with a contingent from Jamaica was received with great rejoicing and seemed to signal an end to the bickering between the War Office and the Colonial Office over West Indian involvement in the war.

Andrew Bonar Law, later to be Prime Minister, succeeded Harcourt on 27 May 1915. Bonar Law was believed by some local West Indian papers to be less prejudiced than his predecessor. This was far from the case, as he believed that the participation of black soldiers on the Western Front, particularly men from South Africa, could create problems for white supremacy after the war.

On 30 August the formation of the West Indian Contingent Committee was agreed at a meeting of former West Indian governors and other officials, leading to approximately £32,000 being raised in England. The West Indian public were impatient at what they believed to be the extreme tardiness of the governors in implementing the contingent, venting their displeasure in the press. Some, including Governor Brigadier-General Sir William Henry Manning of Jamaica, complained to G. Grindle at the Colonial Office that despite being opposed to the contingent, he would welcome the end of the local controversy. Fed up with the delay, even more volunteers left for England without waiting for the contingent to be finalised.

Anger was equally felt on other islands, and against this background of patriotic agitation the negotiations were finally completed and issues of financing, pay and recruitment of the West Indian contingent were agreed on the same terms and conditions as British recruits. It was not the intention of the War Office to make large-scale use of blacks from the colonies in Europe, but as the war progressed, by late 1916 this would become inevitable owing to the loss of life, including two of Prime Minister Bonar Law's own sons.[17] On 26 October 1915 the BWIR was established,[18] an act that would have implications for the recruitment of British-born Black and black settlers long domiciled in the United Kingdom. The first contingent of the BWIR arrived at Seaford Camp, Sussex, on 5 September 1915 for training for the Western Front. Further contingents arrived in 1915 and 1916, and in April 1916 these units left for Egypt.[19]

The WIR and the BWIR

Contributions to the war effort were made by each of the major islands of the West Indies and adjacent British territories: Barbados, Bahamas, British Guiana, British Honduras, Jamaica, Trinidad and Tobago, Grenada, St Lucia, St Vincent and the Leeward Islands. Soldiers from the West Indies of all social classes were trained in English camps for the BWIR, as distinct from the West India Regiment (WIR), which had already been established for over a hundred years and was a veteran regiment in the British service.

Prior to the war, the WIR had recruited mostly in Jamaica and had been an imperial regiment financed by Britain serving in the Caribbean and West Africa. In 1795, eight West India regiments were commissioned, and five more in 1798.[20] Originally recruiting both West Indian freemen and slaves bought from plantations, by the beginning of the First World War in 1914 the 1st Battalion of the WIR was stationed in Freetown, Sierra Leone, a detachment of the regiment's signallers later fighting the German forces in the Cameroons.[21] All troops of the WIR during the First World War were West Indian volunteers with white officers and some senior NCO training personnel. As the enemy in West Africa were German colonial forces drawn from local African peoples, the WIR were black combat troops fighting a black foe, unlike their West Indian fellows in the BWIR on the Western Front, who, faced by a white foe, were restricted to labouring tasks and guard duties. The 2nd Battalion arriving from Kingston in late 1915 helped to capture Yaoundé in January 1916, where the regiment won their battle honour 'Cameroons 1914–16'. In April 1916 they were sent to Mombasa in Kenya to face German colonial forces in the East African campaign.[22]

After the East African campaign, in September 1918 the 2nd Battalion of the WIR was shipped to Suez, then Palestine until the end of the war.[23] In moving to the Middle East, they were joining their fellow West Indian forces of the BWIR, who were also to see action as armed troops against the Turks in the Palestine campaign, a very different position from their BWIR brothers on the Western Front.[24]

Enter Black Tommy: British-based black soldiers

Despite the doubts and fears about the use of black soldiers, it should be said that most of these discussions were centred around the use of colonial troops, rather than the far less numerous British-born or domiciled Black Tommies in the United Kingdom, who never presented any political threat, perceived or real, on a par with the peoples under British colonial rule, who could potentially apply pressure for independence. With the arrival of Caribbean troops, recruitment would seem to change, however, as will be seen later. Differences in recruitment and deployment of black soldiers at home and overseas can sometimes lead one to make the mistake of confusing politics with casual racial discrimination. In his book *Staying Power*, Peter Fryer states that 'black troops' were not allowed to take part in London's victory celebrations, for instance the Peace March of 19 July 1919,[25] but it is likely that this only applied to national units from British colonial countries taking part in parades, rather than black individuals enlisted in mainland British Army units.

By the outbreak of the First World War, despite the fact that small numbers of British-born or domiciled black recruits had been a factor in the British Army since the early nineteenth century, the situation appears to have changed in that they were now no more welcome in the army than those from the colonies arriving to volunteer. In December 1914, Gilbert Grindle, Principal Clerk at the Colonial Office, wrote, 'I hear privately that some recruiting officers will pass coloureds. Others, however, will not, and we must discourage coloured volunteers'.[26] Notwithstanding these official attitudes, local black recruits continued to enlist in what they felt to be their armed forces and the way in which they managed to sidestep the official line will be revealed in the course of subsequent chapters. There was a difference between the recruitment of black people born or resident in the United Kingdom and units raised in overseas British colonies. While overseas black soldiers from Britain's African possessions and the Caribbean usually served together in homogeneous units of men from their own countries of origin (with the later exception of the practice of placing British-born Black recruits into West Indian regiments and the United Kingdom-raised Royal Engineers Coloured Section, as will be mentioned later), British-born Black soldiers originally recruited as individuals could be assigned to units with only a few of their race. Only rarely was the race of the recruit mentioned or indicated in documents relating to his service.

In Liverpool, in order to enlist as many recruits as possible, the Earl of Derby decided to form a battalion of young pals at the outset of the war, allowing them to join up together and, moreover, fight together. Other towns soon produced their own companies or battalions of pals. These 'pals' units had the desired effect of swelling army numbers, but the shortcoming of the measure was that those who fought together often died together; the horrors of the First World War fatalities resulted in the youth of entire streets or villages being virtually wiped out in a way that could not be hidden by wartime propaganda.[27] Young black recruits in such port cities as Liverpool, Cardiff and Newcastle frequently knew each other; groups of friends made a joint decision to join up,[28] but the notion of a 'pals' unit along racial lines was not considered, as their numbers in any particular 'batch' of recruits were never great. Also, many black settlement areas in many old port cities were not separate, isolated communities, an accusation sometimes levelled in our time at more recent immigrant settlements. Therefore, any groups of 'local lads' recruited in a particular area of the United Kingdom were, in most cases, likely to be mixed, crossing racial lines. The nearest to a 'Black Pals' unit would come with the practice of placing British-based black recruits into the above-mentioned Royal Engineers Coloured Section.

The number of black people in the United Kingdom was relatively small compared to some colonial countries' black populations, of course, but this was not the only reason for the lack of homogeneous black units. Prior to the war there had been historical reasons in the *Manual of Military Law* for not keeping black recruits together as a group, still theoretically in effect in the *Manual* at the beginning of the twentieth century, but revised in 1907. In the *Manual* of that year, the 'Enlistment' section gives revisions (or 'relaxations') and the instructions spell out the previous policy towards black recruits. This policy dated back to the days of the Anti-slavery Squadron of the early nineteenth century, when captive Africans were freed from ships of other European powers only to be forced to serve a term of service in His Majesty's forces:

> [...] this provision has been re-enacted in the Army Act (a). An alien so enlisted is by the Army Act made incapable of becoming an officer. A relaxation in favour of negroes and persons of colour was originally made in consequence of negroes captured in slavers being taken into the service of the Crown, and has been continued to legalise the recruiting of natives on the West Coast of Africa for service in the West India regiments and of Lascars in the East; and the relaxation has recently been extended to inhabitants of British protectorates in order to enable troops raised in the East and West African protectorates to serve outside their boundaries (b). It must also be recollected that under the Naturalization Act, 1870, a naturalized alien has the same privileges as a British subject, and therefore is capable of being enlisted to serve His Majesty.[29]

The *Manual* later states:

Special provisions as to Persons to be Enlisted

Enlistment 95. (1.) Any person who is for the time being an alien may, if Negroes &c. His Majesty think fit to signify his consent through a Secretary of State, be enlisted in His Majesty's regular forces, so, however, that the number of aliens serving together at any one time in any corps of the regular forces shall not exceed the proportion of one alien to every fifty British subjects, and that an alien so enlisted shall not be capable of holding any higher rank in His Majesty's regular forces than that of a warrant officer or non-commissioned officer:

(2.) Provided that, notwithstanding the above provisions of this section, any inhabitant of any British protectorate and any negro or person of colour, although an alien, may voluntarily enlist in pursuance of this Part of this Act, and when so enlisted, shall, while serving in His Majesty's regular forces, be deemed to be entitled to all the privileges of a natural-born British subject.[30]

The new provisions in the 1907 *Manual of Military Law* appear to show that the restriction on the number of black recruits in regular army units ('aliens serving together at any one time in any corps of the regular forces shall not exceed the proportion of one alien to every fifty British subject') was no longer applicable, but it is easy to see that a recruiting officer (if, indeed, he consulted the *Manual*) might become confused by the legal language, for the *Manual* rambles on:

NOTE.
See Ch. X, paras. 27, 28.

The proviso to this section enables inhabitants of British protectorates, and negroes and persons of colour, although aliens, to be enlisted without any restriction in point of number, as if they were natural-born British subjects.
 This section will apply to all persons enlisted under the enactments which are replaced by this section.[31]

Some British-born Black recruits from the ports were already 'naturally-born subjects', the focus of this book, and comments relating to rank in His Majesty's regular forces are worth remembering, for this issue will arise later with the commissioning of black officers. Similarly, the rights of serving black soldiers 'deemed to be entitled to all the privileges of a natural-born British subject' were also enshrined within British Military Law, a fact that may have provided a precedent in the case of Private A. Francis mentioned in Chapter Six. In the *Manual*, 'Aliens' and 'negroes' are mentioned in the same breath, as though the notion of 'home-grown' Black British was something of a paradox.

The threat of the impending war coincided with heightened issues of race and nationality. New passport and documentation systems were implemented early in the twentieth century, which occasionally caused difficulties for black residents in the United Kingdom whose country of origin was only recently colonised and lacked the British form of registration and proof of nationality.[32] Laura Tabili says that at this time, 'the reconstitution of racial difference as a political and economic disability took shape in the context of struggles that destabilized and redefined citizenship in relation to nationality, race, and gender'. The growth of the British Empire had brought about a massive displacement of population worldwide, further stimulated by global industrialisation, bringing with it large numbers of migrants to Britain. The definition of British nationality had assumed greater urgency during the last decade of the nineteenth century. A recodification of British nationality resulted in immigration restrictions in 1905, 1914 and 1919, broadening in 1918 and 1928 to include women and dependent men. During this period, any efforts to enforce what Tabili calls 'a race-blind "imperial standard" of citizenship in the Dominions', perhaps similar to the Roman model of antiquity, appear to have failed.[33]

The lack of enthusiasm for black recruitment is also reflected in examples of the attitudes shown by the authorities towards the early arrival in Britain of volunteers from the West Indies, keen to swell the ranks of existing domiciled Black Tommies in what they saw as defence of King and Country. The dockland area of Canning Town in London was under the jurisdiction of West Ham Police Court when in May 1915 nine men from Barbados were charged with stowing away on the SS *Danube* with the intention of volunteering for the British regular army, prior to the arrival of the BWIR. After some attempts to ascertain whether their enrolment was possible, the local police believed that the men were likely to be rejected because of their colour. The magistrate, a Mr Gillespie, scornfully remarked that they had stowed away '[i]n a dark corner in order to enlist in the Black Guards', a clear insult to their integrity. The nine Barbadians were not phased and insisted that they would not return to Barbados as 'They had come to fight, and they were going to fight'. Despite Gillespie's comments, the case against them was discharged. When a group of three Jamaican stowaways arrived with the same intention two years later, among them a sixteen- and a fourteen-year-old, they were sentenced to seven days' imprisonment even though they had worked their passage after their discovery by the ship's crew.[34]

White officers, black soldiers

Besides governmental attitudes, some scrutiny of those commonly found amongst officers serving in black colonial forces at the time helps any understanding of attitudes shown towards comparatively isolated black men enlisted in British regular forces. In 1886, when Lord Dufferin, the Viceroy of India, argued that British regiments in India should adopt 'a more free enlistment of Eurasians', Lord Wolseley, at the time the Adjutant General at the War Office in London, fulminated against the idea, replying:

> I most earnestly hope that no attempt may be made to enlist any Eurasian or other 'man of colour' into our fighting regiments. Those who have actually led our men under a heavy fire in the subordinate position of subaltern or captain will agree with me that we don't want men of any well known cowardly race introduced into our ranks. Of all the dangerous proposals I have ever in my time heard made regarding our army, this is certainly the most dangerous. [...] In fact let them do what they like with their own, but in the cause of all that is dear to us let us keep our British Regiments strictly British whether they be

quartered at home or in India. If ever we begin to fill our ranks with Alien races, our downfall must soon follow.³⁵

This seems strange coming from an officer who had faced the onslaughts of the Sudanese (the so-called 'Fuzzy Wuzzies') and was familiar with such 'martial races' as the Zulus. The War Office replied to the India Office in early 1887 that 'it was a mistaken view that certain men of 3/4 pure European origin were eligible for enlistment in British corps, and also that young men of color [sic] are allowed to enlist in British Regts. at home'.³⁶

At the outbreak of the First World War, a large proportion of British officers had at least experience of serving in the colonies, while many had spent their entire career there. This certainly included Douglas Haig, the Commander in Chief, a wartime figure much maligned by historians. His attitude to black or brown troops is typical of the inconsistencies of the age. Before reaching the apogee of his career, he not only served in India, but in the Sudan against the Khalifa, the successor to the Mahdi, who had defeated the forces of General Gordon in the 1880s. Although the enemy was Sudanese, there were also Sudanese soldiers fighting on the British side. Haig's comment on the black Sudanese troops shows all the prejudices of the time, revealing little empathy beneath that gruff exterior at first glance. While in the Sudan, Haig was dissatisfied with the dishevelled appearance of the British regulars before black troops:

> Saturday 12 March: Egyptian troops lined the road thro' camp at 7.30 am while the British Bde marched between them to Darmali, 2 miles distant! The Egyptian troops cheered louder: Sambo rather bad at it, the sounds sent forth resembled the hoots of a crowd of Apes! The British v. dirty: this no doubt impossible to avoid, but a pity to show them to the 'allies' in this condition! Still the intention was good.³⁷

A sad case was one in which Haig did show compassion. On Saturday 13 August 1898, he noted in a revealing diary entry that a deserter from one of the Sudanese battalions had been caught and shot the night before:

> They have been deserting in some numbers of late, 12 in a week, 25 to 30 in all from 6 Battn, so an example had to be made – still it seems a bit hard to make men who are prisoners of war soldiers, who don't want to do so, and then shoot them if they desert.[38]

It would seem that not all African soldiers were willing volunteers in the colonial forces. In this case, Sudanese prisoners of war were clearly given no choice but to enlist in the British Army upon being captured and paid the ultimate price for transgressions. In Chapter Five, issues relating to the forced recruitment of some African troops are discussed.

During the First World War, however, Haig exhibited the sort of regard for men under his command, and sometimes under the command of others, that reveals a different side of his character not usually recognised. While fighting on the northern banks of the River Aisne, the British Expeditionary Force had dug itself defensive trenches to withstand an anticipated German counter-attack. Haig noted that I Corps was stationed beside a contingent of French Moroccan troops:

> Poor wretches were in cotton clothing and had nothing to eat but wet bread and raw meat for 4 or 5 days in the trenches on our right. It was to improve their fighting efficiency that I arranged to give them the tinned meat rations. [Haig sent them 10,000 British rations of tinned beef, cheese and other items.] General Maud'huy [commanding the French XVIII Corps, which included the Moroccans] was delighted and so were the troops. They will do anything to help us now! The General Commanding the Moroccan Division had one eye on his line of retreat all the time, and his troops were constantly withdrawing, until we gave him a direct order to hold the trenches [...] This order, enlivened with a regular dose of rhum has kept the old boy up to the mark so far.

Haig may have been less than impressed with the resulting note of thanks and a crate of champagne from the French General de Maud'huy, which, apparently, could be more easily procured than proper rations for his own Moroccan troops.[39] Notable for being a brusque character (the cartoon image of Colonel Blimp is thought to have been based on him), it may be possible for Haig to have been misunderstood. The *Daily Mirror* reported a story that may be open to misinterpretation:

> He never failed to be amused when relating what he facetiously termed 'an example of consummate tact.' That occurred when he was reviewing one of the colonial battalions behind the lines. In the ranks he found a coloured man. 'What are you?' he asked. 'A niggah, sah,' was the rather disconcerting reply. But the General rose to the occasion, and said: 'Then see that you remain so, my man!'[40]

There are two ways of interpreting Haig's reply. One is a sharp rebuke to the black soldier, telling him to remember his lowly station, but another way in which his comment might be taken is that although he is said to have been taken aback by the soldier's response, the losses on the Western Front were tremendous and Haig may, in his characteristically unemotional manner, have been merely exhorting him to stay alive, however he chose to define himself. The question remains, however, why did the black soldier respond in that way? Was he being just as facetious or did he feel so browbeaten by his non-commissioned officers into 'keeping his place' that he felt that this was the answer this important officer expected?

Views expressed by some officers further down the line of command, but nevertheless very senior, are far less ambiguous. Brigadier General Wilfred A. White, head of the British Recruiting Mission was sent by the Army Council to New York in mid-1917 to organise the general recruiting of British subjects in the United states and to enlist Black British 'coloured labour' for the military. White was less than enthusiastic about this latter requirement and complained about the lack of firm guidelines regarding black recruitment, particularly as black volunteers had been initially rejected. As by June 1917 it had been agreed that black recruits were to be allowed in the form of a separate battalion,[41] Brigadier General White grumbled to the War Office that further clarification was required. In doing so, he reveals an astonishing level of prejudice, the vehemence of which is still shocking to modern readers aware of the racism of the period. In a telegram to the War Office on 19 February 1918, he makes no attempt to sublimate his feelings in any way, and, perhaps not surprisingly for the times, does not appear to have been admonished by his superiors for the language used. The heading of White's telegram reads – 'Wooly [sic] headed niggers', followed by a protestation that it was not possible to post black recruits to white units and insisting that 'these "niggers" must therefore go to native units'.[42]

'THE MASTER RACE'

The desired image of the natural superiority of Europeans could not be maintained in all circumstances. Although every attempt was made to preserve the mystique of white officers in the presence of non-white servicemen, aboard troopships seasickness struck officers and men alike, irrespective of their race. European officers too ill to appear were said to be detained by 'other duties', as an off-colour officer was considered something not to be admitted. Troops of African descent were not the only ones viewed with disdain; Canadian troops and Chinese labourers were forced to fraternise covertly, one British officer assuring a Chinese labourer that 'he hadn't the beans to become a Tommy in one hundred years'.[43]

Senior officers in the BWIR were exclusively of white West Indian or British origin and shared many of the British officers' attitudes regarding African troops, but, as C.L.R. James complained, some had been recruited from Sandhurst failures and at least one colonel should have been retired long before the war. Although issues of discipline are matters of concern for all officers, power and prestige are often considered important in order to maintain status. Officers of black troops were in a position aided by general societal attitudes of the time in that their troops were considered naturally inferior, both notions of class and racial superiority informing their relationship with their men. Exerting raw power may have had an element of gratification for some[44] and there were occasions when their behaviour could be likened to that of the old plantation overseers in terms of the verbal and sometimes physical abuse suffered by black troops. It is possible that such behaviour may have been a compensatory measure for their low esteem when amongst officers of regular units of white troops, who generally looked down upon officers of the BWIR or of any black troops, but there were occasions when these white officers were considered to have overstepped the mark of acceptable behaviour by their men, who, whilst understanding that levels of discipline had to be maintained, would not take such abuse from men who in daily life on the islands were not their social superiors. Instead of being suitably cowed by rebukes, on one occasion the men of the 4th Battalion of the BWIR retaliated by pouring abuse upon an English officer who had been superintendent of a large cane plantation in Jamaica. Honour, integrity and other attributes of a 'gentleman' were considered a long-standing tradition in the British Army and the officer in question may not have been thought to possess any of these qualities by the men in his command.[45]

Not all white Caribbean officers behaved badly towards their black troops. Officers' personality and leadership style impacted greatly upon the relationship with the black rank and file. Amongst other officers, white Barbadian lieutenants G. Challenor and E.K.G. Weatherhead were publicly praised by Grenadian soldiers who had served under them in Egypt.[46]

Pseudo-scientific racism

Officers' attitudes discussed so far have been those regarding colonial black troops, rather than those shown towards black soldiers in British regular units in the United Kingdom. The United Kingdom-based Black Tommy could not escape this general perception of black people by many Europeans at this time, despite being thousands of miles from the colonies. Although they lacked the support of comrades of the same race available to black soldiers in homogeneous units raised in the colonies, there was the possibility of variability in officers' responses to black soldiers. It is difficult to establish how racist individual recruiting officers may have been when confronted with British-born Black applicants, but there are occasional hints in official documents and letters, as shown in the case of Gunner Albert James, also mentioned in Chapter Two. Like other recruits, Albert was required to undergo the obligatory medical examination upon enlistment. His medical history report reveals just how far race relations at the time were influenced by the development of the pseudo-scientific racism of the late eighteenth and nineteenth century. Beginning during the transatlantic slavery period, this ideology had evolved through Social Darwinism, survival of the fittest, to the even more intolerant eugenics movement[47] which, under the Nazi regime of Second World War Germany, would lead to the brutal removal of individuals or racial groups thought to be inferior and therefore a threat to the genetic inheritance of the European master race. Amongst the usual statistics shown on Albert's medical history report, height, weight, vaccinations, etc., is another comment, written in the hand of the examining medical officer. Under the category 'Slight defects, but not sufficient to cause rejection' is an intriguing entry: 'Is a half-caste'.[48]

Pseudo-scientific racism was also later an integral ingredient in European imperial policies. Authors such as Edward Long had helped develop a strident mythology of race, feeding belief in the innate inferiority of 'lesser breeds', particularly black people. The so-called science of phrenology involved studying the contours of people's skulls to prove a connection between race and culture. The phrenologist Sir William Lawrence wrote in 1819, 'The Negro structure, approximates unequivocally to that of the monkey'. Teleology promoted the notion that black people were put on earth to serve whites. Social Darwinism, which placed whites at the top of a racial hierarchy and blacks at the bottom, was not developed by Charles Darwin, but was a variation of the latter's beliefs developed by Sir Francis Galton, a relative of Darwin, in 1883. Galton's eugenics movement promoted the belief that the qualities of the human species or population could be improved by discouraging the reproduction of persons with genetic defects or inheritable traits perceived to be undesirable.[49]

Eugenic theories were given a boost in the years preceding the outbreak of the First World War when the question of the fitness of the country's young men needed for the forthcoming struggle arose. Following the devastating early military defeats of the British armies during the Boer War fifteen years earlier, the discussion had initially evolved around the notion of 'national efficiency'. Benjamin Rowntree, the British sociological researcher, social reformer and industrialist, had estimated that half of England's workforce was unfit for military service when it was found that three out of every four men attempting to enlist in Manchester were rejected as medically unsound.[50] Mr. Alfred Bigland, the MP for Birkenhead East, near Liverpool, was keen to make a contribution to the war effort and helped set up a committee in Hamilton Square, Birkenhead for the purpose of recruiting a 'Bantam' Battalion of short men. He sought permission from Lord Kitchener to recruit men of a height of between five foot and five foot three, with perhaps a minimum chest measurement of thirty-three inches, one inch above the normal requirements in order to prevent weaker men from enlisting. The aim, Bigland professed, was short but sturdy men, but this did not prevent him from pointing out that Julius Caesar would have been rejected by a recruiting officer in other regiments because of his epilepsy. By December 1914, two battalions, the 15th and 16th, Bantam Battalions of the Cheshire Regiment had been raised and a third reserve battalion added, the 17th.[51]

There is some irony in the fact that the view of non-European bloodlines as inferior contrasted sharply with newspaper reports when West Indian contingents finally arrived and more black soldiers were seen on British streets. Attention was quickly drawn by the press to their physique, and at the Lord Mayor of London's show in November 1915, the *Standard* described the small detachment parading as 'big men all'. Similarly, the *Daily News* had them as 'huge and mighty men of valour', while a local paper in Seaford, East Sussex, reported that the BWIR volunteers, encamped in the south coast town between October 1915 and March 1916, had made a 'splendid impression [...]. Some of them are magnificently proportioned'. This view was not only expressed by the press. Military records of the time regularly remarked on the 'exceptional' or 'fine' physique of both Caribbean regiments, the BWIR and the WIR.[52]

Nevertheless, negative perceptions were still to be found amongst the officer class. The young Winston Churchill had been an officer in the 21st Lancers serving in the Sudan under the command of General Herbert Kitchener and had a poor opinion of black troops fighting alongside the British:

> The black soldier was of a very different type from the fellahin. The Egyptian was strong, patient, healthy, and docile. The negro was in all these respects his inferior. His delicate lungs, slim legs, and loosely knit figure contrasted unfavourably with the massive frame and iron constitution of the peasant of the Delta. Always excitable and often insubordinate, he required the strictest discipline. At once slovenly and uxorious, he detested his drills and loved his wives with equal earnestness; and altogether 'Sambo' – for such is the Soudanese [sic] equivalent of 'Tommy' – was a lazy, fierce, disreputable child. But he possessed two tremendous military virtues. To the faithful loyalty of a dog he added the heart of a lion. He loved his officer, and feared nothing in the world. With the introduction of this element the Egyptian army became a formidable military machine.[53]

In expressing these views, Churchill did not differ from Haig or many other officers of the day. It is interesting that, like Haig and others, there is an element of ambiguity in his real opinion of the black soldier. Churchill is known to have been a member of the group in favour of raising a black army to help with the British war effort, exemplifying the confusion and contradiction sometimes felt at an individual level amongst many Europeans of the period.

Social class

Black British soldiers were not necessarily of the same social class any more than white troops, despite the slave ancestry of some, but there is no doubt that many were recruited in British ports with poor 'sailortown' districts, a term first used by the twentieth-century guardian of the British deep-water sailing tradition, the shantyman Stan Hugill

(1906–92).⁵⁴ Considering the great social divide between the classes during the First World War period, given that black people were at the bottom of the social hierarchy at that time, it is perhaps a little surprising to find that some white middle-class officers, worlds apart in social terms, were linked to some young black soldiers in an unexpected way, their lives caroming off one another. Although such relationships might be viewed as something nearer that of master-servant, employer-employee of the period, it is undoubtedly a reflection of the nature of locally raised regiments that their lives should become in some way intertwined.

While appearing to inhabit the sheltered world of the comfortable middle classes, some officers were from families who regarded it as their social responsibility to try and alleviate the conditions of those in need. Despite the tremendous social gulf, two officers of the 1/10th Battalion of the King's (Liverpool Regiment), the Liverpool Scottish, the unit to which Private Herbert McDavid (see Chapter Two) belonged, were from families every bit as remarkable as that of the latter, bridging the social divide by good works in Liverpool's Toxteth area and other poor districts of the city. Captain Noel Godfrey Chavasse, VC and Bar, MC (1884–1917) was one of only three people to be awarded a Victoria Cross twice. The son of the Rev. Francis Chavasse, the founder of St Peter's College, Oxford, and Bishop of Liverpool from 1900, whilst in Liverpool he became involved with an institution for homeless boys, the Grafton Street Industrial School. After being appointed as a doctor at the Royal Southern Hospital, Liverpool, Chavasse was able to resume his connection to the Grafton Street School⁵⁵ in the Beaufort Street area, later shown to have been a source of black recruitment. Beaufort Street, where both Private Walter Colebourne, also mentioned later, lived and the Christian/McDavid family originated, was situated between Grafton Street and the Royal Southern Hospital in Caryl Street.

The second officer of the 1/10th Battalion of the King's Regiment from a family with a social conscience and a record of service to the poor was Philip St. John Basil Rathbone, later to become famous as the actor Basil Rathbone. Although born in South Africa, his father was the scion of a well-respected Liverpool family descended from William

Rathbone, one of the founders of the Liverpool Abolitionist Movement in the late eighteenth century. After the abolition of the slave trade, each generation of William's descendants continued this legacy of aid to the disadvantaged and philanthropic work in Liverpool. From the beginning of the nineteenth century, in yet another school in Grafton Street, in the dockland area 'adopted' for good works by Noel Chavasse, we find three members of the Rathbone family as school governors contributing to school funds of the Harrington School.[56] It is therefore not so surprising to find that the letter informing Gunner Albert James of the death of his wife Ethel, mentioned later, should have been signed by R. Pierce for E.J. Rathbone, the Officer in Charge of Records, Soldiers' and Sailors' Families Association Liverpool Branch during the war. Once again, this is consistent with the notion of a local community at war, and regiments raised from that community.

Personal/close relationships

The fact that the war had brought European officers and men alike into contact with men of other races, whom they might not have previously encountered, or, at the very least, certainly not in close proximity, had the potential to impact upon and bring about change in attitudes at an individual level. In the mixed forces raised in the United Kingdom, each of the Black British soldiers recruited had their own individual experiences of war and relationships with their fellow soldiers, but examples can be found of a general feeling of unity against a common foe and a responsibility towards the men fighting alongside them, who shared the dangers of the everyday struggle. This sometimes included a measure of respect between officers and other ranks, despite the gulf between them. Norman Manley (also mentioned in the next chapter) appears to have had excellent relations with his fellow recruits, mostly cockneys, in the early days, claiming in his autobiography that, their incorrigible behaviour aside, 'for kindness and generosity, I have never met their equal'. Seen to be able, it did not take long for him to be promoted to lance corporal (bombardier in the artillery) and then corporal by the time he left for France. This did not work out too well, as he encountered violent colour prejudice there: the rank and file may have resented taking orders from a 'coloured NCO', as he described himself, but his fellow NCOs were worse, conspiring to get him into trouble. Once on the Western Front, a sergeant put him on a charge, but Manley was able to find a friendly officer and explain that it was unlikely that there would ever be a peaceful relationship between himself and his antagonists, and voluntarily gave up his stripes. He was moved to another unit and became a gunner once more.[57] Men under fire might have found that expected relational norms of the time based on race might not always pertain when individual soldiers were placed in a position of mutual reliance; in some cases, the man immediately to their left or right on the field of battle. This is summed up succinctly in the diary of the black Glaswegian Private Arthur Roberts, after an incident when he became lost during the Battle of Pilckem Ridge, the main part of the Third Battle of Ypres:

> If I stopped one person for information I stopped a dozen but one seemed to contradict the other while some who had no idea of what I asked just said anything. Yes a soldier may be as welcome as the flowers in May with his own mob, but others help very little a strayed comrade of another battalion.
>
> Throughout the dark dirty night I doggedly splashed about and the dull grey wet morning found me dreamingly plodding, God knows where? I remember walking towards a cluster of tents and timber wagons. The next thing I mind was [sic] I was half lying against a wagon with the rain beating on my face and my own section officer giving me a good drink of rum.
>
> Everybody was pleased to see me but I took most to the post corporal for he had a parcel and a letter for me.[58]

Fellow feeling like this between black and white soldiers could be reciprocal. When Norman Manley's brother was killed at Ypres near the end of 1917, he was not present, but apparently a terrific enemy artillery fire opened up on the wood where Roy and his comrades were deployed, leaving half the unit's men dead or wounded within five minutes.

Norman's brother Roy was a hero, for as the men began running to escape the bombardment, he carried on his back a man he believed to be wounded. In fact he was dead and, soon after, Roy also fell, a shell that burst a little distance off sending a fragment of its casing straight into his heart, killing him instantly. Norman's brother was buried the next day with his fallen comrades, wrapped in blankets and placed in a prepared field near their camp. It is clear that even at the time of writing his autobiography many years later, Norman Manley was still grieving.[59]

Other soldiers' experience of comradeship could be less dramatic. For a hundred years a photograph of a white soldier has been preserved in the family album of Gunner Albert James. The name of this soldier was once known to the family, but with the deaths of older members has become lost. The story is that Albert kept this image after the war as a memento of a fallen comrade. His name might now be forgotten, but his portrait is still in the possession of the family of the black artilleryman Albert James and the story of the photograph is still told.[60] Similar casual references to relationships between men can be found elsewhere. A veteran officer of the First World War, Second Lieutenant William Tobey of the 16th Battalion of the Lancashire Fusiliers, felt moved to comment in an interview with the author Peter Hart that in early August 1918, whilst under fire from the Germans, he had called for three volunteers to go forward towards the German lines to collect a corporal who had been injured. 'Three men stepped forward, one of which was the only black man in the battalion'.[61]

In the course of the war, black troops could be found working behind the lines, frustrated at being unable to engage in combat duties, while others would serve in combat units from the beginning of the war and pay the ultimate price. British-born and domiciled Tommies of African descent, joined by early volunteers from the Caribbean as individuals serving in regular British forces, and later by reinforcements arriving in Britain to swell numbers in the shape of forces raised officially in the Caribbean and Africa, would play an important part in the First World War. At the outbreak of the war, men and women of the Caribbean had answered the call of the Mother Country to seek active service overseas in many capacities. In addition to the Canadian 'Black Battalion', Bermudian troops and the black South African Native Labour Corp (which included men from West Africa), some battalions of the BWIR were to be found in France, working in non-combatant roles, while others from that regiment, including some British-born Black soldiers who had joined the BWIR voluntarily or otherwise, were to achieve their hopes at the time of enlistment and find themselves in direct armed combat with the enemy in the Middle East as troops in armed units.

CHAPTER TWO

THE INVISIBLE ARMY – THE SEARCH

So little research has been undertaken on the part played by United Kingdom-based Black British soldiers in the First World War that as recently as 2009 a newspaper felt moved to publish an article on the discovery of just one image of a Black Tommy rescued from a skip in northern France. The image was one of almost 400 snaps of British soldiers taking part in the Battle of the Somme in 1916. Preserved on glass plates, the photographs had lain undisturbed for more than ninety years in the attic of an old barn some ten miles behind the Somme battlefields and only came to light when the barn changed hands in 2007. They are a poignant reminder of the British Army's part in the Battle of the Somme, the single most murderous battle of the war in which 400,000 British and colonial soldiers died. The image of the single Black Tommy in this instance is just one of many whose memory is preserved only because his image was stumbled upon by military enthusiasts.[1]

Identification of Black British recruits

As photographs of black First World War soldiers in local archives were so rare, in 2013–14 Karen O'Rourke, Curator of the Kings (Liverpool)

Regiment Gallery of the Museum of Liverpool, instigated a project aimed at encouraging local black families to research their First World War family histories in order to collect memories to fill a gap in the museum's archives.[2] In the course of this project, the particulars of some Black British soldiers were found to be already held in the museum's collections, but until families came forward and identified their ancestors, their race had not been known. This was just one of the problems of identification making it extremely difficult to ascertain accurate figures of 'Black Tommies'.

There is perhaps some irony in the fact that researching individual soldiers and military statistics in the First World War relating to black troops from relatively geographically distant African and Caribbean regiments can sometimes be easier than identifying the race of British soldiers born or resident in the United Kingdom at time of recruitment. There are a number of reasons for this archival invisibility, causing the image of the First World War Black Tommy to be considered perhaps something of an anomaly in our time, despite the common presence of black soldiers in the present-day British Army. These include difficulties with the British census, the English- (or, indeed, Scottish, Irish or Welsh) sounding names of many soldiers of Caribbean descent and issues of recruitment of black soldiers. The British census began in 1801, but it was not until 1841 that any substantial detail was recorded. The first four censuses (1801–31) were mainly statistical exercises containing virtually no personal information. In Britain, the census has traditionally recorded only the birthplace, not the race of an individual, unlike the United States, where the census dates back to 1790 and in which race plays a significant part.[3] The British census is therefore unhelpful in identifying the race of a man recording a military profession up to the First World War, and the researcher is hindered further by the fact that census material is not made available to the public for 100 years. This being the case, at the time of writing this book, the last census that can be viewed, 1911, falls short of the 1914–18 war. Another difficulty in tracking Black British soldiers in units raised in the United Kingdom is the likelihood of people of Caribbean ancestry having Anglophone names, a relic of black servitude and slaves being denied their original African names by their owners. This can also apply to some Africans of the period baptised into Christianity by British missionaries, an earlier example, albeit in another branch of the armed forces, being one George Ryan, an African who served on HMS *Victory* at the Battle of Trafalgar.[4] The names of many British-born Black soldiers are therefore not distinguishable from any others listed in British records, making it more difficult to quantify the numbers of serving soldiers of African descent than those of black colonial troops from Africa and the Caribbean. The most obvious source for identifying Black British soldiers is, of course, information held in the National Archives War Office Records or regimental museums, but, once again, unless an issue arose calling attention to the race of recorded individual soldiers, ascertaining this is often difficult.

A decade before the outbreak of the First World War, it seems that black presence in the British Army had been long forgotten when the *Penny Illustrated Paper* of 30 December 1905 reported a young infantryman in the Durham Light Infantry as being the 'the only Soudanese serving in the British army'. 'Jim Durham', as he was known to the men of the regiment, had been recruited in an unusual way twenty years earlier, when the British had fought the troops of the Mahdi in the Anglo Egyptian Sudan. After the Battle of Ginnis, a small black boy named Mustapha was found on the banks of the River Nile and after being adopted as the regiment's mascot was taken to Egypt and later India. Young 'Jim' was formally enrolled into the Durham Light Infantry in November 1898 in Mandalay, Burma, as James Francis Durham, named after Sergeants Jim Birley and Francis Fisher. His battalion moved to Aldershot in 1902 and later to Cork City in 1905, where he attracted the attention of the press. Jim moved from here to Fermoy, Co. Cork in 1909. On 8 August 1910 he died of pneumonia in the military hospital and was buried with full military honours. His headstone, erected by the officers and men, tells the story of his adoption by the regiment.[5]

This early twentieth-century soldier, remembered because he attracted a degree of celebrity status and press attention, did not live to see the outbreak of the war, thus narrowly falling short of the focus of this study, but, as in the cases of other black soldiers, had the press not

2. Marcus Bailey, a First World War sailor in the Royal Navy, with an unknown black soldier. (Reproduced by permission of Marcus Bailey's daughter, Lilian Bader)

chosen to feature the unusual recruitment of this Sudanese soldier serving in Britain's armed forces, we might have had no cause to remember him other than his headstone. In a later chapter, it will be shown that during the 1919 Race Riots the press played a similar role in the identification of black soldiers raised in the United Kingdom in a far less happy way.

In spite of the seemingly insurmountable odds against identifying black soldiers in units raised in the United Kingdom, it is nevertheless possible to establish the presence of soldiers of African descent in the First World War, to bring alive the image of the Black Tommy. Factors that help identify black soldiers include achieving celebrity status; drawing the attention of the media, like James Durham; having a famous relative; or, in some cases, an element of sheer luck, such as a recruiting officer's chance comment about a soldier in his attestation papers.

One of the most powerful means of identification is undoubtedly local community knowledge. Simply knowing the names of the black families in a street in a given area can go a long way to removing the possibility of error when encountering, for example, the bald details of a soldier's name, address and next of kin in the records of the Commonwealth War Graves Commission. In the modern technological age, there are now websites dedicated to individual soldiers and a variety of means can be employed to bring to life the invisible army of Black British soldiers drawn from ports, cities and towns all over Great Britain to serve in the First World War.

'Your Country Needs You': The ports mobilise

Not only did the black Empire rally to Britain's call, but locally born black communities in Britain's 'sailortown' districts, of several generations' standing in some cases, also answered the nation's need. Members of the Liverpool black community, the oldest in Europe in terms of continuous presence, are able to trace their roots from at least the nineteenth century. Other black communities have existed in cities such as Bristol and London for at least five centuries, but have suffered disruption, causing some to die out and rise again in more recent times.⁶ Although only fifteen years of age at the time, and technically well underage, first-generation settler Sierra Leonean-born Ernest Marke demonstrated the patriotism of many people from the British colonies. Near the end of the First World War he was standing on the corner of Stanhope Street and Mill Street in the Toxteth area of Liverpool with an eighteen-year-old friend, Tommy Macauley, also from Sierra Leone, when they chanced upon one of the famous posters depicting Lord Kitchener bearing the caption 'Your country needs you!' Although more than a little late, as the war was coming to a close, Ernest exclaimed, 'That's us', and both boys promptly went along to the recruiting station at St George's Hall. They found themselves in Seaforth Barracks that evening and were later transferred for training to Whitchurch, Shropshire, eventually joining the Preaseth Camp 159th Recruitment Distribution Battalion, according to Marke, but this may be Prees Heath, an army camp also in that area.⁷

There was no coordinated response to the war by the small United Kingdom black population. Many did not live in black communities and most made their decision to enlist at an individual level. Throughout the country, in ones and twos, they presented themselves to the recruiting authorities with varying results in terms of acceptance, depending to the inclinations of the officer in charge.

The Scottish ports were not without their Black Tommies. After nearly a hundred years, the forgotten First World War diaries of a British-born Black soldier were found in an attic in a Glasgow suburb. Private Arthur William David Roberts, who served with the King's Own Scottish Borderers (KOSB) and later with 2nd Battalion Royal Scots Fusiliers, was born in Southville, Bristol, in 1897, but moved to Glasgow with his father David, a black ship's steward, as a small child. His diaries remained in the attic of a house in Mount Vernon until October 2012, when they were discovered by the new owners, a young couple, providing a remarkable memoir and a unique history of a black soldier's experiences on the Western Front.⁸

Always interested in military matters, Arthur had begged his father to allow him to join a scout troop, an act which was to feed his interest and lead to his involvement in the Great War.[9] The quality of his diary seems to show that both Finniston Primary School and the High Grade School on Glasgow's Kent Road served him well. The only reference to racism seems to relate to his army service. Growing up in the crowded communal tenements of the Anderson district, he did not cast himself in the role of the victim and considered Glasgow his home.[10] In a letter written to his aunt while awaiting transportation to France, Arthur commented on the jingoistic feelings of the time:

> I've seen two or three drafts going away since I've been here and it feels so funny while the men are passing. The bands are playing good-oh and [...] it makes one feel creepy especially when the big drum booms and the kettle drums roll but somebody must go.[11]

Arthur described the 'Bull Ring', the training camp where the men were prepared for the front with endless drilling, gassing exercises and bayonet practice.[12] Here, he witnessed his companions fainting through heat and exhaustion, but the reality of the horrors of trench warfare was to be so much worse. Arthur survived a German attack in September 1917 which killed twelve of his pals. He also survived the Battle of Passchendaele, commenting, 'We were shelled to blazes. I had a very narrow shave. One fellow in front of me had his head blew off. I completely escaped. Everyone round me were either killed or wounded. We lost about a dozen all told'.[13]

Throughout the diary there is a strong sense of humour, as can be seen in Arthur's describing enemy shelling with a certain nonchalance: 'Jerry is still noticing us and paying us compliments'. Going over the top at the Battle of Pilckem Ridge near Ypres on 31 July 1917 was, he admitted, terrifying: 'We were over this morning and I saw sights that I never saw before or wish to see again. It was terrible yet it was wonderful. [...] – I got through without a scratch'.[14]

A gregarious man with a love of music, Private Arthur Roberts did not escape racism, despite his popularity. He also tells of being falsely accused of destroying a pair of boots after being picked on by a corporal, narrowly missing being court-martialled,[15] and on another occasion records the comment 'no remarks passed',[16] when put to work in the dining hall whilst recovering from a recurring foot injury, the implication being that he was used to enduring comments of a racist nature. After the war ended, he returned to Glasgow and worked in the engineering firm Harland and Wolff, and married Jessie Finnigan, a widower, in Blackpool in 1956.[17]

Private Arthur Roberts was yet another black soldier who would have been forgotten had his records not been found and publicised by the media. Others are to be discovered through the press or, like the father of the boxer Randolph Turpin in the next chapter, by achieving secondary celebrity status – being related to someone famous. Walter Tull, later shown to be neither Britain's first nor only black officer as widely believed, had a brother serving as a sapper in the Royal Engineers, the same regiment as Yorkshire-based Charles Augustus Williams, the Barbadian father of Charlie Williams, future Doncaster Rovers centre half.[18]

The Tyneside area was another early area of black settlement. In South Shields, Arab and Somali seamen had been settling since the 1860s in the Holborne district near the seafaring area of Mill Dam, and some West African and West Indian seamen in North Shields arrived in the years before the First World War, their numbers increasing fourfold with the outbreak of hostilities.[19] Although the children of those early settlers were available for armed service, many volunteers had arrived from the colonies before the beginning of the war. British-born and thoroughly domiciled black and Asian army recruits known to locals as 'Burnt Geordies', not entirely pejoratively, were soon a familiar sight on the streets of northeastern England. As an old seafaring community, some young black men who had originally begun as sailors were equally keen to enlist in the ranks of 'landlubber' forces when the call came.

It is often difficult to untangle issues of the racism prevalent at the time from stories of the recruitment and service of Black British soldiers, as there were those, like Arthur Roberts, who did not complain or discuss that aspect of their experience. Louis Anchoy was a nineteen-year-old Trinidadian sailor recruited in Newcastle upon Tyne into the Northumberland Fusiliers 1st Tyneside Irish on 6 November 1914. Little more than a month later he was discharged under Kings Regulations, Para 392 (iii), with the comment, 'Not likely to become an efficient soldier. Coloured man'. A medical officer had added a note claiming that he had a 'cardiac weakness'. The connection of his colour with the statement of his rejection might raise a suspicion not entirely unfounded given the experience of others (such as Albert James below), but it is likely that in this case he did in fact suffer from a weakness of the heart, as on 23 September 1918, he died of heart failure at the Seamen's Hospital Greenwich at the age of twenty-two. Having been rejected, Louis had returned to sea as a merchant seaman, determined to play his part in protecting 'king and country'. At the time of his army recruitment, descriptions of his tattoos recorded under 'distinctive marks' report a British flag on his left arm and King George V's crown on his right.[20]

London, capital of the Empire, has had a black presence since Elizabethan times. Prior to the war, Edwardian London could claim a black population of a range of social classes, from professionals to those living in poorer dockland districts similar to those of other British port cities. One soldier, Henry Solomon, was a former pupil of St Paul's School, London, and was old enough to enlist near the end of the war in 1918,[21] while Harold Brown was from a more humble background. Born in 49 Oban Street, Poplar, in the east end of London in June 1899, Harold Brown was the son of John Benjamin, a Jamaican seaman, and Elizabeth Emma, a white Londoner.[22] This British-born Black youth answered the call of king and country during the First World War by serving as a private with The Queen's (Royal West Surrey) Regiment. For his bravery he was awarded two divisional certificates of gallantry, one while serving in October 1917 in the 3/4th Battalion of the Queen's (attached to the 21st Division, signed by the GOC Major General Sir David Campbell) and the other in the 6th Battalion the Queen's (12th Division, signed by the General Officer Commanding Major General H.W. Higginson), and a printed certificate signed by General Sir Henry Rawlinson (GOC Fourth Army). In 1918 he also received the Military Medal. After being demobilised in 1919, he worked as a seaman and a docker at the Royal Albert Docks until his death in 1955.[23]

Another British-born Black soldier from the ports serving on the Western Front was Walter Colebourne, who volunteered early in the war. Walter Colebourne, son of Mrs Catherine Colebourne, was born in 1895 at 60 Beaufort Street,[24] which runs parallel with the dock road in the Toxteth area of Liverpool. Living only four doors away from the house opposite was a young black clerk, George Christian, at number 69. The fates of these two mixed-race neighbours could not have been more different. George William Christian was the son of an Antiguan seaman who had left the West Indies to settle in Liverpool at the age of fifteen and a white Liverpudlian mother. The son of a timber merchant, George appears to have been exceptionally gifted and, after serving as a clerk for Holt Shipping Line, soon established his own merchant trading business in Nigeria and Cameroon, with European as well as black employees. George Christian was to become the first black millionaire in Liverpool,[25] while, like many other young British men of all races, Walter Colebourne was destined to find death in a foreign field.

Walter Colebourne joined the 1/8th (Irish) Battalion of the King's Liverpool Regiment. When the 1/8th Battalion began recruiting in Shaw Street, Liverpool, in August 1914,[26] it was to be part of the Liverpool Brigade, West Lancashire Division,[27] later transferring to the 55th (West Lancashire) Division.[28] Walter was to take part in one of the largest battles of the war, the Battle of the Somme, which took place on both sides of the river of that name in northern France between 1 July and 18 November 1916. Following the invasion of the country in August 1914, the German Army had occupied large areas of France. The British Expeditionary Force responded by mounting a joint offensive with the French Army. Fighting continued until late autumn 1916 and on the first day of the battle alone, the British Army suffered 60,000 casualties, the worst sustained in its history.[29] The Battle of the Somme could perhaps be more accurately described as a somewhat prolonged offensive, rather than a single battle, as it was staged in several phases. Private Walter Colebourne (307589) lost his life on 18 August, almost two weeks before the Battle of Guillemot, one of the big pushes against the Germans during the second Somme offensive. The Somme was the beginning of the end

3. An unknown Black British soldier, posing in front of his unit's group photograph. (Reproduced by permission of Jeffrey Green)

for the Germans, as they never made any further advances, finally retiring in February 1917 to the fortified Hindenburg Line.[30] Walter's body was never recovered, but is commemorated on Pier and Face 1 D 8 B and 8 C of the Thiepval Memorial, near the village of the same name in Picardy, in memory of the British and South African men who died in the Battle of the Somme and have no known grave.[31] Walter received the Victory Medal and British War Medal posthumously.

THE MIDDLE EASTERN FRONT

Like their comrades, United Kingdom Black Tommies served in other theatres than the Western Front. The Ottoman Empire supported the German Empire, facing the British in the Sinai and Palestine campaigns of the Middle Eastern theatre of the First World War. Following Britain's unsuccessful Gallipoli campaign, the Turks invaded the Sinai Peninsula, then part of the British Protectorate of Egypt, mounting a failed attack upon the Suez Canal in 1915.[32] The British Egyptian Expeditionary Force and the Fourth Army in Palestine fought for the Sinai Peninsula in 1916, the Anzac Mounted Division and the 52nd (Lowland) Division succeeding in pushing the German-led Ottoman Army units out of the area. The success of the Battle of Romani led to the pursuit of the Turks in August, eventually pushing the Ottoman Army out of Sinai and into Palestine by 1917.[33]

Born in 1888 in Liverpool, Albert James left a one-year-old son and a daughter two weeks old[34] to serve in the Royal Field Artillery in Egypt and Palestine, while his brother William served in the Merchant Navy.[35] Albert was the son of Edward James, a Bermudan sailor, and Harriet Gates, the daughter of a Cheshire flatman (canal barge pilot). His parents ran a number of grocery and confectionary shops in the Toxteth area of Liverpool, not far from the home of Walter Colebourne. Albert's father, Edward, continued as a ship's steward, whilst his wife and eight children ran the shops. Albert James attended St Cleopas School in Mill Street,[36] before becoming a ledger boy at Liverpool Central Library in William Brown Street at the age of fourteen.[37] By the time of Albert's enlistment on 7 January 1915 at the age of twenty-six,[38] he had occupied other forms of employment and had married Ethel Vernon Jones, a member of the newly formed 'Tiller Girls' dance troupe.[39]

At the time of attestation in Preston on 7 January 1915, Albert was living at 14 Stananought Street, Toxteth,[40] but later gave his address as 141 Windsor Street, the family shop. Gunner Albert James (service number 75119), joined the Royal Field Artillery, 67th Brigade, 10th Irish Division and finally embarked for France on 20 September 1915, remaining there until 30 November 1915.[41] Embarking in Marseilles on 1 December of that year to arrive in Salonica on the 15th,[42] most of Albert's war was spent in the Middle East. Some months after finally arriving in Egypt on 19 September 1917 and enduring the rigours of desert warfare in Palestine,[43] Albert had an attack of malaria, a recurring illness he would suffer for the rest of his life. On 11 January 1918, he was moved back to Egypt and was admitted to the Citadel hospital in Cairo,[44] where he remained until 16 June 1918 before rejoining his unit.[45]

4. Liverpudlian soldier Gunner Albert James with his wife, Ethel. (From the author's private collection)

Black non-commissioned officers were easier to find in the British Army than those of higher rank, which meant that, at least in the forces raised in the United Kingdom, they could be found supervising white troops. Albert James achieved the rank of corporal and was photographed during the war with some of the men in his unit, all white. Albert lost his wife shortly after the war and remarried, adding three children to his earlier offspring. A family story told with some amusement is that his second wife, Catherine (Cissie), would berate him for being the only soldier in the photograph with his tunic undone, giving him what she thought was a 'scruffy' appearance. Albert's excuse was that he had been woken for the photograph after a particularly gruelling spell of duty.[46]

Albert was more fortunate than Walter Colebourne in that he survived the Great War, but not without the tragedy that conflict in foreign parts a long way from home can bring. Throughout his wartime service, Albert's first wife, Ethel, had written several, sometimes desperate, letters to his unit officer to ascertain his whereabouts. Information was slow in coming, and when the letters were answered, they were usually very formal and hardly ever directly from her husband, for security reasons.[47] On 16 June 1919, Albert received the worst news any soldier serving a long way from home could imagine:

Liverpool Local War Pensions Committee
              and
Soldiers' and Sailors' Families Association
6 Sir Thomas Street
The Officer in Charge of Records,
Records,
Blackheath.

Dear Sir,
                re Gunner – A. James. 75119, R.F.A. A. Battery,
                                    67th Brigade, 10th Irish Brigade
We are anxious to communicate with this man about his two motherless children. We last heard of him being in Egypt, but, as it is possible he may have left there, we should be glad if you will forward the enclosed letter

for us.
Yours faithfully,
R. Pierce
for E.J. Rathbone[48]

Far worse than what Americans would later call a 'Dear John letter', informing a serving soldier in a faraway country that his darling back home had found another, Albert's world had fallen apart. His twenty-five-year-old wife had been taken by the infamous 'Spanish Flu', a pandemic that would eventually have a higher mortality rate than the Great War. While awaiting his arrival home, Albert's sisters took it in turns to look after the hapless children.[49] It had been forecast by some extremist religious groups that the Great War heralded the end of the world. For some, including many of the noble houses of England – and Albert and his two tiny children – it may have seemed true. Albert was finally demobilised on 31 March 1920, long after many had returned home, having taken part in the drawn-out political difficulties following victory in Palestine.

There were other soldiers of African descent fighting on the Middle Eastern Front than Albert James and his British-born and resident British compatriots fighting in the British regular Army. By September 1918, the Turks had been pushed from the Suez Canal to Jaffa on the Mediterranean. The British commander in the Eastern theatre, General Sir Edmund H.H. Allenby, protected his right flank against elements of the Ottoman Fourth Army with the troops of New Zealand Major General Edward W.C. Chaytor, intending to attack the enemy on the western side of the River Jordan, while Chaytor's forces prevented any link up with the Ottoman forces on Allenby's side of the River Amman.

In General Chaytor, the 1st and 2nd Battalions of the British West Indies Regiment (BWIR) had a general with confidence in his black troops and who wished to use them in combat as infantrymen. In Palestine in September 1918 his force's strength consisted of the Australian and New Zealand Mounted Division, the 20th Indian Infantry Brigade, the 38th and 39th battalions of the Royal Fusiliers (both battalions of Jewish soldiers) and the 1st and 2nd battalions of the BWIR.[50] On 19 September 1918,

Allenby's British and French troops attacked Turkish forces on the coastal plane. Chaytor's Force dropped patrolling the west bank of the Jordan Valley for a move against the Turks defending the area of Bakr Ridge, supported by the artillery of the 19th (Maymyo) Mountain Battery of the Indian Army on the afternoon of 19 September. Brigadier General William Meldrum, another New Zealander and the commander of the West Indian force, ordered the 2nd BWIR to attack the ridge to the south of the Bakr feature. Three companies of 2nd BWIR assaulted this ridge under heavy artillery and machine gun fire with only thirty-five West Indian casualties, taking Bakr Ridge early the next day. The 1st BWIR, greatly encouraged by the success of the 2nd Battalion, also advanced in artillery formation under heavy-shell fire and seized Grant Hill and Baghalat.[51]

Two men in the 1st BWIR were awarded Distinguished Conduct Medals for gallantry and devotion to duty during these actions: 503 Lance Corporal R. Turpin, a Trinidadian from La Brea,[52] and 6357 Private H. Scott, a Jamaican from St Ann's Bay. Lance Corporal Turpin had not only run a signal wire some two miles from Musallaheh to Baghalat under heavy fire, but returned four times to repair wire damaged by enemy artillery fire. Private Scott had volunteered to carry a message from Baghalat to Grant Ridge, crossing 700 yards (640 metres) of open ground under very heavy shell fire.[53]

Although putting up a tough fight, the Turks were now retreating with Chaytor's Force hard upon their heels. At Jisr ed Damiye, the Turkish Army forced the New Zealanders of the Auckland Regiment back on 22 September, but the 1st BWIR under Lieutenant Colonel C. Wood Hill, was ordered up to march to the Jordan crossing at once. After an artillery bombardment, the enemy rearguard was broken when the West Indians and New Zealanders charged with their bayonets, each trying to get at the Turks first, a competition of comrades that ended in the West Indians overwhelming the Turks. The crossing was taken when a troop of dragoons of the Auckland Regiment, acting as cavalry, swept through the retreating Turks.[54] Men of the BWIR once again received accolades for gallantry: Sergeant W.E. Julian (1454), from St Georges, Grenada, received the DCM for the action at the Damieh Bridgehead, Jordan Valley, on 22 September 1918, which resulted in the capture of two machine guns and a number of prisoners after reorganising his platoon and leading them with great gallantry over broken ground still occupied by the enemy.[55]

In the Palestinian theatre, soldiers of African descent had at last been given the opportunity to prove their worth as infantrymen on the battlefield. Two commanders, Major General Edward W.C. Chaytor and Brigadier General William (Bill) Meldrum, both New Zealanders, had the foresight to use the troops at their disposal to their maximum effect in a manner at odds with many other British officers more prone to prevailing prejudices. It seems an oddity to the modern mind, but the Caribbean troops of the 1st BWIR and 2nd BWIR battalions were happy to be given the right to fight – and the right to die.

Hostility on British streets

It cannot be taken for granted that black soldiers seen on British streets were always regarded with a fellow feeling by the general public back in the United Kingdom. Like black sailors in the ports, there was a confusion about what constituted an 'alien'. Beaufort Street, just one road in Liverpool's Toxteth area of black settlement, has already been mentioned as the home of a Black Tommy. Private Frank Nelson (23508), who served in a King's Regiment Territorial 'supernumerary' company, also lived in Beaufort Street, described in his papers as 'a coloured man aged 30 years 11 months at enlistment'.[56] He was unfortunate in being the victim of a crime that was becoming increasingly familiar even at such an early stage in the war. The *Liverpool Echo* records:

> Black Soldiers.
>
> Protection From Insult In Liverpool Streets
>
> The stipendiary magistrate made it clear today that black men in Liverpool must not be insulted whilst they are wearing the King's

uniform. He administered a scathing rebuke to a man who had indulged in a practice which of late has become far too common in this city. The accused was Robert Starkey, a well-dressed man, who was charged with having been drunk and disorderly in St. Anne Street, and with assaulting Frank Nelson, a black soldier in the King's Liverpool Regiment.

It is an intolerable thing, said his worship. Here are these coloured men putting on the King's uniform—which is more than some white men will do. A drunken blackguard like you comes along and insults them. The magistrate added that he noticed the prisoner was of military age. Asked what his business was, Starkey said he was a ship's waiter. Well, continued his worship, this is one of the most disgraceful episodes that has come under my notice since the war began. You will go to prison for fourteen days, with hard labour on the first charge, and for twenty eight on the second charge. Prisoner,—"Any chance of a fine, sir?" The Magistrate,—"No."[57]

Sadly, Starkey seems to have successfully appealed the next day and paid a fine of 5 shillings. Although Frank Nelson enlisted in May 1915, he was discharged after only three months in July 1915 since he was 'not likely to become an efficient soldier'.[58] Nelson was thus saved from an even worse fate than the beating he received, in the bloodbath he would have faced in the following years of the war.

Black prisoners of war

Although destined to be the richest black person in Liverpool in the early twentieth century, George Christian, the childhood neighbour of Walter Colebourne, was working as a clerk in the service of the John Holt Shipping Line during the First World War in a different part of the war effort, the merchant marine. His nephew Herbert Gladstone McDavid, named after the great Liberal prime minister William Gladstone, who died on the day he was born in May 1898, joined the 1/10th Battalion of the King's (Liverpool Regiment), the Liverpool Scottish, as a private in June 1916 at the age of eighteen. Although remaining a private for the

5. A group of men of the King's (Liverpool) Regiment and an unknown Black British soldier and woman. (Reproduced by permission of Peter Brydon)

duration of the war, as a member of a remarkably gifted Liverpool Black family, Herbert was to rise to spectacular heights in social terms. Not only was his uncle George to become a millionaire, but Herbert's brother Arthur became captain of the British merchant ship SS *Peleus* in the Second World War, remembered by his white crew affectionately, if not politically correctly, as 'Cocoa Mac' (certainly not within his hearing!). Brother Gordon S. McDavid reached the rank of second engineer before losing his life on 11 January 1942 and receiving a posthumous commendation in the *London Gazette* for 'good service in [SS] *Cyclops*'.[59]

Following his initial training, the young Herbert McDavid was sent to France to join his comrades of the Scottish Regiment, which was destined to play a part in the Somme Offensive only a few weeks later. After a short time at the front, Herbert was captured and sent to a prisoner of war camp in Germany. Undaunted, he learned the German language, which he used to negotiate better conditions for his fellow prisoners after an unsuccessful attempt to escape. The family story that he eventually ended up virtually running the camp is upheld by his receipt of the Meritorious Service Medal, given for exceptional service 'whilst not under enemy fire', at the end of the war. After the war, this astonishing young man went on to rise through the ranks of the John Holt Shipping Line, like his uncle George Christian, becoming director, and eventually general manager, of Glen Line, the London branch of the firm. During the Second World War, Herbert was awarded the CBE for his services to the Normandy landings in 1944 after being seconded to the Ministry of War Transport and later he was to play a part in the family's fortunes by eventually becoming the first Knight of the Realm from the Liverpool black community for services to his country after the Second World War.[60]

Herbert McDavid was mixed-race and very light-skinned and it is likely that his African roots were not recognised by the German prison camp personnel, but another 'black' prisoner mystified his guards, who found him difficult to categorise, despite his dark skin, in an age when race and social rank mattered. Many would be surprised to know that indigenous Australians have served in virtually every conflict since the nineteenth century. Theoretically, non-Europeans were officially barred from serving in Australia's armed forces, but some 500 Aborigines and a few Torres Strait Islanders managed to enlist during the First World War, a situation not dissimilar to variations in the recruitment of soldiers of African descent at this time – to say nothing of the Kings Regulations policy of not commissioning black officers. Like 'black' officers who managed to find their way into the army, sometimes it was a case of their skin being deemed 'white enough'. Some Australian Aborigines arrived home with appalling wounds while others were captured. One such was Private Douglas Grant, 13th Battalion.

After being captured by the Germans, Grant was separated from the other Australian prisoners of war for study by German doctors and anthropologists. As mentioned elsewhere in this study, although in the period of the First World War the race cult was yet to reach the extremes of the years leading up to the Second World War, the eugenics movement was nevertheless exercising an influence upon the thinking of German scientists, medical men and anthropologists. Private Grant shared something of the experience of Herbert McDavid in that he was placed in charge of a camp of black prisoners (as opposed to McDavid's white prisoners), perhaps French colonial or Indian troops, for his German captors were apparently bewildered by his ethnicity despite purporting to be experts on racial issues. When he finally returned to Australia, Douglas Grant involved himself in ex-service affairs but, like many of his fellow Aborigines, was continually frustrated by racism and lack of recognition.[61]

The deploying of black battalions on the Western Front by France had been met with horror and indignation by the Germans, who claimed that this was a violation of military law. The Germans retaliated by shelling black troops of the South African Native Labour Contingent and threatened black troops directly by dropping leaflets warning that they had no right to be involved in a European war and would be treated with special severity. One West Indian soldier, Norman Manley, was destined to become Jamaica's first prime minister and recalled in his autobiography his feelings when he believed that the Germans were about to overrun his detachment's position:

> I loaded my rifle, the rifle I had thought never to use, with care and prepared to sell my life dearly, not in the cliché sense, but for the practical reason that I was half-Negro and the stories of what happened to coloured men taken prisoner of war were very grim and of course believed by all of us implicitly.

In the event, his unit managed to evade the advancing enemy.[62]

Throughout the war, black men from the colonies, United Kingdom residents or British-born were accepted or rejected by the army in a haphazard way, volunteers continuing to be accepted into the ranks as individuals. Several men who served in the British Army were listed by the *Sierra Leone Weekly News*, once again an example of the press helping to identify those with English-sounding names as black servicemen. Four from West Africa or with West African backgrounds mentioned were J. Egerton Shyngle, the son of a Lagos lawyer and a white mother, who served on the Western Front; Patrick Freeman from Freetown, who originally joined the French Navy then enlisted in the British Army, and ended up wounded and sent to recuperate in a hospital in Liverpool; Bob Collier and George Williams, the latter twice wounded and gassed in France.[63]

Since the outbreak of hostilities, the British-born or raised black soldiers attempting, and succeeding, to enlist were joined by many volunteers from the colonies. Black men in the West Indies particularly regarded themselves as free members of the British Empire determined to act out their perceived rights in every way. These displays of patriotism were not welcomed by local island governments, the Colonial Office or the War Office, who took an adverse view, intent on keeping these men in their place, as the historian Glenford Howe says, 'socially, politically, economically and psychologically' as a dependent population.[64] Attempts to dissuade black West Indian patriots from volunteering for the British forces were found to be futile and while waiting for a West Indian contingent to be raised, many sailed to Britain at their own expense. These volunteers would increase the smaller numbers of British-born Black Tommies considerably.

CHAPTER THREE

BLACK VOLUNTEERS – THE EMPIRE AND BEYOND

Since the beginning of hostilities, there had been other black soldiers waiting in the wings to join Black Tommies in the United Kingdom. The men of the British West Indies, Canada, and Britain's African possessions were all a potential source of manpower in her hour of need, but each had their own difficulties to overcome in order to fulfil what for many was a patriotic desire to serve the Mother Country. British-born Black and black volunteer Tommies, not only from the West Indies, but from other parts of the Black Diaspora, were to find themselves bound in a brotherhood based on race, rather than nationality, conjoined by the machinations of the Colonial Office and the War Office. Although the practice of casual dispersing black troops throughout the British Army could be found in operation at the beginning of the war, as it progressed and with the arrival of the British West Indies Regiment (BWIR), some individual British-born or domiciled black soldiers would be placed into homogeneous units of this regiment or other 'coloured' units, such as the Royal Engineers Coloured Section mentioned below. The historian David Killingray comments that it is unlikely that black recruits were always refused, owing to individual recruitment officers being either ignorant of, or disinterested in, policy, not to mention Colonel Abdy, a commissioning officer seen in Chapter Four, who chose to ignore it. This is borne out by the black soldiers recruited in the previous chapter even before the war had begun, such as Mustapha/James Durham, who was formally attested in 1905, and others.

Later inconsistencies in the recruitment of black soldiers in the United Kingdom are difficult to understand without some scrutiny of what was happening in the West Indies. At the beginning of the war, the intransigent War Office resisted the argument for the use of blacks in the war effort, preferring to continue the call for more white soldiers, whether enlisted or, later, conscripted. One of the most bizarre arguments originally put forward was the view that the Germans might object to the use of black soldiers. Even though the Colonial Office shared the prejudices and concerns of the War Office, it was very conscious of the widespread public agitation in the West Indies for a black contingent. While many of Britain's colonies with non-white inhabitants showed loyalty to what had become the 'Mother Country', black reformers in those countries had their own agendas with a long-term vision of what would happen when hostilities finally ceased, the spectre of a more worldly wise, military trained, black population arising before the eyes of the colonial governing bodies. Reformers opposed to crown colony government in the West Indies saw the war as an opportunity to advance the movement for representative government, which was rapidly gaining momentum in the region by the beginning of the war. The war offered opportunities for middle-class Caribbean blacks in their struggle for political and constitutional change. Their protestations of patriotism and their support for the war effort was linked to the grant of the reforms they desired and, increasingly, pressure by the local media and a vocal population caused island governors to petition the British government for participation in the war.[1]

The question of black West Indian volunteers who had come to England through their own efforts had to be dealt with by Colonial Office officials even before the offer of a West Indian contingent was formally made by the West Indian governors. Whilst some were able to gain acceptance into British regiments in a variety of mainly non-combatant roles, others were rejected in spite of a middle-class background in the

West Indies. One example was W.A. Moore, the manager of one of the larger stores in Trinidad, who had paid what was then the large sum of £25 for the privilege of travelling to England only to be rejected by the military authorities on the grounds of his colour. Mystified as to why this should be when others were accepted, he appealed to Colonial Office officials, who were aware of this random approach to acceptance in the armed forces and were undecided as to how to deal with this issue. In Chapter One, Principle Clerk G. Grindle, later Assistant Under Secretary at the Colonial Office by 1916, is seen to have minuted on 21 December 1914 that he had heard that some military officials were prepared to accept black volunteers and felt that this should be discouraged.[2] Although this was not the first time the recruitment of black soldiers had been discussed in governmental offices, this may be a significant communication in the formulation of a policy of enlisting black soldiers into the BWIR when they arrived, without choice, irrespective of whether they were West Indian or British-born, bearing in mind the variability of decisions of individual recruiting officers 'on the day'. The absorption of black recruits into the colonial Caribbean forces would have the effect of making the 'invisible army' of British-born Black and domiciled Tommies even more invisible, with the additional effect of rendering recognition of the notion of Black British by the wider British public more difficult.

One of the difficulties was that black West Indians had undergone a cultural 'brainwashing' over centuries during and following their emancipation from slavery. The names of the descendants of slaves were never those of their original African families. The experience of black slaves in the West Indies and the Americas generally was designed to deprive them of their own language, seen as a way of facilitating rebellion; a family life, as emotional ties through marriages or even permanent relationships made the sale of individuals more difficult; culture, art forms, religion, education and even music, all being seen as understandable by the slave only at the master's expense. The result of this acculturation was that by the First World War, black West Indians had come to see themselves as black Englishmen, in spite of the existence of a hierarchical class system based on race in the Caribbean. Memories of Africa had long disappeared, only to be revived by such leaders and thinkers as Marcus Garvey with his 'Back to Africa' movement and, later in the twentieth century, with the Black Freedom movement sweeping over the Black Diaspora in the United States. West Indians readily rejected any idea of being considered as 'natives', a name they knew only too well to be associated with primitive savages, rather than simply a term denoting birthplace. They were no more native to the Caribbean than their white West Indian fellows, the true natives of the islands, the Caribs and Arawaks, having virtually disappeared.

The Colonial Office was reluctant to take up the matter of the enlistment of British-born Black men into the BWIR with the War Office and opted for suggesting to the governors what the War Office's negative response would probably be. The approach of covertly discouraging the enlistment of local blacks in regular regiments without raising the colour issue was adopted, the governors having to make excuses, citing, for instance, economic reasons.[3] Although shrinking from confrontation with the War Office, in an effort to appease the West Indian public, the Colonial Office communicated to the military authorities the West Indian desire for a contingent overseas on 28 August 1914, only for the idea to be immediately rejected. The issue would not die, however, and the governors again raised the matter in December, the Secretary of State for the Colonies, Lewis Harcourt, suggesting that such a West Indian contingent might be used on the Middle Eastern Front against the Turks. A concession was made by the War Office that a West Indian contingent might be allowed to serve as a peace-keeping force in the territories captured by the Allies in West Africa, but Harcourt and the Colonial Office made the point that this would not fulfil the West Indian desire to fight for the Empire and this peace-keeping role would be resented by the public.[4] While the governmental offices' procrastination dragged on, the volunteers continued to sail, impatient for a solution to their increasingly angry protestations of patriotism and the need for a black West Indian military unit to be added to the war effort.

In some West Indian islands, the government had thought it necessary to restrain newspapers from being disloyal to their society in the Empire's hour of need. As far as much of the black West Indian public was concerned, such fears were hardly appropriate, as even those organisations agitating for better treatment of black subjects rallied to the Allied cause in a way that should have shamed those who were for maintaining oppressive elements in the governance of the West Indies. Black nationalist fraternal organisations, such as the Universal Negro Improvement Association and African Communities (Imperial) League (UNIA-ACL), founded by Marcus Garvey (1887–1940) in August 1914 as a means of uniting all of Africa and its diaspora into 'one grand racial hierarchy', would rise to prominence after the war, but at the beginning of the war, Garvey and his followers sent a resolution to the Colonial Office emphasising:

> That we the members of the Universal Negro Improvement and Conservation Association and African Communities League, assembled in general meeting at Kingston, Jamaica, being mindful of the great protecting and civilizing influence of the English nation and people of whom we are subjects, and their Justice to all men, and especially to their Negro Subjects scattered all over the world, hereby beg to express our loyalty and devotion to His Majesty the King, and Empire and our sympathy with those of the people who are in any way grieved and in difficulty.

Although Garvey was a Jamaican, some British-born Black and early black Empire volunteers resident in the United Kingdom would have been aware of his ideas, as Garvey had lived for a time in England as a young man prior to the war, before returning to Jamaica to found his organisation. He left England on 14 June 1914 aboard the SS *Trent* and reached Jamaica three weeks before the declaration of war.[5] Amongst his contacts in the United Kingdom was Dusé Mohamed Ali, an activist who was certainly an influence upon Garvey's thinking. Ali is thought to have been an Egyptian Sudanese, but this has recently been questioned by researchers, who believe he may have been British-born Black.[6] Black Tommies in the United Kingdom were therefore not entirely isolated from the wider Black Diaspora as it might sometimes seem.

In March 1916, Garvey travelled throughout the United States, inaugurating the New York Division of the UNIA-ACL in 1917. At first it had only thirteen members, but this would soon rise. Near the end of the war, *The Negro World* was founded as a weekly newspaper expressing the organisation's ideas. UNIA-ACL reached the height of its influence in the 1920s, but after Garvey's deportation from the United States its influence was to wane, the organisation splitting in two in 1949.[7]

Private A. Francis, mentioned in Chapter Six as being long domiciled in Britain, is described in an official letter as 'a coloured man who worked in the shipyard at Liverpool, volunteered under the Derby Scheme' and posted to the BWIR because 'great difficulty was found in posting men of colour to ordinary British units', which seems to have been a way of dealing with similar cases.[8] The Derby Scheme, officially called 'the Group Scheme', began very early in the war as a voluntary recruitment policy created in 1915 by Edward Stanley, the 17th Earl of Derby. It was abandoned in December of the same year, however, and was superseded by the Military Service Act in 1916, which introduced conscription. There is no real explanation for the fact that both these policies – allowing some black recruits to sign up for regular British units, while others were effectively barred and consigned to the colonial BWIR – seemed, in some cases, to be running concurrently. This leads perhaps to the conclusion that issues of race were largely dealt with on an *ad hoc* basis, depending on the opinions of the recruiting officer in charge on the day. More will be said about these differences between stated policy and instructions on implementation in a later chapter dealing with the commissioning of black officers. All in all, these inconsistencies and the prevailing racial attitudes of individual recruiting officers meant that black volunteers would meet with varying degrees of success in joining regular army units. Because the Army Service Corps served in an auxiliary role, rather than on the front line, some were enlisted in this unit, whilst others joined infantry regiments, a number even electing to transfer to the BWIR when it finally arrived in Britain.[9]

At the beginning of the war, whilst being the only black recruit or one of few in a unit might have its disadvantages in terms of facing the racist attitudes prevalent at the time, it also had its positive aspects (or at least perceived benefits) in that black soldiers were allowed to carry arms and fight in the same way as their fellows for what they thought of as their 'Mother Country'. Established communities in English ports were not the only source of soldiers of African descent. Isolated black families from other parts of the United Kingdom also played their part. In addition, black volunteers from the Caribbean not only found their way to British ports; some settled and found homes in English towns far from the sea. Lionel Fitzherbert Turpin of British Guiana (now Guyana) was the father of boxers Dick (1920–90) and Randolph Turpin (1928–66), the world middleweight boxing champion. Lionel was disturbed by the delays and the reluctance to allow units of the West India Regiment (the distinction between the WIR and the BWIR being made in Chapter One) to be directly involved in armed combat, in spite of its combat history. His answer was to make his way to Britain where, as an individual recruit, he enlisted in the Royal Warwickshire Regiment. For his pains he almost lost his life after being gassed during the war. Settling in Leamington, Warwickshire, after the end of hostilities, he suffered for some years before dying when his younger son Randolph was nine months old.[10] Lionel is nevertheless remembered as the father of two eminent boxers and the fact that he was a black soldier in the First World War has, once again, come down to us in the course of press and other media pursuing his celebrity children.

Inconsistencies of official policy in the recruitment of black soldiers appear to have continued throughout the war, and in different branches of the armed forces. Two lighter-skinned Jamaicans able to enlist in the Royal Flying Corps (RFC), then a unit in the British Army, were Sergeant L. McIntosh, a former solicitor's clerk who had been sponsored by his employer, and Flight Sergeant W. 'Robbie' Clarke. Sergeant McIntosh became an aerial observer and was injured in a plane crash in 1916. He later became a flying instructor. Flight Sergeant Clarke was also seriously wounded after being shot down over Ypres.[11] However, when Roy Manley and his brother Norman (both light-skinned Jamaicans) attempted to join the same formation, the RFC, Roy's application was refused, while Norman was enlisted in the Royal Field Artillery. These inconsistencies and issues of 'shadism', recurring factors in the recruitment of both men and officers, are discussed more fully in Chapter Four. The Manley brothers had been studying in Britain when they volunteered in 1915. At first, Norman had joined a mounted unit dealing with ammunition supply, as he had grown up with horses and horse-drawn vehicles. Norman Manley, destined to be the first Jamaican prime minister after independence from Great Britain, fought on the Somme and at Ypres, and his twenty-one-year-old brother Roy managed to get himself posted to the battery in which Norman was serving after being wounded. Near the end of 1917, Roy was killed at Ypres in a German bombardment. Norman was demobbed in 1919.[12]

Some volunteers felt themselves to have the social class and physical requirements to apply for enlistment in the elite regiments. Private Harman, a Barbadian, was six feet eight inches tall and wished to join the Life Guards.[13] Egbert Watson, another Jamaican, had enlisted in January 1916 in the Royal Garrison Artillery as a gunner, after settling before the war in Camden Town, London, where he worked as a leather-worker. He served in France for two months before being discharged on medical grounds at the end of 1917 suffering from epilepsy and myalgia.[14] An African American newspaper, the *Indianapolis Recorder*, recorded on 4 April 1915 that a Jamaican, James Slim, had enlisted as a private in the Coldstream Guards. The paper proudly stated, under the heading 'Effects of the European War on Colour Prejudice':

> Before the war [...] it would have been impossible for a negro to join a white regiment in England, let alone one of the proudest and most famous of the crack regiments. The fact of Slim's acceptance is a strong indication of the democratic effects of the war. Slim was in France when the war broke and joined the French foreign legion. Wounded in battle, he was sent to a hospital, where he expressed the wish to join Kitchener's new army. Word was sent to Kitchener, with the result that he was allowed to enroll in the Coldstreams. Slim is now (March 29) training with the reserve battalion at Windsor.[15]

This newspaper might have been surprised to learn that James Slim was certainly not the first black soldier to join a 'white regiment' in England

and perhaps a little disappointed to find that he had not lasted very long in the Coldstream Guards. The historian Richard Smith suggests that his discharge under instructions from the War Office must have been on the grounds of his colour, as his conduct was good and no mention was made of any medical condition.[16]

Facing the enemy

Young West Indians were living in an era when war still held the promise of glory and romance for many, a notion soon to be dispelled as the First World War progressed. Even those recruits who knew that their role in the BWIR was likely to be in a non-combatant capacity were keen to associate themselves with action on the battlefield and tales of daring. Under the caption 'A Native of Falmouth Fought at Chapelle', a photograph of a young black Jamaican, Alonzo Nathan, a volunteer serving in a regular unit of the British Army, appeared in an issue of the Jamaican newspaper, *Daily Gleaner,* in October 1915 with a white comrade beside an article reporting that, having enlisted together, both had been wounded in the Battle of Neuve Chapelle in March 1915 and were now recovering from their wounds in a military hospital in Aldershot. The truth behind the article, drawn from Nathan's letter back home, was somewhat different, as although he appears to have been keen to show himself in a heroic role back home in Jamaica, his service papers show that it was not until the end of August 1915 that he had enlisted in the Army Service Corps (ASC) at Aldershot after serving as a ship's fireman.[17]

The Caribbean arrives

The arrival on British soil of black soldiers from the Empire would have the effect of heightening awareness of issues of race in the British High Command, as did the involvement of the United States. When the British Army rejected the training of African American soldiers after their arrival in late 1917 (some of whom were eventually incorporated into the French Army as combat troops),[18] race had already long been an undercurrent in British military circles.

When the BWIR finally sailed, volunteers from the Caribbean had the opportunity to join their own national force, rather than British regular forces. Alonzo Nathan transferred to the BWIR after its arrival, possibly because he thought it might increase his chances of seeing front-line action. It was not unusual for volunteers who had enlisted before the formation of the BWIR to be posted to the ASC as this was a non-combat unit involved with similar duties of supply and logistic support. Many men, particularly the young, saw themselves directly fighting the enemy; the truth of the daily grind participating in what they considered menial duties often leading to frustration. When confronted by a civilian audience, it was tempting to cast oneself in a heroic role. The Jamaican press was involved in the propaganda machine, actively seeking out soldiers' stories to encourage others by promoting an image of volunteers serving on equal terms with their white comrades. This was closely bound up with notions of nationhood and strengthening the right for an emergent nation-state to make demands from the Mother Country, which, some felt, could lead to eventual independence. One poet living in Jamaica even suggested that Jamaicans making the ultimate sacrifice, dying for the cause, would find immortality, an example to others to respond to the call of the Empire.[19] When the West Indian contingent finally arrived on the Western Front, following the delays mentioned in Chapter One, many young men answered the call of the Empire, believing the stories, such as that of Alonzo Nathan, that had been seized upon by the West Indian press. Although the BWIR was a non-combatant regiment, when moved up to the front, a West Indian soldier could be 'in harm's way' as much as any other Tommy.

It was not unusual for young recruits to lie about their age, few imagining what was in store for them, but some volunteers found the reality too hard to take. Jamaican Private Herbert Morris (7429) was just seventeen when his service ended tragically. He served with the 6th Battalion of the BWIR stationed close to the front line. Raised in Jamaica

6. This photograph of men of the British West Indies Regiment at work, stripped of their formal dress uniform, shows the reality of their wartime service. (Reproduced by permission of © Crown Copyright. IWM)

between November 1916 and March 1917, the battalion's duty was to service a battery of eighty-pound guns at 'Essex Farm' near Poperinghe in the Ypres Salient. In the course of fifteen days preceding the main Allied thrust on 31 July, 2,297 British guns fired over four million shells, an enormous barrage four times the size of that fired prior to the attack on the Somme. Morris's battalion suffered daily casualties as the Germans responded, adding to the hellish cacophony. A local Catholic priest commented that the West Indians were often bewildered and disorientated during the shelling, which is confirmed by Alfred Horner, one of Morris's comrades who had joined the battalion at the beginning of September and claimed that the full range of German 'heavies' made day and night alike a terror to all. Faced with such a horrific experience, the young West Indian went absent without leave, only to be given fourteen days' field punishment after being picked up at Boulogne. His fears were not imaginary, as he absconded again on 20 August having seen seven of his comrades become casualties, this time by jumping from the lorry returning him to his battery. There was no escape, however. Morris was arrested again whilst trying to enter a rest camp without authorisation, and pleaded at his subsequent court martial, 'I am troubled with my head and cannot stand the sound of the guns. I reported to the Dr. and he gave me no medicine or anything'. Although obviously showing signs of 'shell shock', the court did not attempt to adjourn the case for medical reports, relying instead on character witnesses who claimed that he was of a general nature, no trouble, a willing worker and of above average intelligence.

Morris was found guilty of desertion and after the subsequent death sentence was confirmed by Field Marshall Haig, he was made an example of and paraded in front of the battalion. On the morning of 20 September 1917 Herbert Morris was executed by a firing squad composed of seven West Indians and three white soldiers. He had dictated a letter to Padre Horner for his parents,[20] William and Ophelia Morris of Riversdale P.O., St Catherine, Jamaica, and is buried in Grave II F 45 at Poperinghe New Military Cemetery, Belgium.[21] Morris was one of the youngest soldiers to be executed, and it is possible that the board had no idea as to his age, though they might not have bothered to note it.

There were others who did not give their true age. George Blackman served in the 4th Battalion, exchanging the shores of the Caribbean for the mud and gore of the battlefields of the Western Front. Like many young men all over the Empire, the seventeen-year-old George lied about his age to the recruiting officer. In an interview with journalist Simon Rogers of the *Guardian* in 2002, then aged 105, speaking in patois he recalled, 'Lord Kitchener said with the black race, he could whip the world. We sang songs, "Run Kaiser William, run for your life, boy"'.

Kitchener's private views on black soldiers at the front alongside white soldiers were very different from the image suggested by George Blackman's interview, but the intervention of King George V in the face of enormous losses made the use of black colonial troops inevitable. George Blackman emphasised the prevalent widespread enthusiasm: 'We wanted to go. Because the island government told us that the king said all Englishmen must go to join the war. The country called all of us'.²²

Eugent Clarke, another BWIR veteran, at the age of 105, was one those who lived to received France's Légion d'honneur in 1999 for meritorious service in the First World War. Due to the dominance of German U-boats in parts of the Atlantic, Clarke remembered his ship putting into Halifax in Nova Scotia, where many of his BWIR comrades experienced snow and frostbite for the first time. No thought had been given to moving the men from the tropics to Europe in the middle of winter and this oversight led to illness and fatalities as, dressed in tropical lightweight khaki uniforms, the West Indians were not allowed to use the heavier weight uniforms of the British soldiers stored aboard ship until the loss of half of the battalion. One of the 200 lucky survivors, Clarke was sent to Bermuda to convalesce before finally arriving in Europe. Conditions there were not much better. Digging trenches, carrying supplies to the frontline and hard labour, all continued to suffer from severe weather conditions, frostbite, measles and mumps. Over ten thousand had left Jamaica in the BWIR; one thousand never returned to their place of birth.²³ Frederick Chandler, a white veteran of the Great War still alive in the 1980s, told the historian Jeffrey Green that he had seen West Indian soldiers near Béthune in France 'freezing' in the winter of 1917.²⁴

The incident of hundreds of soldiers succumbing to severe frostbite as a result of army bungling, as winter uniforms had been left locked up leaving them to freeze in thin summer clothes, were not their only troubles. Upon arriving at the Western Front, the BWIR were assigned to labouring duties, although certainly in the line of fire from the enemy. Climate and conditions remained a constant problem to the West Indians. George Blackman complained: 'It was cold. And everywhere there were white lice. We had to shave the hair there because the lice grow there. All our socks were full of white lice'.

Nevertheless, some Caribbean soldiers seem to have been involved in actual combat in France. BWIR soldiers sometimes found themselves in the position of fighting off enemy attacks, one group fighting off a

German assault with the only weapons in their possession – knives they had brought from home. Although Caribbean troops were not officially supposed to be engaged in combat, contemporary photographs show black soldiers armed with British Lee Enfield rifles and oral accounts from veteran soldiers such as George Blackman tell another story. He remembered taking part in trench fights alongside white soldiers:

> 'They called us darkies, [...] but when the battle starts, it didn't make a difference. We were all the same. When you're there, you don't care about anything. Every man there is under the rifle. [...] The Tommies said, "Darkie, let them have it." I made the order: "Bayonets, fix," and then "B company, fire." You know what it is to go and fight somebody hand to hand? You need plenty nerves. They come at you with the bayonet. He pushes at me, I push at he. You push that bayonet in there and hit with the butt of the gun – if he is dead he is dead, if he live he live.' [...] George Blackman leaps up, brandishing his walking stick. 'Like this,' he breathes, imitating the thrust of a bayonet. 'Like that,' he says, mimicking the butt of the rifle. 'I still got the action. I'm old now, but I still got the action [...].' He points to a scar above his left eyebrow. 'That is a bayonet cut on the eye.' He touches his hands. 'This is from the blow of the rifle butt.'
>
> The West Indies Regiment experienced racism from the Germans as well as the British. 'The Tommies, they brought up some German prisoners and these prisoners were spitting on their hands and wiping on their faces, to say we were painted black,' says Blackman.
>
> He didn't make friends. 'Don't have no friend. A soldier don't got friends. Know why? You believe that you are dead now. Your friend is this: the gun. That is your friend.'[25]

By no means all the First World War black volunteers in the British Army were originally from the Caribbean. Nor were they of the same social class any more than their white fellows, as mentioned earlier. Charles Alexander F. Calvert was a 'Cape Coloured' from South Africa and not only seemed to be well-educated, but also well connected. After the war, Calvert wrote to Harriette Colenso, the daughter of John William Colenso, the first Anglican Bishop of Natal. His letter was sent on to her sister and annotated with the words, 'From a half Bantu half

Irish Cape boy – such a nice fellow – was in the "Imperial" Army in War (R. Artillery) & has been studying engineering'. In his letter, he wrote that he planned to return to South Africa, sailing for the Cape in autumn 1922.[26] Calvert was not in the Royal Artillery, in fact, but had been a private in the Machine Gun Corps (service number 10858). He was enlisted on 17 June 1915 and discharged on 5 October 1919, his incident report listing only sickness. He received the three medals sometimes irreverently called by veterans Pip, Squeak and Wilfred: the Victory Medal, also called the Inter Allied Victory Medal was awarded to all who received the 1914 Star or 1914–15 Star and, with certain exceptions, to those who received the British War Medal. It was never awarded alone.[27] Calvert attended the University of Loughborough Department of Engineering after the war, perhaps another indication of his social class, and appears in a class photograph of 1922.[28]

Another South African volunteer was Melrose Goda Sishuba (c. 1893–1964). Volunteers who came directly from the African continent generally present less difficulty of identification than black soldiers of Caribbean ancestry who are likely to possess English-sounding names, but this is not always the case. Mixed-race Cape Coloured also had European names and during the nineteenth century particularly it was not unusual for Africans to adopt European names as a token of their conversion to Christianity, often the name of the missionary who converted them. Born in Eastern Cape, Melrose Goda Sishuba was the son of a missionary of the African Methodist Episcopal Church, possibly the Rev. Isaiah Goda Sishuba, head of the church at Queenstown in the United States. Melrose sailed to New York for an American education in 1910 as a student at the Roger Williams University, Nashville, Tennessee, but volunteered to fight for the British, serving in the South Lancs. Regiment as Private 48178 from 1914 to 1918.[29] After the war, Sishuba returned to the US, the African American newspaper *California Eagle* reporting a 'stereopticon lecture' (a lecture aided by a 'magic lantern', a sort of projector) given by him at St Andrews Church on 13 November 1923, no doubt one of many in the United States.[30] He lived in the US from 1919 to 1929, returning to South Africa to become one of the leaders of the Ethiopian Church of

South Africa and was later involved in the Cushian Church,[31] as well as being active in the African National Congress in the Eastern Cape.

Frederick Njilima was from Malawi, then colonial Nyasaland. Perhaps rather paradoxically in view of his own allegiances, he was the son of Duncan Njilima, a rebel against British rule who was hanged by the colonial authorities for his part in the Chilembwe rising in Nyasaland in 1915. Originally, Frederick had received an education in the United States, but travelled to England to continue his studies at Cambridge not long after the outbreak of war. Visiting London and, to use his own words, 'struck by war fever, I decided to join the white war!' He changed his name to Frederick Graham (96624) and enlisted in the Irish Rifles. After training in Winchester and Nottingham, Njilima joined the 150th Battalion, Machine Gun Corps, at Ypres and was wounded near Reims on 27 May 1918. After months in a Cambridge hospital, he was awarded the Military Medal and repatriated to Nyasaland at the end of the war with a twenty per cent disability pension.[32]

West African volunteers include the Nigerian father and uncle of the British-born footballer Roy Brown, Eugene and John Brown (Roy Brown was a teammate of Stanley Matthews at Stoke City in the late 1930s). Eugene and John served in the 5th North Staffordshire Regiment having originally come to Britain to attend college. Roy's father Eugene was killed in action, while his uncle John ended his war days in hospital.[33] Eugene's other son, Douglas, was to became the first black mayor of Stoke on Trent in 1983.[34]

Whilst the *Manual of Military Law* tended to lump 'Negroes &c.' with 'aliens',[35] there were, in addition to British-born, domiciled Black Tommies and volunteers from the Empire, some genuine 'aliens' from non-British countries. One of the strangest to enlist in His Majesty's Forces was African American Joseph Howard Lee, born in Baltimore in 1887, a travelling entertainer, vaudeville artist and lecturer, who chose to be known by the African name Bata Kindai Amgoza Ibn LoBagola. A somewhat unwholesome if colourful character, he appears to have voluntarily adopted the status of 'alien' in his home country and modified his racial origins and life story throughout his life. He claimed to have been born a black Jew in West Africa who ran away from home, finding his way to Glasgow as a small boy in 1896,[36] but no evidence has been found to substantiate his Scottish childhood. Having enlisted in the US Army on 3 August 1918 as an alien in the US, which he was not, LoBagola now applied for naturalisation, which was granted. LoBagola lasted only five weeks with the US Army before being 'honourably discharged' under somewhat unsavoury circumstances. LoBagola's discharge was not the end of his military career. Within a very short time he enlisted in the British Army under his adopted name in a Jewish Regiment as, following the Balfour Declaration, a British recruiting office in New York City had begun enlisting Jewish recruits for the 38th, 39th and 40th battalions of the Royal Fusiliers.

LoBagola claimed that it was his rejection as a black Jew which caused the social isolation that would lead him to his later conversion to the Roman Catholic Church. When things began to go wrong, LoBagola blamed his stay in the Tanta Roman Catholic School for the heavy drinking that would blight his later life and once more went on his travels, first to Cairo for a time, West Africa and later to New York in early 1925.[37]

Australian Aborigines are mentioned in the previous chapter, but there were other non-African groups deemed 'black', sometimes with uncertainty, by the various colonial European administrations. Pacific Ocean groups, including the Polynesians, the Maoris of New Zealand being the most well known, and South Sea islanders such as the Fijians, were also amongst volunteers. George Betts, a private in the 312 Brigade of the Royal Field Artillery Regiment remembered a Fijian volunteer in his unit during the war. Although unable to remember his name, he recollected an unlucky incident that occurred when the men were relaxing around a camp fire one evening. 'There were four or five blokes squatting around the fire waiting for their chips to cook in an old petrol tin when a discarded rifle round concealed beneath the fire, detonated'. The Fijian was struck in the leg, from which 'blood spouted out like a tap'.

Possibly the only Fijian artilleryman to be accused of a self-inflicted wound, he was never charged or convicted, according to George Betts, but was certainly confined to a hospital for self-inflicted wounds.[38] The fact that the Fijian escaped punishment shows that the circumstances in which his injury was sustained showed the lack of feasibility of his wound being engineered. It was not unheard of for soldiers faced with death or permanent disability to shoot or otherwise injure themselves in the hope of being sent home with what was known as a 'blighty wound'. Those found guilty of such self-inflicted wounds (SIW) could theoretically face execution by firing squad, but none of the 3,894 men in the British Army convicted of SIW appear to have been executed, serving prison sentences instead.[39] Gunner George Betts does not appear to be wrong in thinking that his Fijian comrade was placed in a special hospital for those with self-inflicted wounds, for a soldier in another unit was suspected of SIW after being shot by mistake by his own men. Puzzled to find himself the only casualty in an ambulance car, after arriving at the 39th Casualty Clearing Station he found that none of the nursing staff appeared friendly, particularly the matron. He discovered that he had been classed as a suspected SIW case. Unknown to him, 'SIW?' had been written on the label attached his chest.[40]

A unique British-raised unit

As the war progressed, race consciousness on the part of the British authorities seems to have increased, spreading to the British-born Black community and Caribbean troops who had volunteered before the arrival of formally raised units of their countrymen. The Royal Engineers Coloured Section is quite unique, in that this unit was a homogeneous 'coloured' unit raised in the United Kingdom, rather than overseas, and yet appears to have endured all the difficulties experienced by West Indian and African units. The men of the Royal Engineers Coloured Section were enlisted into the Inland Water Transport and Docks Section to be employed as crane drivers, clerks, motor boat drivers and as part of ships crews. Sent to Mesopotamia under Captain D.J. Marriot, RE as a single draught, the unit comprised 224 men taken on strength on 31 December 1916, returning to the United Kingdom in April 1918.

In order to develop transport on canals and waterways of France and Belgium, the Inland Water Transport and Docks Section of the Royal Engineers formed in December 1914 was originally operated under the Director of Railways, but by October 1915 had its own directorate to deal with the rapid development of Inland Water Transport. The Inland Water Transport Directorate was responsible for all non-transport work in Mesopotamia by the summer of 1916 and the following year its scope was extended to cover Inland Water Transport and Dock Working in Egypt, Salonika and other theatres of war. By the end of the war, some 42,000 workers from India, Egypt, West Africa and China supplemented Europeans and, it would seem, black personnel recruited in the United Kingdom and British Honduras. During 1917, over 600 officers and 8,000 men were drafted overseas to theatres of war and by the end of the year some 1,100 officers and nearly 30,000 men were serving in the Inland Water Transport Section.[41]

The following letter to the Colonial Office, quoted verbatim, is from the unit described as 'the Royal Engineers Coloured Section'. Although it is clear that the men were originally seafarers from British ports, it would seem that they were from those colonial countries already providing homogeneous units. This is also borne out to some degree by the language in which the writer expresses himself (mistakes remain uncorrected), but some may have been British-born:

Mesopotamia Expeditionary Force
Royal Engineers Coloured Section
13th Division
Marquil Depot
Mesopotamia
29th January 1918.

Dear sir in sincere honour

We have hereby taken the prividge of writing you, whereby we have asked your apology for not knowing you personally but we have known your authority, office and honour, and on only you can we state our grievances to, Sir, we humbly ask, please to take our troubles in great earnest, which we are going to relate to you, as we afore said its only you we call on, and please you may represent us to your abilities, as all things lie in your power.

Its true we have not born in England, but shall always boast on ourselves as true British subjects and have volunteered ourselves to serve King and Country but please note sir, when we have first enlisted in the Army in Cardiff, Liverpool, Manchester, and various towns in England we told the recruiting masters that we are all seafaring men and would do our bit in the Inland Waterways Transports. Who then promised to give us 3 shillings a day as soon as we should get overseas.

Luckily we leave Sandwich Kent our training Depot for Mesopotamia, where Thank God we had arrived in safety on the 31st December 1916. Where the first thing or action grieved us, all our officers that came out with us were sent away in different regiments and units leaving the Coloured sections only with Lance Corporals to represent us, where all advantages are now taken on us, and only giving us for pay 1s 21/4 pence per day, and have changed our ranks from sappers when we were in England to pioneers and Coloured labour section where as all other Indian labourers are contracted men for a fixed salary, and even the Infantry Men are getting more than us. When we asked to see the General They wont allow us, when we asked an officer to petition for us they refused us also, we are not allowed to go nowhere, whilst the rest of the soldiers are at privilidge to go, in case we write letter its torn up and out of the 1 shilling 2d ¼ farthing when ever we goes to draw fortnightly 3 or 4 rupees are stopped by the pay Master, and all of us are employed in skillful jobs and when night is nigh, there is no books, Chest Boards, or even a pack of cards to pass the time away, and the food we gets is most miserable, we only get 1 loaf a bread daily, 1 tin of Bully Beef and a drink of tea every days meal, and We no knows that lofts of goods gifts been always sent out but we are not receiving anything.

Dear Sir, our grievances are so great that we have partly [?] driven to dispair. The megarity of us are married men leaving six-pence a day for wifes allowance and have received our letters that they are not receiving it and that money is always being stopped from us out here, and we does not believe that is the way a poor soldier should be treated who has left his home far away came to England in ships to maintain our families who have no other to depend on, and yet we have deprived ourselves from Bread and our families to serve our King and countrys cause and yet for all we are treated worst than the Turkish prisoners. Pardon me sir, we know that there are many evil carrying on an oppression to soldiers out here, what you all does not know about, and are innocent and would not allow it only get to your notice, but they have kept us so prison like and tear all our letters in suspicion, and promised even to shoot a man who writes to any representative. We know that there are lots of coloured men serving in the Navy and admiralty ships where in we would promise to fulfil our duty and are much more capable of seafairing than soldiering or manual labouring for one reason to be near our Colonial homes where we can send better aids to our poor families and for better health. Please sir may you grant us the pleasure of interceeding for us whilst we obediently awaits your answer as it lies in your grace and always be faithful comrades, obedient and humble servants.

The Coloured Sections and suffering Pioneers
Marquil Depot
Mesopotamia[42]

Many of these men would have been from British Honduras, as a large part of the 534 men serving with the Honduran Contingent joined the Mesopotamia Inland Water Transport corps on the Tigris.[43] Before the war, British Honduras had been a wealthy colony supplying timber and fruits. When the volunteer force of one officer and 128 men was called for military service,[44] the governor's concern that they might encounter difficulties in a cold climate[45] led to the rejection in October 1916 of the men being sent to France to join a labour battalion. Sending some of the Hondurans under Lieutenant Furness overseas with the BWIR and others accompanying The Inland Water Transport Corps to the Middle East[46] was certainly in line with the king's suggestion to use black troops from the general Caribbean area (British Honduras being on the Central American shore of the Caribbean Sea) to Egypt and Palestine.[47] A further contingent of 406 men and four officers was sent to the front in July 1916.[48]

As this unit was largely raised in the ports of the United Kingdom, it was not impossible for British-born Black soldiers to find their way into this unit. At this time, the notion of black people born in Britain was not widely recognised. In the first year of the war, a private of the Oldham Pals or Lancashire Fusiliers might perhaps have viewed the isolated Black Tommy on the Western Front with an interested curiosity, but by the end of 1915, the numbers of British-born and domiciled soldiers of African descent, including the early Caribbean volunteers to regular regiments, would be added to considerably by the arrival in the United Kingdom of whole units of black soldiers from the West Indies, a situation that would be a game-changer for British-born Black soldiers and earlier volunteers. The arrival of the BWIR would have a greater impact on the British-born and domiciled Black Tommy than any other black group from the dominions. The Liverpool-born Black merchant George Christian, mentioned earlier in Chapter Two, had a similar problem to those enlisted men finding themselves placed in West Indian units, when trading in the Cameroons before the war. The German authorities tried to treat him as a 'native' and fined and eventually expelled him for not registering a title to land. George managed to enlist the support of the MP for Toxteth, Robert Houston, who had the Foreign Office appeal to Berlin, complaining that although George was, indeed, 'a mulatto', he was a British subject and should not be treated as a German colonial subject.[49]

Although the members of the Royal Engineers Coloured Section in the letter above clearly stated that they had not been born in the United Kingdom, the sight of Black Tommies, some British-born, others domiciled for some years in British ports were becoming far more familiar to the British public as the Empire responded to the call of king and country. It would later seem that the apparent 'swallowing up' of British-born and resident Black Tommies by the BWIR might suggest the end of the image of the lone Black Tommy, but, as in the case of the pioneers of the Coloured Section, their voice would still be heard even after the war had been won. In Chapter Six we hear the voice of Private A. Francis, who had been forcefully enlisted in the BWIR, complaining that his pension rights had been violated owing to veterans of the BWIR being paid a lesser amount, a battle he fought and won.

Many men seem to have continued to be rejected because of their colour throughout the war, but many are seen to have succeeded in enlisting nevertheless. Constant variables were the attitude of individual recruiting officers and the skin shade of the recruit.[50] In Liverpool, the home of Britain's oldest and possibly largest black community at the time, to name just a few, West Derby Cemetery houses the grave of R. Cole (15801), who died in July 1918, and Anfield Cemetery those of W. Clarke (15720) and Edwin Ebenezer Facey (15813), who both died in November 1917. And graves of black colonial soldiers are not only to be found in such ports as Liverpool. In Seaford Sussex Cemetery is the grave of Private Harold Grubb (2239), aged eighteen. They are all listed as men of the BWIR, but the identities of Black Tommies born and bred in the United Kingdom for generations, those who settled before the war began, and those from the Empire who answered the call even before the forces of their home countries were officially raised, would mingle. The possible transfer or direct enlistment of British-born Black soldiers into the BWIR make it difficult in some cases for the researcher to establish who is who and where they originally came from. Cemeteries all over Great Britain are likely to hold graves of soldiers who fell in the Great War whose Black British families were lucky enough to have their bodies repatriated and are now to be found lying not only alongside the early black recruits who joined them in the UK at the beginning of the conflict, but with later soldiers of the BWIR. During the course of the First World War, besides Caribbean troops, there would be further arrivals of men of African descent, Canadians, Bermudans and an African labour force, all willing to play their part.

CHAPTER FOUR

BLACK OFFICERS, WHITE SOLDIERS

During the First World War, colonial African troops and those of the West India Regiments have been shown to have served under white officers nearer the apex of the command chain, with black non-commissioned officers occupying other positions. Although British-born Black servicemen raised in United Kingdom regiments seemed to have been in a similar position to their colonial cousins, it would appear that during the First World War some very small inroads were being made into the commissioning of officers of African descent, intended or otherwise. Moreover, those officers, though few in number, would be leading European troops.

In recent years, Second Lieutenant Walter Tull has often been credited as the first black officer in the British Army. Daniel Tull, his father, was the son of a black slave in Barbados. In 1876, Daniel came to Folkestone and married Alice Palmer, a local white woman. Walter was one of six children, but was left an orphan at the age of ten when his parents died within two years of each other. His mother died in 1895 and was soon followed by his father, who had already remarried, with Alice's cousin Clara. When he had first arrived in the United Kingdom, Daniel had joined the local Methodist church, which now came to the relief of his struggling widow by arranging for a Methodist orphanage in London's Bethnal Green to take care of the boys.[1]

Having served an apprenticeship as a printer after leaving school, Walter's passion for football led to him being spotted by a talent scout for Tottenham Hotspur while playing in Clapton in 1908. His initial experiences were not good. In 1909 Bristol City fans jeered and cat-called Tottenham's first black outfielder to the extent that both Walter and his team were traumatised for the remainder of the season.[2] He never got fully into the rest of the season and was sold the following year to Northampton Town, where he became a firm favourite. Walter played over a hundred times for the first team, who recognised the young player's star quality.[3]

At the outbreak of the war, instead of taking an opportunity to sign for Glasgow Rangers, Walter joined the 17th (1st Football) Battalion of the Middlesex Regiment, commanded by Major Frank Buckley, a Boer War veteran and an ex-Manchester United and Aston Villa player who later became famous as the stern disciplinarian manager of Wolverhampton Wanderers.[4] The 17th and 23rd battalions of the Middlesex Regiment were made up of players who would have known, or even played against, each other, so Walter was less likely to be amongst strangers. In May 1916, however, Walter suffered from post-traumatic stress syndrome and was sent home to recuperate. He returned to France fully recovered on 20 September, in time to take part in the Battle of the Somme, July–November 1916. By Boxing Day, he was back in England, his period of duty completed, but did not return to his unit, instead being sent to Scotland to begin training for a commission as an officer on 6 February 1917.[5] It would seem that his superiors were prepared to break the rules for him as this was clearly against Army Regulations. The *Manual of Military Law* of 1914 clearly forbade black or mixed-race officers leading Europeans in the British Army:

> Commissions in the Special Reserve of Officers are given to qualified candidates who are natural born or naturalised British subjects of pure European descent.[6]

Walter Tull was commissioned as a second lieutenant in May 1917, later serving in Italy, where he was mentioned more than once in dispatches

7. Second Lieutenant Walter Tull, often erroneously credited with being the only Black British officer in the First World War. (With kind permission of the Walter Tull Archive, part of the Finlayson Family Archive)

for 'gallantry and coolness' under fire. Once back in France, fighting this time with the 23rd (2nd Football) Battalion of the Middlesex Regiment, he led from the front once more in the second Battle of the Somme. Near the end of the war, Walter was shot early in the advance while leading part of an attack on the German trenches at Favreuil. He was almost killed instantly by a bullet in the head.[7] In the British Army it was normal for the men to try not to leave their fallen comrades on the field of battle, if it could be helped, but, it was also a point of honour for units not to leave the bodies of their officers on the battlefield. Despite crushing machine gun fire, Leicester Fosse goalkeeper Private T. Billingham and another man bravely attempted to recover Walter's body without success. Walter

Tull was destined to become one of the many brave soldiers recorded as missing in action. Today his name is listed on the Arras Memorial in the Faubourg d'Amiens Cemetery, on the Boulevard du Général de Gaulle, in the western part of the town of Arras.[8]

Given the heart-wrenching task of writing to Walter's brother of his death, his commanding officer commented on the popularity of Walter throughout the battalion and his bravery and commitment, ending with words he did not have to add to the usual tortuous letter of commiseration to the family of the fallen: 'and personally I have lost a friend'.[9]

Walter Tull has been described as the first, and sometimes the only, black officer in the First World War, but, however worthy he may have been as an individual, there are other contenders. It might be argued that some other officers of African descent were 'not truly black' being very light-skinned mixed-race, but then so was Walter Tull, though his African ancestry may have been more recognisable than some others. In that class-conscious age, it is also possible that Walter's lowly origins were more likely to cause him to be associated with the placement of blackness on the social scale in a way that mixed-race officers higher on the social scale may not have been, their origins politely ignored, or at least not commented upon, by their upper-class peers.

Since the beginning of the transatlantic slavery period, a social hierarchy had developed in the West Indian islands, North America and other parts of the African Diaspora, based on the shade of a person's skin. Female slaves were at the mercy of their wealthy owners, who often took advantage of them and fathered children. The mixed-race offspring, if recognised by their fathers, sometimes came to occupy an intermediate social position, particularly following the abolition of slavery, between the descendants of the ruling white classes and the black under-caste of former slaves.[10] Further racial mixing often resulted in individuals who were hard to categorise even by those determined to adhere to the strict racist social codes relating to perceived acceptable interactions between black and white. This social system based on a segregated society reached its height first in the United States of America with its strict 'passing' laws of the early twentieth century[11] and much later in South Africa, also under a European hegemony, where the infamous Apartheid system in which mixed-race people were classified as 'coloured', a separate class between black and white.

It would seem that at the onset of the First World War, public perceptions of race were such that one was extremely unlikely to find an officer of African ancestry, however diluted, in the British Army on the Western Front, but not impossible. It did happen – by bending the rules, so to speak, through commissioning officers 'turning a blind eye' to regulations, or light-skinned individuals applying for commissions, taking the initiative themselves and 'passing', as it was known in the United States: pretending to be wholly white in the hope that nobody would notice that they had what was pejoratively referred to in those days as 'a touch of the tar-brush'. Obtaining a commission by these means was not unknown, but there is yet another factor that could impinge upon the success of black or, more likely, mixed-race applicants – social class. A non-military example is Andrew Watson (1857–1921), a mixed-race civilian born in Demerara, British Guiana and widely considered to be the world's first black association footballer to play at international level. Capped three times for Scotland between 1881 and 1882, Andrew Watson was the son of a wealthy Scottish sugar planter, Peter Miller Watson, and a local Black British Guianese woman named Anna Rose. He was educated at King's College School in Wimbledon, London, and later studied natural philosophy, mathematics and engineering at the University of Glasgow. The fact that Andrew Watson was from a wealthy middle-class family seems to have allowed him a degree of social mobility denied to other black and mixed-race people living in less fortunate circumstances. He does not appear to have experienced much prejudice from his peers or from the Scottish football Association.[12] Similar experiences to this late nineteenth-century black civilian can be found amongst military men and serve to show the impact of class and position on social acceptance and that, perhaps more surprisingly, social class could occasionally be as important as race at that time.

Nevertheless, social status alone could not always be relied upon, as many middle-class black professionals who sought commissions in the army would discover, and some found strategies to deal with this prejudice. Governor Manning of Jamaica gave the Jamaican government veterinary officer G.O. Rushdie-Gray his official blessing and six weeks' paid leave to travel to England on the official understanding that he would be accepted as an officer. Although Rushdie-Gray had previously served as a vet to the West India Regiment (WIR) and had impressive credentials, he was refused a commission in the Army Veterinary Corps. Rushdie-Gray was offered veterinary employment in the civilian sector by the Colonial Office and War Office and, more enthusiastically, a paid return passage home. It seems clear that Rushdie-Gray was considered too dark; correspondence between the Colonial Office and the Veterinary Department of the War Office suggests that he may have been accepted had he been of a lighter shade:

> Mr Gray called today, he is presentable, but black [...] I am surprised at the Gov[ernor] recommending a black man without previously informing us of his colour. I have spoken to the Veterinary Dept of WO and understand that there is no absolute bar against coloured men for commissions in the Vet. Corps, but that they did not expect Mr G to be the colour he is.[13]

The interpretation of a recruiting officer or an interviewing board could determine a man's acceptance into the ranks, or whether he was offered a commission. Some white individuals tried hard to champion the cause of young black candidates seeking commissions in the army, an example being a Mr H.S. Cox who maintained a lengthy correspondence with the Royal Military Academy at Sandhurst and the War Office in an effort to secure a place on an officer training course for 'a young British West Indian subject [...] a public school boy, twenty years of age, and a good athlete, but he is not of pure European descent which is apparent by his colour'.

The War Office also applied this rule of 'unmixed European blood' to British West Indies Regiment (BWIR) officers, the benchmark being whether an applicant 'looked coloured'.[14] One Colonial Office official minuted in December 1915 that some Trinidadians of the Merchant's

Contingent accepted by the United Kingdom Officer Training Corps (OTC) were 'practically white men', while a later minute made the plea, 'I trust that the Governors won't interpret the [White officers only] decision so strictly as to exclude sixteenth and thirty-seconds'.[15] The official was referring here to the fraction of Sub-Saharan African blood in an applicant's lineage.

The colonial official writing that minute was only too aware of the current thinking on racial matters. During the war, the eugenicist Madison Grant commented in *The Passing of the Great Race* that:

> The cross between a white man and an Indian is an Indian; the cross between a white man and a Negro is a Negro; the cross between a white man and a Hindu is a Hindu; and the cross between any of the three European races and a Jew is a Jew.[16]

Grant was, of course, subscribing to the 'one-drop rule' behind the American Passing Laws, which meant that any person with 'one-drop of Negro blood' was considered black. The colonial official knew that the governors were likely to exercise the principle of 'hypodescent', the assignment of children of a mixed union of different socioeconomic or ethnic groups to the group with the lower social standing.[17] Between 1910 and 1924, the 'one-drop rule' was adopted as law in several American states, first in Tennessee and last in Virginia under the Racial Integrity Act of 1924.[18]

Shadism in the Black Diaspora was not restricted to mainland North America. The British West Indies had also developed its own racial hierarchy based on skin shade as a legacy of the slave trade. In her study of present-day attitudes towards skin colour among young black women, JeffriAnne Wilder found that light skin is still viewed as ideal and of the most value, shaping the belief in an individual's behaviour and attractiveness; while women with light skin are viewed as pretty, girls with dark skin are seen as 'ghetto'.[19] The effects of shadism go far beyond mere fashion considerations: an individual's skin-tone could have a bearing on educational and job market outcomes whether male or female. Although Aaron Gullickson believed that shadism was less in evidence after the

1940s,[20] this factor was certainly an issue during the First World War and beyond in most of the English-speaking Black Diaspora and a factor not only in the commissioning of black officers, but also the recruitment of black men.

GEORGE EDWARD KINGSLEY BEMAND

George Edward Kingsley Bemand (1892–1916) came to Britain on the *Lusitania* in 1908 at the age of sixteen. The fact that he is recorded as 'African' in the 'race or people' column of the passenger list would not normally be discernible in the passenger lists of British vessels, but a record of his race appears because his journey with his mother and brother Harold was not direct from the West Indies, where George junior was born, but via the United States, where the recording of race was much more salient than in British territories.[21]

Born at 3 Musgrave Avenue, Kingston, Jamaica,[22] George's father appears to have been white, living between the United Kingdom and Jamaica. After arriving in England, the now reunited family lived at 26 Woodville Road, Ealing by the time of George's admission to school. George Bemand had a good education, attending Dulwich College in South London and later studying engineering at University College, London in 1913. After joining the University of London OTC in November 1914, in May 1915 he applied for a commission in the 30th (County Palatine) Divisional Royal Field Artillery.[23]

Despite George's relatively affluent background, compared with Walter Tull, the spectre of prevalent aspects of race crops up again, a sad reminder of the 'shadism' derived from the racial hierarchy of the time. George's application form for a temporary commission in the regular army is revealing. When the form signed by Bemand on 7 May 1915 asked 'Whether of pure European descent,'[24] George answered 'Yes', in spite of his appearance in the photograph used in the Dulwich College War Record 1914–19 and comments in other records, such as the *Lusitania* passenger lists. He was very light-skinned and the commanding officer of

8. George Edward Kingsley Bemand, second lieutenant in the Royal Field Artillery. (With kind permission of the Governors of Dulwich College)

the artillery division, Brigadier General A.J. Abdy, stated, perhaps a little cryptically, 'I am willing to take him', possibly suggesting that he had noticed what might have been considered undesirable traits[25] but, as in the case of the medical officer signing Gunner Albert James's enlistment papers in the previous chapter, chose to make his own judgement. George was accepted as a second lieutenant in the Royal Field Artillery. Researching the British Navy, rather than the army, the historian Marika Sherwood discovered that during the Second World War, this bending of the rules was also in operation. In correspondence with the Head of the Naval Historical Branch, she received the reply '[...] there is to the best of my belief no way of identifying without inordinate effort the ethnic origins of RN personnel during the Second World War.' Sherwood's own comment on this reply was:

This exchange ought to warn us of the possibility of vast gaps between stated policy and instructions on implementation, and of the ignorance of heads of departments who know only of policy![26]

What is interesting, though not surprising, is that George Bemand himself appears to have been aware of his 'handicap' in gaining a commission, in view of his affirmative answer to the question about his racial 'purity'. At first glance, this appears to be a clear case of what was described in the United States as 'passing', until one considers the appalling pressures that might cause an individual to do this; at a time when being black was likely to curtail professional advancement considerably, as shown below. On the other hand, however unlikely during this period, in view of his privileged environment, he may have genuinely considered himself white, being unable to see any difference between his own lifestyle and that of his white acquaintances.

On 30 December 1916, Bemand's mother received a telegram saying that on Christmas day he was wounded in action, but had remained on duty. He was killed the following day.[27] A later letter from the War Office stated that he was buried in Le Touret Military Cemetery, Richebourg l'Avoue, his grave marked with 'a durable wooden cross'.[28]

George was not the only son of the Bemands to pay the ultimate price. Six months later, their second son, Harold, was also killed on active service. The Commonwealth War Graves Commission provides the all too familiar stark announcement:

> Bemand, Harold Leslie, United Kingdom, Gunner, Royal Field Artillery, 'X' 8th T.M. Bty., Age: 19, Date of Death: 07/06/1917, Service No: 107838, Son of George and Mary E. Bemand, of St. Michael's Villa, 1, Bow St., Kingston, Jamaica. Grave Reference: No.2 I. F. 15, Bedford House Cemetery.[29]

John Albert Gordon Smyth

John Albert Gordon Smyth was another who, like Bemand, answered 'Yes' to the question 'Whether of pure European descent' when applying for a temporary commission in the regular army,[30] when clearly he was not. John Smyth was the son of the Rev. Henry Armstrong Smyth, born in Sierra Leone, and the grandson of John F. Smyth, from Antigua, who served as Colonial Secretary although he was passed over for the governorship due to his colour. When John's grandfather died in 1859, his widow Mrs Eliza Smyth (born Antigua c. 1822) was left with a family of five children aged between fifteen and two, and an annual government pension of £100. She decided to move her family to London, where Henry (1855–1937), John's father, became employed as a bank clerk. In 1878, Henry had been admitted as a student to Gloucester Theological College and, after many years of itinerant clerical life, became Chaplain to the Lewisham Union and later Chaplain to Lewisham Infirmary until 1932. There is no question about Henry's black heritage. In July 1900 he attended the Pan-African Conference convened in Westminster Town Hall, and in December of that year joined Henry Sylvester Williams on a visit to the Reform Club, Manchester to help win support for a local Pan-African Association branch in the city. Henry Sylvester Williams was a Trinidad-born law student who had helped form the African Association in 1897, of which he was secretary. Henry Smyth married locally born Clara Elizabeth Nuell and his son John Albert Gordon was born on 13 April 1886.

Like some other black officers in the regular British Army, John Smyth came from a family that was relatively well-heeled, compared to Tull. His father left an estate of £3,522 and had shares in the Great Western Railway.[31] John was a bank cashier and unmarried at the time of his commission in the 1st Cadet Battalion Royal West Kent Regiment in October 1914. In March 1916 he joined the Royal Fusiliers and was given a temporary commission as a second lieutenant in the 5th Battalion Machine Gun Corps (Infantry) on 19 December 1916, which interestingly is some six months earlier than Walter Tull, who was commissioned in

May 1917. Smyth is yet another officer of black ancestry who predates the commission of Tull.

John Albert Gordon Smyth was attached to the 11th Battalion of the King's Own Royal Lancaster Regiment from April 1917 and then in April 1918 was transferred to the Machine Gun Corps. He was killed in action on 29 June 1918 and is interred at the Merville Community Cemetery Extension.[32] His name – 'J.A. Gordon Smythe [sic]', is inscribed on the war memorial of St Margaret's, Lee, in south London. According to the *London Gazette*, at the time of his death, his parents were living in 16 Clarendon Road, Lewisham, London.[33] He left an estate valued at £606.[34]

Reginald Emanuel Collins

Unlike the mixed-race officers George Bemand and John Smyth, when Reginald Emanuel Collins filled in the official form asking that critical question: 'Whether of pure European descent', Collins told the truth and wrote 'No'.

Born in Kingston, Jamaica, on 31 May 1894, Reginald Emanuel Collins attended New College, Jamaica. At the outbreak of the war, he was working for the police, but left for England and joined the 19th Battalion of the Royal Fusiliers in London. After training from August 1915 to April 1916, he and his colleagues moved to France on 13 April. He was held in high regard by his officers, who approved his application to be admitted to Officer Cadet Unit training to serve as an officer in the wartime British Army.

Having completed the forms in May 1916, Collins left France on 18 May to train in Oxford. He had heard that a third Jamaican contingent was being organised for the BWIR, and had requested to join it as an officer. This was recommended by those superior officers who knew him, but his file shows the stark comment: 'not suitable to be an officer owing to his colour' dated 11 September 1916.[35]

'Shadism' has been discussed as a way of contravening King's Regulations, along with arbitrary decisions by sympathetic commissioning officers on the day, but Collins appears to have had the backing of officers who knew him. They may have been incredulous that Collins was not even allowed to lead an all-black West Indian unit, his own people. Collins had done his training – longer and more realistic than many officers in the BWIR – and had been recommended by the officers of the Royal Fusiliers. As a result, he was, in fact, appointed second lieutenant with the 6th Battalion of the BWIR on 30 March 1917 and his commission was valid until 11 November 1920, serving in Egypt, Palestine and Italy. He survived the war, unlike many of the black officers mentioned in this study, travelling back to Jamaica via New York City (where he was at the end of April 1919). Henry Collins of the Republic of Panama is given as his next of kin in his file.[36]

Brigadier General Horace Somerville Sewell

The Hon. Brigadier General Horace Somerville Sewell, CMG, DSO (and bar), Légion d'honneur (1881–1953) surpassed all other officers of African descent in the First World War, not only in terms of rank, but also in his membership of an elite branch of the British armed forces, the cavalry. This British-born officer was the grandson of a prominent Jamaican planter, William Sewell, who had married a former slave, Mary McCrea.[37] His father, Henry, married in England, settling on the Isle of Wight at Steephill Castle, near Ventnor, though Horace was born in Wales. When Horace's father inherited William's rich Jamaican plantation, he appears to have relocated back to that island, his son Horace also spending a good deal of his life in both the United Kingdom and Jamaica, where he served as a Justice of the Peace (JP).[38]

Once again, unlike Walter Tull, Horace received a privileged education appropriate to his social class, attending Harrow School and Trinity College, Cambridge. In 1900, he joined the 4th Royal Irish Dragoon Guards.[39] Horace appears to have been very light-skinned, but any physiological differences do not appear to have been missed by his subordinates, who nicknamed him 'Sambo'.[40]

After being seconded to the West African Frontier Service in 1907, Horace was soon promoted to captain. By 1914, he was serving with the British Expeditionary Force and promoted to major. From 1915 until the end of the war, he had command of the 1st Cavalry Brigade. Following the First World War, Horace commanded another cavalry regiment, the 7th Queen's Own Hussars, until 1923, when he took command of the Midland Cavalry Brigade of the Territorial Army, a post he held until 1928.[41]

Horace married the daughter of the New York gypsum magnate Jerome Berre King in 1916 and when he retired in 1940 he settled in Tysoe Manor in Warwickshire. Like his father, he divided his time between England and Jamaica. During his military life, he had been twice wounded and five times mentioned in dispatches, earned the DSO in 1915 and the French Légion d'honneur in 1916. The following year, he received the bar to his DSO after the Battle of Cambrai, followed by the CMG in 1919.[42]

David Louis Clemetson

Like Walter Tull, David Louis Clemetson enlisted in a sports unit, the Sportsmen's Battalion of the Royal Fusiliers. The eldest son of David Robert Clemetson of St Mary, Jamaica, David was born at Port Maria, St Mary, in 1893, receiving an education at Potsdam, Jamaica, and Clifton College, England. At the beginning of the war he was an undergraduate at Trinity College, Cambridge, and like many young Jamaicans, volunteered for service in Kitchener's Army.

While serving with the Royal Fusiliers in Salonika he was invalided to England. Upon his recovery, he was transferred into the 24th Welsh Regiment of the Welsh Hussars.[43] The *London Gazette* of 4 November 1915 states that David was commissioned as a second lieutenant on 27 October, 1915, before Walter Tull.[44]

Lieutenant David Louis Clemetson lost his life near Péronne on September 21 1918.[45] Like most of the other 'black' army officers, such as Bemand or Sewell, Lieutenant David Louis Clemetson belonged to the emerging mixed-race 'plantocracy' class in the Caribbean, the children produced by unions of former African slaves and their European masters. Recognition by white, usually male, parents granted them a lifestyle not so very different from 'well-heeled' white peers, such as private (so-called 'public school') education in the United Kingdom. Almost, it would seem, but not quite. As can be seen in the photographs of David Clemetson in Clifton College Officer Training Corps,[46] George Bemand and others, rather than an early European approximation of skin colour, the term 'black' had come to represent a social assignation not dissimilar to that endured by victims of the American passing laws of the 1920s and the infamous South African Apartheid laws, which classified as 'coloureds' many visibly white, or near white, citizens. Despite the advantage of wealth, the 'almost white' class in the Caribbean still faced discrimination and the strictures of military laws.

There is another reason for some senior officers apparently showing more flexibility than others, which may not have been simply bending the rules. Many had served in the Indian Army (including the Commander in Chief, Douglas Haig) and it is possible that this may have influenced their view of how the issue of non-white officer candidates should be dealt with. Some senior officers may have been simply drawing upon their own military experiences and previous interpretations of army regulations. This is not as fanciful as it may seem, as 'coloured' or 'native' were used as catch-all terms to refer generically to many non-white inhabitants of the Empire, irrespective of their nationality or race. Caribbeans may have been seen as little different from Indians. The *Manual of Military Law* 1914 states:

> Europeans in the Indian forces are subject to the laws and regulations for the government of the British Army. Half-castes and persons born in India, but of certain degrees of European descent, specified in the Indian Articles of War, are, for the purposes of this Act, Europeans. It will be observed that the Indian Articles of War are by this sub-section expressly extended to the natives of India belonging to the Indian forces in whatever part of the world they are serving.[47]

Senior officers may have referred to this section of the *Manual* when required to make a judgement on the thorny issue of whether to allow a mixed-race officer, albeit one of partial African rather than Indian ancestry, drawing upon their own early service experience in the Indian Army. It is interesting that Bemand, Smyth, Collins and Sewell predate Walter Tull, who is usually perceived as being the first black officer in the British Army, a sad reflection of the fact that ignorance of the historical contribution of Black British people can mean that visible individuals are presented as 'firsts' or even unique, such as Mary Seacole, the Jamaican nurse in the Crimean War or Olaudah Equiano, the black abolitionist and author. An extreme error is the case of the press presenting James Durham as being the only back soldier in the British Army[48] as seen in Chapter Two (in 2004, the BBC Local Black History Month programme *Tyne Roots* even claimed that he was the first Black African to join the British Army as a fully enlisted soldier).[49]

Medical officers

A number of black medical practitioners resident in the United Kingdom, or who had returned to the West Indies, were graduates of British universities and applied to join the Royal Army Medical Corps (RAMC). This would have entitled them to a commission in the army as doctors, but they faced the problems encountered by other black applicants. The War Office and Colonial Office were keen to stress the futility of black men applying to join as medical officers, officially documented in May 1915, when the Colonial Office was told that only government medical officers from the West Indies of 'pure European descent' were likely to be accepted as officers in the RAMC.[50]

Dr Jenner Wright, Dr S.J. Allwood, Dr James Jackson Brown and Dr James Samuel Risien Russell
The British-born Dr Jenner Wright, the son of a prominent Sierra Leonean lawyer, was brought up in Britain by his mother. Newly qualified

at the outbreak of the war, he joined his fellow doctors at the recruiting office to volunteer as a medical officer. His white contemporaries were accepted, but Wright was told to wait. After a time, he received a letter from the authorities telling him to go 'home' to Sierra Leone and seek employment there. He took this advice, and was forced to serve in West Africa with the inferior rank of 'Native Medical Officer', an experience that left him a greatly embittered man. Similarly, Dr S.J. Allwood of Jamaica was told by the War Office in August 1915 that he should apply to the Commanding Officer of the Jamaica contingent for employment in his field. A particularly sad case was that of Dr James Jackson Brown, who had not only studied medicine at the London Hospital, but practiced in London. The only post he was offered in the RAMC was as a Warrant Officer, which he accepted, tired of arguing that his qualifications entitled him to a commission.[51]

It is worth remembering that by no means all officers and other military personnel served overseas during the First World War. Dr James Samuel Risien Russell (1863–1939) was yet another son of a white plantation manager and a black mother. His father, William Russell, had successfully run the Leonora sugar plantation in Demerara since the 1840s, presiding over the change from what he called 'old time labour', meaning workers who had been freed slaves, to the newly indentured Indian and Chinese 'coolies', as he calls them in a letter to a British-based agent, perhaps a reflection of the racist linguistic norms of the time considering his marriage to a black, or at least mixed-race, woman. In the same letter, William Russell seemed to show an interest in the health and well-being of his charges (for very good reason in that post-slavery period), possibly providing the germ of medical interest picked up later by his young son.[52] James and his brother William (born 1867) were sent to the Academy in Dollar, Scotland. Dr James Samuel Risien Russell studied at Edinburgh University from 1882 to 1886, adding a gold medal-winning Doctor of Medicine (MD) (1893) to his Bachelor's degree (MB) and his Certificate of Medicine (CM). He became a fellow in 1897 and was awarded a BMA scholarship in 1895, studying in Berlin and Paris. He also taught at the National Hospital.

9. Dr Risien Russell, who was commissioned with the rank of captain in the Royal Army Medical Corps during the war. (Image courtesy of the Queen Square Library, Archive and Museum. Copyright National Hospital for Neurology and Neurosurgery)

In 1908, Dr Risien Russell received a commission as captain in the Royal Army Medical Corps, lasting until 1918. As his skill included the diagnosis and management of diseases of the nervous system, it is likely that the war provided ample opportunity to apply his knowledge in a practical way to the healing of men who were seriously damaged, but physically intact as a result of their wartime experiences. His clientele were drawn from the more affluent members of society, possibly including young officers of 'good family' brought home from the field of battle, whose relatives desired the best treatment available.[53] For some forty years, Risien Russell was considered a solid and respectable professional in London, with a private practice (44 Wimpole Street from the 1900s) comprising 'a large proportion of chronic psychotics and psycho-neurotics'.[54] The explorer Sir Henry Stanley and the best-selling novelist Mrs Humphrey Ward, niece of the poet Matthew Arnold and granddaughter of Thomas Arnold, the famous headmaster of Rugby School, were numbered amongst his high-society private patients. He served on the management board of the Hospital for Nervous Diseases until 1928.

Unlike some other black officers, there does not seem to have been any ambiguity over whether Risien Russell showed evidence of his African ancestry (via the Caribbean, of course) or not. He was described as being 'of mixed racial stock' in a 1960 study of the National Hospital where he taught and Macdonald Critchley, his house physician from 1923, recalled his 'dark skin' and thought 'he was one of the most important and colourful figures within the medical profession of Great Britain'.[55]

The similarities between Risien Russell and Sewell stretch to their marriages to women from 'respectable' families. In July 1892, Risien Russell married Ada Gwenllian Michell, daughter of a JP in Truro, Cornwall. Ada's eldest brother studied at Cambridge, then Barts, became an FRCS (Eng) and MD, dying of wounds received in France in July 1916. Ada divorced Risien Russell in 1915, and he remarried, to another Ada, the widow Ada Hartley, who, with her son Anthony, survived him.[56]

The variability of black medical officers' commissions meant that some black West Indian doctors who were accepted could be subjected to the most blatant forms of racism from British officers. One such case was J. McDowall, a doctor from St Vincent who was given a commission by the War Office in spite of the earlier restrictions mentioned above and enlisted in England in November 1917. At first, he served with the 6th and 9th battalions and later with the base depot of the BWIR, but was attached to the Staff Marseilles Stationary Hospital in September 1918 and subsequently transferred to Ambulance Transport. Major F.F. Middleweek, the officer commanding the transport, was deeply offended by his placement and requested his transfer, which was refused. Middleweek was adamant to have Dr McDowall transferred and wrote to the surgeon general, Sir William Donovan, reiterating his objection to Dr McDowall's presence:

> I wish to let you know that when we left Marseilles on February 15, Captain J. McDowall, RAMC, – a West Indian Negro – was put on board by the Assistant Director of Medical Services, (Base) Marseilles for permanent duty. I greatly resent this and consider that an Ambulance Transport is not a suitable unit for him to belong to, where the limits of space are so circumscribed, and where his presence on deck and in the dining saloon is greatly resented. Moreover, it is not at all pleasant for Nursing Sisters in having to work with him in the wards. I should feel greatly indebted to you if you would kindly transfer this Officer to another sphere of duty.[57]

Normally, officers were entitled under the King's Regulations to be shown such reports before they reached the level of the War Office, but the first McDowall knew about it was when the assistant director of Medical Services at Marseilles sent him a copy, possibly attempting to rectify what he may have thought was a procedural error. McDowall was greatly distressed by the letter and protested to the West Indian Contingent Committee, as no mention had been made of any professional misconduct, lack of ability or conduct unbecoming of an officer and a gentleman. McDowall was deeply insulted and could not understand why members of the Indian Medical Service were allowed to serve on the ambulance transports while he, a West Indian holding the King's Commission, had encountered this response. He was clearly unaware that part of the pseudo-scientific racism that had developed during the nineteenth century, fed by social Darwinism and the later eugenics movement, was a particularly pernicious racial hierarchy which ranked humankind with northern whites at the top and African blacks at the bottom, with a sliding scale in between rating Asians and Arabs higher. As this was based on skin shade, light-skinned mixed-race 'black' officers and soldiers seeking rank or employment fared better than their darker-skinned compatriots.

The Colonial Office was warned by the West Indian Contingent Committee that news of this incident would cause considerable resentment among members of the BWIR and the people of the colonies. By the time this protest was made, McDowall had already been removed from the ship, having made only two voyages.[58]

A Black Canadian officer

Canada adopted a similar policy to Great Britain insofar as the white officers only rule was concerned. Like the United States, black Canadians were in a different position to British-born black people in that their numbers were far greater and nearly all were 'home grown'. More will be said in Chapter Five of the general reluctance in Canada to recruit black troops at all in spite of a similar pressure from black leaders to that experienced by the British West Indies authorities, but a compromise was made by the establishment of a labour battalion, the No. 2 Construction Battalion, Canada's 'Black Battalion', on 5 July 1916.[59] The battalion's chaplain, Rev. Captain William A. White, was a prominent Baptist minister in Truro, Nova Scotia, and one of many black leaders who had led the drive for a black unit. All of the officers were white with the exception of the Rev. White, who had been given the rank of honorary captain. Originally an American student from Williamsburg, Virginia, White had studied at Acadia University in Wolfville, Nova Scotia, obtaining Bachelor of Arts and Bachelor of Divinity degrees. By the beginning of the war, he was the minister of the Zion Baptist Church in Truro, Nova Scotia. White was prepared to enlist as a private in the 106th Battalion, CEF, but the authorization of Canada's first black battalion resulted in him being taken on as Chaplain of the newly formed No. 2 Construction Battalion. As chaplains held the rank of captain, the Rev. White is yet another wrongly thought to be the first black officer in the British armed forces during the First World War. White served in England and France, returning to Canada to become Pastor of the Cornwallis Street Baptist Church in Halifax. A few months before his death in September 1936, he did succeed in achieving a first when he became the first Black Canadian to receive an honorary degree from his old university.[60]

It would seem that although, officially, an apparently 'strict' adherence to a racial code still blocked black officers, the exigencies of war had helped overcome both the race and class elements, at least in some cases, a change that would go a long way to explain the fact that as this chapter has shown, Walter Tull was not the lone black officer in the British Army many think. In September 1917 the Army Council had conceded, albeit not publicly, that commissions in the BWIR might at least go to 'slightly coloured persons [...] at the discretion of the Governors of the Caribbean colonies.'[61] One West Indian who had earlier been rejected by the War Office because of his colour, despite being admitted into an OTC unit in the Inns of Court, was later allowed a commission in the BWIR, as was Ivan Shirley from Jamaica, who was dark-skinned, which shows the tremendous variation in actual recruitment practice. Shirley had attended Dulwich College, London, like George Bemand, another gentleman student, and became a lieutenant in the 9th Battalion BWIR.[62]

Retrospective suppositions are always contentious, but it is tempting to ponder upon the course the lives of some black soldiers might have taken had military career prospects presented themselves. Two examples mentioned in earlier chapters that stand out are Herbert McDavid, in the British forces, and Norman Manley of the BWIR. Herbert McDavid went on to become director of a British shipping line and a knight of the realm, while Norman Manley later became Prime Minister of Jamaica. Neither was directly concerned with the military after being demobbed, but perhaps serve to show the folly of not recognising human potential.

CHAPTER FIVE

THE BLACK EMPIRE ARRIVES – CONSCRIPTION

The British West Indies Regiment (BWIR) would not be the only black unit from the Empire to arrive in Europe during the war years. Manpower was so sorely needed as to require conscription in the United Kingdom by the beginning of 1916, so further black troops from the Empire should, in theory, have been welcome. The Atlantic slave trade had produced a far-flung African Diaspora beginning in the fifteenth century, the dispersal of people of African descent through the slave trade representing one of the largest forced migrations in human history. The descendants of black slaves formed the basis of many of the British dominion troops who would answer the call, including black Bermudians and Canadians as well as servicemen directly from the African continent. The next to arrive after the BWIR in late 1915 was a black contingent from the tiny island of Bermuda in March 1916, followed by the South African Native Labour Contingent, arriving in France in October 1916 and black Canadians arriving in Britain in March 1917 prior to being shipped off to France. Each of these countries of the British Empire would have to deal with their own issues of black recruitment and conscription.

Black Bermudian troops

Situated in an isolated position off the coast of the United States, north of the Caribbean islands, the Crown Colony of Bermuda was Canada's nearest British neighbour. With the outbreak of the war, this tiny island was determined to make a contribution. The Bermuda Volunteer Rifle Corps (BVRC) had been an all-white, racially segregated reserve for the Regular Army infantry component of the Bermuda Garrison since 1894,[1] but calls for the formation of a corps of coloured volunteers were heard in the *Royal Gazette* as early as November 1906. In March 1916, the first of the Bermuda Contingents of the Royal Garrison Artillery (BCRGA) taking part in overseas service during the war comprised four white officers and 197 largely black troops similar to the West Indian model. Initially, there seems to have been some resistance to volunteer recruitment, which the Commanding Officer of the BCRGA, Major Thomas Melville Dill, blamed in a letter to Governor Sir George Bullock written in France on 1 April 1917 on the African Methodist Episcopal Church working behind the scenes to discourage black recruitment. He also blamed black Bermudian women for objecting to their men joining the previous year, possibly believing them to be, in some way, agents of the church. His praise was reserved for black Bermudian men he named as 'Cann, Wilson and others of that type', who seemed to have had a different view of black recruitment. In this correspondence, Major Dill advocated conscription, but a second volunteer contingent was raised under Lt. Wrigg, RGA and sailed from Bermuda on 6 May 1917, without the necessity of conscription. In the same letter to Governor Bullock, Dill wrote that 'our men, who were the first African troops to serve in the British Army in France soon got a good name for ammunition work'.[2] In this he was wrong, as the BWIR had been on the Western Front since the end of 1915. When the first contingent arrived in France in June 1916, they were allowed three months to recuperate in Marseilles, and appear to have suffered a great deal from the weather during the following winter.

Major Dill's war diary provides an excellent account of the sort of duties undertaken by most non-combatant troops of other British

THE BLACK EMPIRE ARRIVES — CONSCRIPTION

territories and their general experiences. Arriving at Plymouth on 19 June 1916, the Bermuda Contingent travelled to Folkestone before sailing to Boulogne on 21 June, where they were issued with gas masks and trained in their use. Two days later they arrived at Heilly, where they were divided into four parties of an officer and fifty ordinary ranks for service at Bouzincourt, Raincheval, Dernancourt and La Neuville. The men were put to loading ammunition at Acheux, those at Bouzincourt arranging the Royal Artillery advanced ammunition dump before travelling by lorry to Aveluy Wood, Mesnil to supply the guns. The men were shelled during the night and the following day were occasionally shelled at Northumberland Avenue, near Martinsart Wood. Two men of the Bermudian force were killed at Bouzincourt on 30 June.

Other duties were special jobs, such as sign painting, carpentry and preparing positions for howitzer batteries such as the 9.2 Howitzer Battery (55 (Australian) Siege Battery) on Albert Road. Men were put to work digging ditches around gun batteries and strengthening and sandbagging the telephone exchange, where a Bermudian telephonist was killed at 11 pm on 11 July. They were shelled throughout from Beaumont-Hamel and at other locations such as Thiepval. During most of July, the men were engaged in ammunition work at the railhead until the 24th, when they were relieved by parties of Royal Scots. When after three days there was a request that the Royal Scots might be relieved, the Bermudians returned to ammunition supplies. On 25 July, Major Dill succeeded in uniting some Bermudian detachments, but less than a month later, four men broke down under the strain of long hours of hard labour, causing Dill to change the work hours to three shifts of four on and four off per day. These new arrangements were also adopted for a working party of Australian infantry and found to give fifty per cent better results. Dill continued to press for the reuniting of the Bermuda Contingent, which he believed would be far more economical and efficient than simply drafting in small parties of infantry to assist when the demand became too much to deal with.

Throughout September and October, the Bermudians, now divided into two parties, worked at Puchevillers, Becourdel, Longueval and Dernancourt, where they camped near the 3rd Battalion of the BWIR. By

21 October, men suffering the effects of the bitter cold were admitted to hospital and on 24 October Bombardier G.J. Steed was also hospitalised after suffering a crushed leg caused by a falling girder in the battery. The Longueval contingent was then sent by train to a warmer climate on 30 October. From November 1916, Dill's war diary shows the effects of the cold weather. At Abancourt, there were several cases of pneumonia as the winter wore on, Br. G. Wears dying on 19 November, and in mid-April, they were still experiencing heavy snow. On 19 May Sergeant Tregaskis was seriously wounded and Br. Stowe was killed in an explosion. The Bermudians continued their ammunition work and other labour duties after moving to a camp near Poperinghe and later Vlamertinghe, attached to XIX Corps and administered under 52nd Labour Corps. Carrying on to Musso Camp (Marseilles Stationary Hospital) via Rouen, the Bermudians were also employed at cargo work and care of the boatswain's stores, and also provided plumbers, painters and artificers who were employed permanently by the Royal Navy.[3]

African recruitment and conscription

As the war progressed, Europe would become more familiar with South African non-combatant forces than their West and East African comrades who had been directly engaged in combat with the enemy since the outbreak of the war. But some mention should be made of other African theatres in order to understand British attitudes and policies of recruitment and conscription on the African continent, which, as shown earlier, invariably had a bearing upon the lives of black soldiers in the United Kingdom.

As previously mentioned, the dilemma of whether to allow black troops to fight did not apply in the African theatres of war for, unlike on the Western Front, the enemy was also black, the Germans deploying their own colonial forces. Much of the war in Africa involved African units led by white officers as British, French and Belgian colonial forces faced their German counterparts. The conflict between the British Empire and Germany served to bring many of the separate African nations together under British protection, forgetting their traditional quarrels. In most African territories, including West Africa earlier in the war, each village contributed to the war effort as a token of loyalty to the king, a sentiment repeated in East and South Africa, where the contribution of the Basuto State in the early part of 1917 was used to build early aeroplanes.[4] The chiefs were by no means the child-like, subservient figures often portrayed by contemporary British media sources and were often politically astute. In Western Nigeria, local rulers pledged men and much-needed supplies, and thousands of men were sent to the carrier recruitment depot at Sapele by the Oba (ruler). In Northern Nigeria, the traditional elite had benefited under British rule and were happy to see an expansion of their own influence, many considering themselves indispensable to the war effort.[5]

The British used a number of methods to recruit soldiers in their African colonies. The most obvious was a direct appeal for volunteers, but one of the most important measures was recruitment through local leaders and chiefs, who used their influence to raise the troops and carriers needed. Without their cooperation, the British would not have succeeded. Following the South West African phase of the war, in addition to contributing £817 to the war fund, King Khama of Bechuanaland ensured that every crossing and railway bridge of the Rhodesian trunk line passing through Bechuanaland to Central Africa was guarded, as these were a vital means of reinforcing and victualling the British Rhodesian armies continuing the fight against Germany in Central Africa.[6] Similarly, the Bugandan chief Samwiri Mukasa (Buganda is now the largest subnational kingdom within modern Uganda) claimed that his assistance was one of the most important services he had rendered 'for the peace of the protecting government and of the whole world'. He felt that a war against Britain was a war against Buganda, and promptly left for Kampala with 5,000 men. Mukasa was adamant that he kept in contact with the British armies for, as he put it, he 'did not want the enemy to get to our city London'.[7]

Regrettably, despite the loyalty shown in many British African territories, the British were certainly not alone amongst the other European colonial powers in resorting to forced recruitment in their own territories, such as Northern Rhodesia.[8] In East Africa too, the British instituted a compulsory service order in 1915 covering all males aged eighteen to forty-five, which was extended to the Uganda Protectorate in April 1917.[9] The French had a similar policy of enforced conscription and the Belgians in the Congo conscripted some 260,000 men to work as porters of soldiers, equipment and provisions.[10] From mid-1916, the war in East Africa was essentially 'black on black', largely conducted between African soldiers fighting for their respective colonial masters. Theoretically, signing up for British service was voluntary, but in practice Africans of lower status found themselves in situations with little choice. While soldiers enlisted for armed service were usually voluntary, the British relied on conscription for enlisting military porters. By the beginning of the war, the British had a good deal of experience of what was termed 'carrier recruitment', in reality little more than forced labour. In West Africa, an official passing through a village might demand men and sometimes women and children.

As the war progressed, however, distinctions between the recruitment of soldiers and carriers and other non-combatants became blurred. Although Britain did not follow the example of France in adopting a formal policy of enforced conscription, large numbers of Nigerians were abducted for service in the army and the Carrier Corps. Men believing they had volunteered for one form of service often found themselves in other roles, soldiers being used for porterage or carriers finding themselves in combat ranks. Similarly, those enlisting for garrison duties were shipped overseas, whilst others on plantations, in the railways or mines, were impressed by the military for service in the army or Carrier Corps; the designation 'volunteer' lost much of its meaning as the war progressed, largely because men were 'volunteered' by their chiefs for military duty.[11]

THE SOUTH AFRICAN LABOUR CORPS (SALC)

It was, however, to Southern Africa that the British turned for manpower on the Western Front, though individual British-domiciled West Africans were also to be found amongst black volunteers in British-based regular units, adding to the numbers of British Black Tommies. The Union of South Africa, part of the British Empire rather than a sovereign state during the war, offered to help Great Britain at the outbreak of hostilities by releasing the imperial garrison in order that those white troops could be used elsewhere, including the Western Front, should they be required.[12] The South African General J.C. Smuts had declined African and coloured officers the right to fight, determined to keep it a 'white man's war', but 83,000 Africans and 2,000 coloured men served in a non-combatant capacity nevertheless. Black South Africans were as determined to prove their worth as much as their British West Indian comrades. Despite continuing its agitation against the 1913 Natives Land Act, which put restrictions on the land that could be owned by the 'natives', the South African Native National Congress (SANNC), the predecessor of the African National Congress (ANC), passed a resolution of loyalty to the Empire and promised not to publicly criticise the government during the course of the war.[13] Although these measures might have been intended to encourage volunteers, it is unclear to what extent the decision to serve was an individual one or was undertaken on the orders of local chiefs as in North East and West African. A South African Labour Corps was formed in Africa to assist the Boer generals Louis Botha in German South West Africa and Jan Smuts in German East Africa, serving as civilian batmen and support. By 1916, their work was appreciated enough to form another force, the South African Native Labour Contingent, recruited for service overseas.[14]

The South African Native Labour Contingent (SANLC)

As the war progressed, despite the desperate shortage of manpower in Europe, the widespread fears of arming colonial forces among the authorities meant that British government policy preferred to employ the African troops shipped to the European front in non-combatant service roles. Africans were recruited from all over South Africa, including many from Pondoland and other peoples; Nguni speakers with similar cultures and traditions, like the Zulu and Xhosa, were recruited to serve overseas as labourers supporting the British Army in France and Italy. This force of 21,000 men from the SANLC left Cape Town for France between October 1916 and January 1918. They were to be put to work labouring in quarries, laying and repairing roads and railway lines, and cutting timber. The majority were employed in the French harbours of Le Havre, Rouen and Dieppe, unloading supply ships and loading trains with supplies for the battlefront. To the lasting shame of the wartime authorities, the volunteers of the SANLC, allies in the wartime effort, were housed in closed compounds little different from the camps used to hold German prisoners of war, who were also employed as labour in France. In spite of this apparent nervousness on the part of their European allies, the SANLC's work was held in high esteem, those employed at the harbours earning especially high praise.[15]

When the SANLC first arrived in France, the public were not unimpressed and the sight of these men from Britain's overseas empire helped to raise morale at a time when it was sorely needed. The press played its part in this wartime propaganda; the correspondent of the *Newcastle Daily Journal* writing in March 1917:

> I do not think I have before been so impressed with the sense of why the Allies are winning and are bound to win this War than I was today, [...] it was the sight of a double line of South African natives linked up for me to see in one of the many gangs which are already occupied by the South Africa Labour Corps in various parts of the War area. In the ranks of this motionless array, standing rigidly to attention, were splendid-looking Zulus [a nephew of Cetywayo – the former King of Zululand – and a grandson (son of Dinizulu) are serving in the ranks of one of these battalions], sturdy Basuto, [...] and deep-chested Pondos – willing volunteers every one of them, who have exchanged their sunny luxuriance for the bitter cheerlessness of this particularly severe winter in order to do their bit towards winning the war. I was told, and quite readily enough believed, that they would very much rather be fighting than digging and carrying; but as that was not to be, they had come overseas to set free White men for the trenches [...] The success of the step has been so great and so unqualified that the War Office is asking for it to be expanded manifold beyond the original limit.[16]

THE BLACK EMPIRE ARRIVES — CONSCRIPTION

Besides logistical problems, there were also worries about the change of climate, Percival Phillips, a correspondent of the *Daily Graphic* stating that the military authorities had anticipated 1,000 hospital patients from the six or seven thousand Zulus and Basuto in France between October 1916 and February 1917. The fears that these forces could not stand the cold of a winter in northeast France turned out to be unfounded: in the event there were only 124 hospitalisations due to the climate. In Chapter Six, Caribbean troops are seen to have suffered a good deal more, not least because of their enforced stay in Halifax, Nova Scotia.[17]

There was also some nervousness at the arrival in France of the first contingents of black African auxiliaries singing weird versions of British soldiers' songs, such as 'It's a Long Way to Tipperary', but when a South African administrator was asked how many guards would be required to stand over the 'natives', he replied, 'Not one'. The Africans were put on their honour:

> [...] to show the White man that they knew how to conduct themselves without outside interference [...] When their work is over, they smoke or sing together or laboriously copy English words on their slates. They have a simple, childlike trust in the White officers, who talk to them in their own language, and their one desire is to do what they can to help in the war. They dig a ditch or mend a road or build a hut with cheerful willingness.[18]

THE LOSS OF THE SS MENDI

The SANLC's first taste of danger and loss of life was not on the Western Front, where they theoretically had a non-combatant role; the long journey north was not without its hazards. The SS *Mendi* troopship (4,230 tons) was carrying the last SANLC contingent from Cape Town to La Havre in France when, upon reaching the English Channel on 16 January 1917, the heavier SS *Darro* (10,000 tons) rammed her with no warning signals, sinking the *Mendi* in minutes.[19]

The men of the SANLC were accompanied by their own chiefs

and headmen acting as interpreters and just when the ship's company realised that all was lost, an astonishing act of bravery is said to have occurred. One of their leaders, the Rev. Isaac Wauchope Dyobha, a Xhosa, exhorted the doomed men to remember their tribal traditions and die like warriors, whereupon they promptly removed their boots and uniforms and stamped the death dance as the *Mendi* sank, fighting the waves as they slid from the slanting deck, some even leaping into the water. The truth of this story has been questioned, the historian Albert Grundlingh doubting its veracity[20] while the writer Norman Clothier is inclined to disagree, suggesting that there is no reason to disbelieve black South African oral tradition any more than any other and that the tale may have a basis in fact.[21] To be fair, Grundlingh's argument is that the story seems to have been seized upon by the press before and during the Second World War, precisely the time when both wartime propaganda and elements of African nationalism were very much in evidence, each pursuing their own agenda, and such a story had the right patriotic tone for the time. If Grundlingh is saying that the press published an existing story, however, this would seem to invalidate his argument.

Some 616 African men and thirty-nine Europeans drowned in the tragedy, and much of the blame was attributed to the actions of the captain of the SS *Darro*, H.W. Stump, who gave no fog signals and was travelling at a dangerously high speed. He appears to have failed to act even when the crew of the *Mendi*'s escort, HMS *Brisk*, were picking up survivors as many as they could. Sadly, the Rev. Isaac Wauchope Dyobha was amongst those who lost their lives, along with many white members of the *Mendi* crew who bravely gave up their lifeboat seats to the African labour force, considering it their duty to put their African civilian passengers first. At the subsequent Court of Inquiry, Captain Stump had his licence suspended for a year, a punishment considered far too lenient, but it has been suggested that he may have simply lost his nerve due to the enemy submarine presence, and that it was this rather than racial prejudice that made him abandon any idea of rescuing the drowning men.[22]

Black Canadian troops

Canada had adopted the United States' model of recruitment in that black recruits were largely formed into homogeneous units of their own race. Perhaps characteristic of Canada's relationship with both the United States and Great Britain, her armed forces adopted a policy towards her own black troops somewhere between the two in that they favoured all-black units, under white officers, like Britain, the US Army having black officers, but of a lower rank than their white peers, some 600 African American officers serving during the war.[23]

Despite the great need for manpower in 1916, racial prejudice was such that Canadian recruiting officers often refused black volunteers into their regular forces. As in Great Britain, some individuals had managed to join up in the opening years of the war and, like the Caribbeans, many black Canadians were keen to play their part on a wider scale, pressurising the government. As the black population of Canada was numerically far greater than that of the United Kingdom, cases of individual rejection were likely to be more widely known, presenting the Canadian authorities with the dilemma of what to do with black Canadians responding to the country's call. In a letter dated 7 September 1915 to Sir Sam Hughes, the Minister of Militia and Defence, a George Morton of Hamilton pleaded the case of black Canadians:

> [...] As humble, but loyal, subjects of the King trying to work out their own destiny, they think they should be permitted in common with other peoples to play their part and do their share in this great conflict.
> So our people, gratefully remembering their obligations in this respect, are most anxious to serve their King and Country in this critical crisis in its history and they do not think they should be prevented from so doing on the ground of the hue of their skin.[24]

This letter, like others, met with denials and prevarication, including the mooted possibility of a mixed-race regiment, whites voluntarily enlisting to serve alongside blacks. The Canadian Chief of the General Staff Major, General W. Gwatkin was cynical, replying, 'in the last extremity we might organise a company or two. But would the Canadian Negroes make good fighting men? I do not think so'. After the rejection of twenty fit and able new black recruits when they reported to the military camp at Sussex, New Brunswick, in order to join the 104th Battalion Canadian Expeditionary Force (CEF), the issue of the rejection of black recruits began to have repercussions across the country.[25]

Major General W. Gwatkin wrote on 22 December 1915, 'It would be humiliating to the coloured men themselves to serve in a battalion where they were not wanted [...]'.[26] However, on 11 March 1916, Brigadier General E.A. Cruickshank, the officer commanding Military District 13, Alberta, suggested the formation of a segregated battalion to serve overseas, as he believed that it would be inadvisable to enlist 'Negroes or other coloured men' in a white battalion. In answer to this suggestion, Gwatkin produced a memorandum that began with extremely disparaging comments on the loyalty and combat capabilities of black men, including even more strange and inexplicable remarks about problems of their use on the firing line: 'It would be eyed askance; it would crowd out a white battalion; it would be difficult to re-inforce'.

Gwatkin's solution was the establishment of an all-black labour battalion and the continuation of the existing system of leaving recruitment decisions to the discretion of commanding officers (not that much different from what was happening in the United Kingdom). The No. 2 Construction Battalion, Canada's 'Black Battalion', headquartered in Pictou, Nova Scotia was formed on 5 July 1916. More than 600 men were eventually accepted,[27] recruits coming from across Canada and including 165 African Americans.[28] The battalion's chaplain, Rev. White, a prominent Baptist minister in Truro, Nova Scotia, was one of many black leaders who had led the drive for a black unit. All of the officers were white with the exception of Rev. White, mentioned in Chapter Four, who had been given the rank of honorary captain, possibly the only black commissioned officer to serve in the Canadian Army during the war.[29]

Black Canadian troops found their way into British ports prior to being shipped to the Western Front, tasked with non-combat support roles. After serving in Canada, the No. 2 Construction Battalion, under the command of Lieutenant Colonel Daniel Sutherland, 605 men and nineteen officers, left Halifax on 28 March 1917 for Liverpool.[30] The sight of black Canadian troops landing in the British port must have been a source of curiosity for the Liverpool public and strongly reminiscent of a similar unusual event involving black voyagers a century earlier. Liverpool had been the capital of the slave trade until its abolition in 1807 and only four years later, on 2 January 1811, the African American sea captain Paul Cuffe sailed to Great Britain to seek the help of the African Institution in settling free African Americans in the Sierra Leone Colony. He arrived in Liverpool on 12 July 1811 to an astonishing sight as a welcoming crowd lined the dockside for a glimpse of Cuffe's brig, for the *Traveller* not only had a black captain, but an all-black crew. The second of Cuffe's fleet of four ships, the *Alpha*, which arrived the day after, also had an all-black crew.[31]

The role of some soldiers of the No. 2 Construction Battalion was to change soon after arrival. Because it was understrength, the battalion was redesignated as a company in May 1917 and attached to the Canadian Forestry Corps, a specialised organisational corps of the CEF, serving in France on the Swiss border. Most men served at Lajoux in the Jura Mountains, others joining forestry units in Péronne and Alençon. A number would nevertheless take part in trench combat, joining fellow black Canadians who had been accepted into regular line units.

Commended for its faithful service and discipline, the unit returned to Canada in early 1919, following the Armistice of 11 November 1918. Canada's 'Black Battalion' was disbanded on 15 September 1920.[32]

Black expatriate recruits

Owing to the machinations of the War Office, some British Black Tommies found their way into Canadian forces by a circuitous route – through the United States. The official stance of the War Office's opposition to the enlistment of black soldiers into British units (regardless of what was actually happening in the recruiting offices) seemed, at one point, about to change as a result of attempts to raise volunteers among the thousands of British subjects living in the United States. An agreement between the British and United States governments held that if British subjects in that country were not conscripted into the British forces then they were eligible for the US armed forces.[33] The terms of the Military Services Convention Act 1917 were put into action soon after America entered the war with the Army Council sending Brigadier General W.A. White to New York in mid-1917 not only to organise the general recruitment of British subjects, but to enlist 'coloured labour' for the military. The War Office understood that something in the region of 2,000 men could be found amongst the many Caribbean migrants in the United States: enough to form a separate non-combatant battalion on the lines of the Canadian Black Battalion. The numbers enlisting were disappointing at first and the Army Council was against the idea of putting 'coloureds in white units'. An embarrassing incident occurred in September 1917 when sixteen 'coloured persons' were erroneously enlisted in Chicago for the British Army. The War Office was faced with having to cancel the men's attestation, which General White felt would damage Britain's image in the United States, not to mention the message it would send to black colonial subjects, whose support was sorely needed.[34]

Lord Reading, Ambassador and High Commissioner in Washington, pointed out the danger for Anglo-American relations and the effects of negative propaganda on the Allied cause should a racist recruiting policy be made known. By early 1918, the hoped-for 2,000 or so blacks had come forward, and Reading urged the British authorities that the 'recruiting mission be authorised to enlist and send forward all coloured men registered here who are medically fit', a move supported by Balfour at the Foreign Office.[35] The War Office had the idea of declaring those black recruits who had presented themselves and been registered for military service exempt from duty until they could be enlisted into the British Army, using the excuse that there were logistical difficulties in transporting the men to Europe.

There was some embarrassment that Black British subjects rejected for the British Army might be conscripted into the US forces under the terms of the Military Convention. Finally, after holding out for so long amidst the pressing need for manpower, the War Office officially agreed, with some reluctance, to lift the colour bar in June 1918. Was this decision definitive? So long as they did not present any difficulty of food and language, the Army Council were to allow British subjects of colour to be permitted to enlist into British units, combatant or otherwise. This proved to be a ploy to deal with the embarrassment of the earlier mistake whilst trying to recruit in the United States for, despite this ruling, there were still complaints about would-be black recruits being excluded by the War Office. In correspondence from the Colonial Office to the governors of the British West Indies, the latter were requested not to send British subjects to the United Kingdom for enlistment as it was not desirable to post coloureds to regular British units,[36] and that those who did present themselves were to be placed in the BWIR. Those who had enlisted were now also posted to the 'Black Battalion', the Canadian battalion specially raised for black troops.[37]

Conscription in Canada

The Canadian forces died in their thousands on French battlefields, approximately 60,000 dead or missing and 173,000 wounded. Measures had to be taken to replace losses and on 29 August 1917 Ottawa passed the Military Service Act, making most British subjects between the ages of twenty and forty-five resident in Canada since the outbreak of the war liable for active military service.

An annoying aspect of this Act was that those black Canadians who had been trying in vain for some three years to enlist only to be rejected were now legally obliged to present themselves for service. There were some who now refused to respond to call-up notices, causing a further souring of relations as, perversely, blacks were now stopped on the streets and required to show exemption documents, being forced into the army should they fail to produce them. One such was the father of Hilda Lambert of Halifax, Nova Scotia, a man in his late forties who was returning from work when he was approached by the military police, promptly taken to the armouries to be conscripted into the army. After he protested that he had two sons serving overseas, they released him. John Crawley of North Preston, Nova Scotia, also narrowly missed being 'pressed', to use the naval term, into the army on an errand with his brother-in-law Harry Sparks to Dartmouth to pick up some groceries. They were both taken to Halifax. Harry explained that John was too young, and the latter was held until his father came to collect him. Harry Sparks was conscripted into the army and sent overseas.

Black conscription was a complete reversal to the previous policy of refusing black recruits – or so it seemed. Having being told, 'We don't want you. This is a white man's war', blacks were now obliged to enlist. Their conscription seemed to have caused as much confusion for the military authorities, who would have preferred to maintain the status quo of racial segregation. Isaac Phills of Dartmouth, Nova Scotia, was one of approximately sixty conscripted blacks in one unit who received training alongside white conscripts in Canada, but upon arrival in England he found that he and his black comrades were placed in a segregated unit and assigned to fatigue and labour duties. The confusion was such that, though black conscripts had been trained as infantry, they believed they would be posted to the segregated No. 2 Construction Battalion, CEF. At the end of the war, black conscripts were to be used as reinforcements for the 85th Battalion, CEF, a combat unit, but they were spared this service by the signing of the Armistice.[38]

Conscription in the Caribbean

Although conscription was introduced in Grenada and Jamaica (on 4 April 1917), most recruits continued to be volunteers, enlisting largely for economic reasons, and the measures were never enforced. There had been a feeling in Jamaica that in some cases service was being avoided by some able-bodied men, as a result of which resolutions in favour of enforced military service were passed by some Parochial Recruiting Committees. At the March 1917 meeting of the Legislative Council, the governor stated:

> I have received from time to time reports concerning the services of the Jamaica units of the British West Indies Regiment, and these reports have been of a very satisfactory nature. The services of the soldiers sent from Jamaica have been very highly spoken of, and their steady conduct under severe artillery fire has been much commended [...] I am able to announce that the Army Council desires to raise as many battalions as possible in Jamaica to reinforce those battalions now serving at the front, and that His Majesty's Government relies upon the patriotism of the people of Jamaica to ensure that this call for men for the service of the Empire in these critical days shall be fully met. I have had no hesitation in replying that the call will be fully met, relying as I do upon the patriotism of the people, and upon the services of those who have already done so much in the cause of recruiting.[39]

A resolution requesting that a bill rendering military service compulsory should be introduced was passed and on 22 March, the Attorney General introduced 'a bill entitled a Law to make provision with respect to Military Service in connection with the present War'. The bill, passed by a majority of twenty-one to four, aimed at the registration of every male in Jamaica between the ages of sixteen and forty-one, approved by the Governor on 1 June, made Jamaica the second colony, after New Zealand, to pass a conscription law. Despite opposition expressed in the newspapers, some 135,601 persons were registered. Enforced conscription was unnecessary; the men joining the war effort from Jamaica were volunteers.[40]

At this time there was nevertheless some public resistance to recruitment in Grenada and Jamaica and, as in Bermuda, in Trinidad recruiters had accused women of encouraging their menfolk not to volunteer.[41] Some areas of British Honduras failed to recruit any men for active service. In early 1916 there was an unprecedented exodus of young men from the district of San Estevan after calls for men to enlist, some fleeing into the bush while others crossed the border into Mexico.[42]

It is not the case that Hondurans did not play their part in the war effort however. As seen in Chapter Three, Honduran men under Lieutenant Furness served overseas as volunteers with the BWIR and the Inland Water Transport Corps to the Middle East.[43] It was the Governor of Honduras, rather than potential conscripts, who expressed concern about the climate on the Western Front,[44] a view initially supported by the king, who felt that black troops might be better deployed in the warmer climes of the Middle East.[45]

Resistance to conscription in the Caribbean does not appear to have been dealt with harshly. One of the few West Indian conscientious objectors to encounter any level of severe punishment seems to have done so in England, rather than the Caribbean. Skilled carpenter Isaac Hall had arrived in Britain shortly before the outbreak of the war. The grandchild of a slave on a Jamaican sugar plantation, Isaac was unlucky, as conscription had been introduced earlier in Britain than in Jamaica, in 1916. When Hall was ordered to report for military service he ignored the summons and was arrested and taken to a training camp. This was only the beginning of his problems, for he was dragged around the parade ground until he fell unconscious after refusing to obey orders. Still he resisted commands to work on soldiers' haversacks, earning himself a spell in solitary confinement on a diet of bread and water.[46]

After the First World War had failed to reach an early conclusion, on 27 November 1914 The No-Conscription Fellowship (NCF), a British pacifist organisation, was founded in London by Fenner Brockway and Clifford Allen.[47] According to Fenner's account, a Quaker visitor at Pentonville Prison alerted the NCF to Hall's case, who was visited by a doctor and the Labour party activist Alfred Salter. Hall was described as being 'a living skeleton [...] gaunt, bent, starved [...] a coal-black man with ashen lips and sunken eyes'. He was taken by a taxi to Salter's own home until he was able to return to the West Indies nine months later.[48]

In the pacifist newspaper *Tribunal*, a Jamaican who may have been Hall is attributed with saying:

> I am a negro of the African race born in Jamaica. My parents were sent in bondage to Jamaica. They were torn from their home. My country is divided up among the European powers (now fighting each other), who in turn have oppressed and tyrannized over my fellow-men. The allies of Great Britain ie., Portugal and Belgium, have been the worse oppressors, and now that Belgium has been invaded, I am to be compelled.[49]

As the author is simply described as 'a negro', it is possible that he is not Hall. Another West Indian could well have found himself in similar circumstances, and it is even possible that the words were not penned by the absentee 'negro', but by a zealous journalist equally anxious to plead the case for the pacifist cause.

Conscription in the United Kingdom

Back in the United Kingdom, as general wartime losses in the army rose and volunteer figures fell, British Prime Minister Herbert Asquith was forced to introduce conscription in January 1916, Parliament passing the first military conscription laws ever passed in Great Britain, the 'Military Service Act' of 27 January 1916. These dire circumstances did not stop the continued rejection of black men by recruiting offices in the United Kingdom; those who were accepted were often enlisted at the discretion of the recruiting officer on the day or because of their skin tone. Because of the ignorant and haphazard way in which race was treated, British-born Black men and blacks resident in Britain often fell foul of the conscription laws, sometimes even those who wished to enlist. One such was a black actor playing the part of a servant in *Romance* at the Theatre Royal in Nottingham, Obadiah Coles, who found himself considered an absentee from military service after being rejected because of his colour.

Not only men of African descent were rejected, but also Asians and other 'people of colour' who had come over to enlist. When Robert Reubens, a twenty-year-old Indian from Singapore, was called up in February 1917 and failed to report, he was summoned to Brighton Magistrates Court in July. So muddled was the official thinking that when he stated that he was a student, he was convicted anyway, even though the Ministry of National Service told the court that he should not have been called up. When the government of the Straits Settlements (now Malaysia) sent engineer Kenneth Oehlers, of unknown origin and identified only as 'Eurasion', to Britain in order to enlist, he was turned down in March 1918 'on grounds of colour' and his fare home paid by the Colonial Office.[50]

Black Tommies, even when officially discouraged from enlisting, were still to be found on the battlefield in one capacity or another. The restriction of black recruitment was looked at again as the war progressed, when losses were at their peak. A memo from Prime Minister Lloyd George to the War Cabinet on 18 April 1917 stated that it should keep:

> the War Office short [of men] to compel the soldiers to adopt tactics that will reduce the waste of man-power. [...] Further, they desire the War Office to work out their own salvation by a careful substitution of elderly and partially fit men and coloured men for fit men in all services behind the lines.[51]

Lloyd George has been accused by some historians of starving the Commander in Chief, Douglas Haig, of reinforcements in early 1918, using his powers to control the manpower available for military reinforcements, but in June 1918, at a time of severe shortage, the War Office officially agreed to lift the colour bar. The Army Council 'decided that British subjects of colour may be enlisted into combatant or other units of the British Army' provided they were able to fit into British units as regards food and language. Despite the paper rulings, some blacks were still excluded from the army after the lifting of the colour bar in mid-1918 however.[52] Nothing had really changed and the random system of recruiting blacks into regular British units continued to the end of the war.

CHAPTER SIX

THE RETURN OF THE HEROES

Melt, melt away ye armies—disperse ye blue-clad soldiers,
Resolve ye back again, give up for good your deadly arms,
Other the arms the fields henceforth for you, or South or North,
With saner wars, sweet wars, life-giving wars.

(Walt Whitman, 1867)

American poet, essayist and journalist Walt Whitman's eight-section poem *The Return of the Heroes* was written some decades before the First World War at the conclusion of another bloody conflict on another continent, the American Civil War. Though acknowledging the patriotic glory of a fight well won, Whitman's poem was a reminder amidst the jingoistic fervour, medals and military honours accompanying marches through the newly reunited nation's capital city of the ambiguity of victories, the difficulties of reconstruction and the transition these men would have to make to civilian life.[1] Black soldiers who had fought for Britain would also have their medals after the greatest war the world has ever known, but would face their own hardships upon their arrival back home.

Medals and accolades

By the end of the war, many soldiers of African descent fighting for the British cause had earned medals in many theatres of the war. Attitudes shown by the British authorities to black United Kingdom-based soldiers were very much a reflection of how soldiers of African descent were treated throughout the Empire. One such was Sergeant Major Ebrima Jalu of Gambia, described by the author and colonial administrator Sir Harry Johnston as 'a full-blooded Negro of Mandingo race' who served in the West African Frontier Force. In an action in the Cameroons, Sergeant Major Jalu was in command of one of the hottest parts of the firing line following the death of his European superior officer Lieutenant Markham Rose. In January 1916, he was recommended for the Distinguished Conduct Medal by his commanding officer, General C.M. Dobell, for holding the British position against German troops. Perhaps a little surprising is the low expectations evident in the reason given for the award: 'Although deprived of the support of any European for several hours, he displayed the greatest coolness in controlling his men and directing the fire of the guns'.[2] It would seem that the prevalent belief in a racial hierarchy reveals itself even in the most positive, congratulatory of circumstances.

A similar story appeared in the *Buluwayo Chronicle* telling of the heroism of an Angoni sergeant in the Northern Rhodesia police. The sergeant was involved in the early fighting on the Anglo-German frontier in East Africa. A surprise German attack killed a European officer and five African soldiers, and others were wounded. Although in considerable force, the Germans faced strong resistance from the British African soldiers. The white officer, a Belgian who had been wounded twice, had refused to leave the firing line and fallen in the long grass. The African sergeant stood over his officer's body, firing his rifle and calling to his comrades not to let the 'bwana' fall into the enemy's hands. The refusal to leave the body of an officer behind is a recurring theme with British troops, black or white, who considered it a matter of honour to retrieve their fallen officers, if not their wounded or dead comrades. The 'native' sergeant was recommended for the Distinguished Conduct Medal. It is unfortunate that the prevalent race consciousness and paternalistic Eurocentric attitude of the period once more reveals itself when the newspaper correspondent reporting the incident comments, 'I have heard of men with dusky skins being pure-white inside, and I have certainly had proof of that on more than one occasion on this border'.[3]

During the First World War, the highest British award that could be conferred to a soldier of African descent was the Distinguished Conduct Medal – one step below the Victoria Cross (VC). This effectively meant that only white soldiers could receive the VC. This is an unexpected reversal of previous policies for there had been black recipients of the VC during the nineteenth century. Originally, the VC was not awarded to Indian or African troops; white officers leading native troops could receive it while their troops could not. There were restrictions related to social class or rank upon the award of medals for gallantry in the British Army and Navy prior to 1856. Some awards, such as the Order of the Bath, Brevet rank and Brevet promotions recognised only officers' gallantry, other ranks restricted to 'a Mention in Despatches', but during the Crimean War (1854–56), a groundswell of opinion from the public at large to Queen Victoria herself led to the creation of the VC, 'for valour in the face of the enemy'.

William Edward Hall, AB, RN, a Nova Scotian marine and the son of an African slave, was the first black recipient of the VC, only two years after the first investiture, along with two other British medals with the Sebastopol clasp and the Inkerman clasp respectively, and the Turkish Medal.[4] The first black soldier to receive the VC was Samuel Hodge, who served in West Africa in 1866. He won the award at Tubabecolong on the Gambia River, where he and his men used axes to chop their way through the enemy defences. Hodge was wounded, but the men of the 4th West India Regiment (WIR) were able to enter and clear the town. Hodge died in Belize shortly after receiving his VC.[5] Other black recipients followed but, by the time of the First World

War, there seems to have been something of a retrograde step insofar as attitudes towards awards for black troops are concerned.

Like VC winner Samuel Hodge, members of the Caribbean Regiments earned their accolades also. At the beginning of the First World War in 1914, the 1st Battalion of the WIR was stationed in Freetown, Sierra Leone, a detachment of the regiment's signallers later fighting in German Cameroons. Several men were mentioned in dispatches and Private L. Jordon earned a Distinguished Conduct Medal (DCM).[6]

Another battle honour, 'East Africa 1914–18', was added to the WIR laurels for their service in Africa, as well as eight Distinguished Conduct Medals. The column that took Dar es Salaam on 4 September 1916 included 515 officers and men of the 2nd Battalion, who later played a notable part in the Battle of Nyangao in German East Africa in October 1917.[7]

Back on the Western Front, British Black Tommies had also made their mark. Private Frank S. Dove (91658), the eldest son of a Ghanaian lawyer, was born in Brighton and joined the Royal Tank Corps in 1915. He was awarded the Military Medal for his bravery in action at Cambrai in November 1917.[8] After hostilities ceased, an article in the *African Telegraph* told the tale of another soldier, John Williams:

> 'The Man Whom White Soldiers Call "The Black V.C.";
> Though Undecorated'
>
> Private John Williams, age 20 years, joined the British Army in 1914. He has won the D.C.M., the M.M., the French Military Medal, the Cross of St. George, and the French Legion of honour. Among many brave deeds, which would earn any European the V.C., his greatest feat was the killing of three German officers who, disguised as British, were acting as spies. He wears four wound stripes.[9]

THE MAN WHOM WHITE SOLDIERS CALL "THE BLACK V.C.," THOUGH UNDECORATED.

Private John Williams, age 20 years, joined the British Army in 1914. He has won the D.C.M., the M.M., the French Military Medal, the Cross of St. George, and the French Legion of Honour. Amongst many brave deeds, which would earn any European the V.C., his greatest feat was the killing of three German officers who, disguised as British, were acting as spies. He wears four wound stripes.

10. John Williams 'The man whom white soldiers call "the black V.C."' (Reproduced by permission of ©The British Library Board. All Rights Reserved, c12343-01)

The return of British Black soldiers

At the end of the war, many Black British soldiers returning from the battlefields would have a good deal more to worry about than the status of the medals they received. During the year following the cessation of hostilities, like their white comrades, some black soldiers, particularly British-born Black soldiers, believed that they would return home into the welcoming arms of a grateful public, eager to help their heroes readjust to civilian life after the horrors of war. The sight of these disciplined black servicemen in their uniforms on the streets of the United Kingdom, at the Western Front and later as casualties in the hospitals should have improved the general public awareness of the part played by the black soldier during the war, but some returning Black Tommies were to be sorely disappointed, as many of the British public, including those in their own home cities, did not recognise them or what they had done in their name.

Soldiers returning to their homes after this global conflict would find that the world had changed, perhaps frightening in its scope with newly emerging patterns of social class, gender issues, and even new countries created. There were, however, other reasons for the Black Tommy returning to the United Kingdom to be more immediately alarmed. In anticipation of the task of rebuilding national life after the war was over, Lloyd George created a Ministry of Reconstruction to deal with a range of issues in post-war Britain, including housing, employment, labour relations and the economy. In view of the disruption to normal life the war had caused and the numbers of men involved, this was to prove extremely difficult. Shortly before his replacement in the Cabinet reshuffle that followed the electoral victory of the Lloyd George coalition on 14 December 1918, War Secretary Lord Milner commented:

> The difference is that while the war is on, people mind less. The sense of national danger, national necessity, submerges complaints. Men are ashamed to nurse grievances when their country is in peril. But when danger is over, or thought to be over, there is at once a reaction.

Men are, quite naturally, less patient, more critical, more exacting. Grievances are made the most of, and there are plenty of people about, who make a business of stimulating the sense of grievance, collecting instances of everything that goes amiss, exaggerating it, and putting it all down to the negligence, or slackness or mismanagement of officials, to red-tape, to departmental dawdling and so forth.[10]

There was also a search for scapegoats for post-war hardships endured by the population. If ever the poet Rudyard Kipling's famous poem *Tommy* applied to any British soldiers in peacetime,[11] it was to the returning Black Tommy after the war. At the end of the war, there were approximately 20,000 black people living in Britain, the majority in the ports because of the influx of much-needed sailors, originally welcome additions to the navy.[12] Many black soldiers had also been demobilised in Britain, increasing the country's black population. Wounded and crippled black soldiers were brought back to Britain for treatment in military hospitals and some fifty of the 2,000 wounded soldiers in Belmont Road Military Auxiliary Hospital, Liverpool, were black. Most of these patients had been in the British West Indies Regiment (BWIR) and had lost limbs. The good relations between patients were seriously damaged by the arrival of white soldiers who had served in South Africa. When the newcomers started taunting the black soldiers, a fight erupted in which a sledgehammer was flung at a group of black men, two of whom had lost lower limbs and could not move away. After another incident of abuse in the concert room, two black soldiers decided to leave, hobbling out on their crutches to a white soldier's cries of 'Make room for the swine to pass'. The response of the hospital authorities was to put the concert room out of bounds to black troops. John Demerette (known as 'Demetrius'), a black sergeant who had lost both legs, had heard a rumour that the ban had been lifted and crawled towards the guard to ask. He was promptly seized by the guard and thrown into a cell, his shouts alerting ten crippled black soldiers. With the cry of 'The niggers are fighting the guard', some 400 to 500 white soldiers began beating the fifty black soldiers with crutches and sticks and throwing pots, pans, and kettles, knocking down a white nurse in the melee, who later died of pneumonia after going into shock. The one uplifting aspect of this deplorable incident, which would be by no means isolated in the years immediately after the war, was the behaviour of those white soldiers who did their best to defend their black comrades.[13] And comrades they were, in many cases, for a contemporary report said:

> Some of the British Tommies who had fought side by side with these coloured soldiers in the trenches [...] took sides with the coloured soldiers [...] When the Provost Marshal arrived on the scene with a number of military police to restore order, there were many white soldiers seen standing over crippled black limbless soldiers, and protecting them with their sticks and crutches from the furious onslaught of the other white soldiers until order was restored.[14]

The 1919 riots

Any promises of improved conditions, 'homes fit for heroes', were slow to be fulfilled after the war. The return of black and white soldiers set the scene for conflict only months after the end of hostilities, with demobilised black servicemen facing competition once again with poor whites, many of whom considered black settlers as aliens or at the very least latecomers, despite some being British-born. The sad irony was that 'while whites viewed blacks as foreign, different and inferior, blacks viewed themselves as citizens and defenders of the British Empire'.[15]

In 1919, the Cambrai veteran and medal winner Mercantile Marine Officer Fred W. Dove from Glasgow wrote of 'a greater number [of Blacks] who have fought and bled in Flanders and elsewhere',[16] and noted that 'An angry feeling appears to exist among those [Blacks] who have served during the war in France and at sea'.[17] During the riots, several soldiers are mentioned in newspaper reports as black victims of the race riots in Cardiff, Liverpool and Glasgow and of the 700 blacks who took shelter in the city Bridewell (police station with cells) in Liverpool, eighty or so were discharged soldiers or sailors from the Royal Navy.[18]

A meeting of Black British seamen on the beach in Glasgow early in

1919 was followed by others in ports throughout the United Kingdom. Their grievance was that labour exchange managers had secretly been given instruction by the Ministry of Labour's Employment Department to keep unemployed black seamen of British nationality in ignorance of their rights: 'The majority of these are eligible for out-of-work donation, but they have apparently not realised this, and it is not considered desirable to take any further steps to acquaint them of the position'.[19]

In January 1919 a riot ensued in Glasgow harbour after the national seamen's unions and their local delegates claimed Black British colonial sailors were unfair economic competitors.[20] This was one of many disturbances that year as members of the white working class and ex-servicemen took to the streets in violent demonstrations of dissatisfaction with post-war conditions. Since competition for jobs between white and black seamen was the main reason behind the race riots in Britain's port cities, black soldiers were invariably dragged into the disturbances in 1919. Leaders of the seamen's unions promulgated the idea that blacks were accepting lower wages than whites, an oversimplification seized upon by the most illiterate and deprived sections of the white working class,[21] who soon focused upon soldiers and sailors of African descent. Thirty Sierra Leonean seamen were arrested by the police in Glasgow and, as the press would point out, many of the white mob were not British, to the annoyance of the black seafarers.[22] Although at least some of the press may have blamed the many white foreigners sailing under British flags, the main body of the rioters attacking the East Holborn Arab quarter of South Shields had been residents of South Shields.[23] Despite union membership and long records of service, not to mention war service, the seamen's union did not allow black sailors to sign on. *The Africa Telegraph* of May–June 1919 remarked:

> If the labour market is glutted, why employ Scandinavians, Russian Poles, Danes and Swedes, and not a Britisher? If a white Britisher is not available – although it is said that the market is glutted – why not a black Britisher before foreigners?[24]

The Arab and Somali seamen settlement in Tyneside dated from the 1860s and was joined by West African and West Indian seamen in North Shields before and during the First World War. Once again, the unions treated local ethnic minority seamen poorly, in this case, mostly Arab seamen – all British subjects – who were asked to pay to clear their union books, then denied work.

In Liverpool, white employees refused to work with old black workmates, causing them to be dismissed.[25] Severe riots broke out in which individual blacks and their homes and lodgings were attacked by white rioters.[26]

Little was done by the police to protect black seamen, who chose to raid boarding houses used by black seamen. The Elder Dempster shipping line's hostel for black seamen, the David Lewis Hostel for black ratings and many houses were sacked in the heart of the black community.[27] Among the black soldiers under attack in the spring of 1919 was the West Indian Robert Bessesseur, serving in the Dorset Regiment, and four other black men who were involved in an affray in London's Edgware Road.[28]

Intermarriage

In the search for other scapegoats, as the troubles became more widespread, relationships between black men and white women were seized upon, particularly in the old areas of black settlement in Liverpool and Cardiff. In Cable Street, in the dockland area of London, some locals had objected to English girls visiting an Arab eating house. A number of ex-soldiers entered and a fight broke out in which some shots fired. A crowd gathered outside became increasingly hostile, making it difficult for the police to gain entrance to free the imprisoned men, some of whom had been wounded.[29]

Few black settlers in the ports had brought their wives with them from their homelands, resulting in many marrying white wives. Prior to the war, a good deal of prejudice was often shown towards mixed marriages, an idea encouraged by the growing Eugenics Movement, mentioned in earlier chapters.[30] The popular belief in a racial hierarchy provided the theoretical underpinnings and justification of antipathy towards people of African descent in Britain and in the first half of the twentieth century intermarriage between black and white was often seen as absolute anathema.

As attitudes had hardened towards black people as the nineteenth century progressed, by the beginning of the twentieth century negative views could also be found amongst churchmen.[31] In 1920, the Rev. James Hamilton addressed the first meeting of the Liverpool board of the Eugenics Society under its new title 'The Liverpool Hereditary Society', emphasising the eminence of the British nation over others by virtue of inherited powers and 'its own great, common blood-stream, always differing more or less from all others'.[32] Hamilton clearly believed in the right of Anglo-Saxon might, which should be kept free by selective breeding:

> [...] as far as possible from pollution, and, especially from certain foreign admixtures [...] if, for example, the policy of keeping an open door for every foreigner, and especially allowing such alien and inferior breeds as Negroes, Chinese, and Japanese to enter, marry and settle down in great numbers, while young people of pure British blood emigrate to other lands, this country will in a few generations have so much foreign and undesirable blood in the national veins as cannot fail to have a deleterious effect on the national character, and, as a consequence, on all those national ideals, endeavours, and achievements which we value so highly in the present day.[33]

Cardiff, another source of British-born Black Tommies, came under fire in February that year from the Rev. George Hopper, a Wesleyan minister in Bute Town, the black settlement area, who protested that he had received several requests to solemnise marriages between white girls and men of colour: 'Speaking at a meeting of the Public Morals Committee of Cardiff, Mr. Hopper stated that he refused to have anything to do with these matches'.[34]

Relationships between white women and black men were claimed to be one of the explanations for the riots by one Liverpool police officer, who stated that there would have been no such trouble without such intermarriage. As many seamen long settled in the ports had white wives (the parents of some Black Tommies), a former British colonial administrator wrote to *The Times* that he believed that 'sexual relations between white women and coloured men revolt our very nature [...] What blame [...] to those white men who, seeing these conditions and loathing them, resort to violence?' He felt that while British subjects of good character could not be forcibly repatriated, steps should nevertheless be taken to prevent the employment of large numbers of 'men of colour' in such ports.[35]

Laura Tabili points out that it is perverse that strict taboos existed in the empire inhibiting sexual or romantic relationships between white women and black men, in spite of white men's exploitation of black women being routine since the days of slavery; a reflection of attitudes back home, where women were certainly seen as objects in their male relatives' possession. The colonial authorities considered race, class and gender barriers necessary to maintain colonial domination otherwise the mystique of European difference and superiority would be eroded.[36]

On 11 June, a brake carrying coloured men and white women attracted the attention of a hostile crowd in Cardiff, made even more aggressive by the arrival of a number of other vehicles containing mixed parties. This soon developed into a full-scale riot involving 2,000 people, possibly the worst disturbance of 1919, the shops and houses of black people attacked in a similar manner to Liverpool. These disturbances continued the next night, involving a number of white colonial troops, possibly from Canada, Australia and South Africa.[37] A white soldier, John Donavan, described by the press as a veteran wearing his Mons service ribbon, was shot by the occupants when 59 Millicent Street was attacked and set on fire by these ex-servicemen.[38] Much was made of the medal of the white attacker who was shot, as though attempting to raise his status from hoodlum, and it apparently did not occur to the press that the occupants may also have been servicemen.

Similar disturbances in Liverpool led to the death of Charles Wotten, a young Bermudian who was chased by a large white mob after running from 18 Pitt Street in the dockland area. A crowd of several hundred cornered him, tore him away from the pursuing police and stoned him to

THE RETURN OF THE HEROES

death in Queen's Dock.[39] The *Evening Express* pressed for an end to what amounted to racial war in Britain's ports:

> The negroes by the hundred have thrown themselves upon the mercy of the authorities. In dozens they presented themselves at the bridewell yesterday afternoon and evening, and before today's dawn broke there were between 600 and 700 black men safely housed at their own request in the main bridewell (local gaol) at Cheapside. During the day this number has been considerably increased.

Reporters witnessed the sad spectacle of 400 black men, women and children being marched through the streets by the police when all was quiet between one and two o'clock in the morning.[40]

The newly demobbed Sierra Leonean soldier Ernest Marke tells in his autobiography of being chased by a baying crowd in the Brownlow Hill area of Liverpool shouting, in his words, 'Niggers, niggers. Stop them niggers'. He and a West Indian friend were saved by a white woman who opened her front door and allowed them to run through the house. Unfortunately, they were spotted by another gang who caught his friend as they both tried to jump on a passing tram. He was beaten unconscious. Ernest had a similar lucky escape when he and another black friend ran into a mob on another occasion. They tried to escape but were caught by a second gang and beaten mercilessly, only to be saved by the timely intervention of female workers who came pouring out of a nearby factory at lunch hour, screaming and shouting at the mob. Ernest felt that his life and that of his friend was saved by these white women.[41]

Ernest was not alone in valuing friends and allies at this time. Agnes Brew, the sister of Private Albert James, mentioned earlier, remembered an experience which took place during the 1919 riots in Liverpool. She was walking along Park Road with a white girl when a gang of men across the road began calling things to them, running towards them. Hindered by the dresses of the time, tight-waisted and tight at the knee, the young women found they could not run and began to panic. The white girl was a very refined vicar's daughter, but picked up a brick and threw it at the first of the men who were gaining on them. When the others saw that he had been hurt, they stopped to see to him, allowing the girls to escape. Agnes never forgot her friend.⁴²

Some former members of the BWIR may have chosen to go about the streets of Cardiff with their uniforms because it afforded them some protection, but this was not always the case. On 14 June 1919, the *Western Mail* described one black ex-serviceman as 'a well-set-up young fellow' who 'proved to be a brave man, and in perfect English appealed to the crowd not to molest him, but this did not prevent him receiving several blows before police escorted him away'.⁴³ The fact that he is described as speaking 'perfect English', implying a lack of any *patois*, suggests he may have been British-born, a factor that many had yet to come to terms with. The British-born Black former Mayor of Battersea (1913), John Archer (1863–1932), proved an able champion of the well-established Liverpool black community. In a powerful speech to the African Progress Union's Inaugural Meeting in 1918, he complained in a manner that presaged the future independence movements in the colonies:

> Side by side with the British army, for the first time, our compatriots from Africa, America and the West Indies have been fighting on the fields of France and Flanders against a foreign foe. A war, we have been repeatedly told, for the self-determination of small nations and the freedom of the world from the despotism of German rule […]. The people in this country are sadly ignorant with reference to the darker races, and our object is to show them that we have given up the idea of becoming hewers of wood and drawers of water, that we claim our rightful place within this Empire. That if we are good enough to be brought to fight the wars of the country we are good enough to receive the benefits of the country.⁴⁴

There were newspapers putting forward the cases of black servicemen. One West Indian ex-soldier stated in the *Daily Record* that 'every man who is under the British flag has done his share to secure the country'.⁴⁵ Five days later, another correspondent remonstrated:

> Did not some of these men fight on the same battlefields with white men to defeat the enemy and make secure the British Empire? Why

can't they work now in the same factories with white men? Did they not run the risks of losing their lives by the submarine warfare in bringing food for white women and children in common with white men?[46]

Black soldiers faced other issues besides encountering difficulties on the streets. In some cases, volunteers who were not British-born or domiciled wished to return to their country of origin, expecting the promised equality of pension, even if promises of equal pay during the war had not been forthcoming. In June of 1919, the month when the civil disturbances reached their height, the *African Telegraph* displayed a photograph of a smart volunteer on the streets of London, accompanied by a plea for fair play on the part of the British government:

A West African Soldier 'Walking Out' In London

> They pay special attention to their uniforms and personal appearance, hence they are nick-named the 'Coloured Army Knuts'. [Knut being a slang term for showy young men]. This one wears a good conduct stripe, overseas chevrons and two wound stripes. Some of these young men left their studies to join the British Army upon the outbreak of hostilities and rendered a very good account of themselves in the trenches and fields of Flanders, many of them wear coveted distinctions, and one from Oxford University won the M.C. for a particularly daring deed with the Tank Corps. Now that the war is over, the mandate has gone forth from the authorities that they are not to receive the same benefits as other British soldiers because they are coloured men. Their life is made almost unbearable by Americans and South Africans in England, because they are popular with the British public everywhere they go.[47]

Not only did black soldiers returning to the United Kingdom encounter difficulties as a group, some individuals found that badly thought-through recruitment policies created problems. In Chapter One, a Private A. Francis is mentioned as a volunteer under the Derby Scheme who was posted to the BWIR rather than an ordinary British unit. Francis was described as 'a man of colour who was discharged after two years seven

THE RETURN OF THE HEROES

A WEST AFRICAN SOLDIER "WALKING OUT" IN LONDON.

They pay special attention to their uniforms and personal appearance, hence they are nicknamed the "Coloured Army Knuts." This one wears a good conduct stripe, overseas chevrons, and two wound stripes. Some of these young men left their studies to join the British Army upon the outbreak of hostilities and rendered a very good account of themselves in the trenches and fields of Flanders, many of them wear coveted distinctions, and one from Oxford University won the M.C. for a particularly daring deed with the Tank Corps. Now that the War is over the mandate has gone forth from the authorities that they are not to receive the same benefits as other British Soldiers because they are coloured men. Their life is made almost unbearable by Americans and South Africans in England, because they are popular with the British Public everywhere they go.

11. 'A West African soldier "walking out" in London'. A soldier of the British army who served during the First World War. (Reproduced by permission of ©The British Library Board. All Rights Reserved, c12343-02)

THE RETURN OF THE HEROES

months service on account of amputation Right Arm sustained on active service in France.'⁴⁸ The problem, as the Ministry of Pensions put it in a letter to the Treasury 9 February 1920, was that:

> coloured men of the British West Indies Regiment are pensioned according the European Scale of the Royal Warrant 19114, Article 1162, and Mr. Francis was accordingly awarded a life pension the rate of 1/6 a day. It has however now been presented that the pensioner has been resident in this country since 1898, when he came from Canada, and prior to war was earning good wages in a Shipyard of Liverpool.
>
> In December 1915, he had voluntarily enlisted under the Derby Scheme and in the following March he was mobilized and, apparently without being offered any choice in the matter, was drafted to the British West Indies Regiment. He was discharged in October 1918 and has again taken up residence in Liverpool, but, in consequence of his disability, he is unable to return to his former employment.
>
> His present rate of pension is considerably lower than that to which he would have been entitled had he been posted to a British Line Regiment, and Sir Laming Worthington Evans is of the opinion that so long as the man is resident in this country he should not be prejudiced by the accident of his original posting, but should be pensioned according to the scale laid down in the Royal Warrant of 1914, which is admittedly drafted with reference to the cost living in this country, I am therefore to request that their Lordships may be pleased to sanction the issue of a pension under that warrant, which would be at the rate of 28/- per week, for such time as the man shall be resident in the British Isles.⁴⁹

At first, the question of granting Francis a higher pension bewildered the government offices, as any concession might affect all BWIR veterans. A further letter stated:

> Great difficulty was found in posting men of colour to ordinary British units and the British West Indies Regiment was constituted a Corps in order that a unit might be found for bona fide West Indian Negroes, who happened to be resident in this country before the war. No difficulty was foreseen in their being posted to a Corps with special rates of pension.

> There might be a number of other cases like that of Mr. Francis and if you approve the proposal of the Ministry of Pensions, it may lead to a number of consequential demands. Could you not get over the difficulty by giving Mr. Francis an alternative pension? This would take into account his comparatively high earnings before the war.
>
> The application of alternative pensions to the British West Indies Regiment was, I think, approved in your letter 21841/19 of 31st May, 1919, to the Ministry of Pensions.[50]

Further correspondence urged that the treasury should pursue the suggested 'Alternative Pension' in Mr. Francis' case,[51] but the outcome and the payment agreed upon is not known. The crux of the matter seemed to be that he was a long-term resident of the United Kingdom and, as claimed by those pleading his case, 'without being offered any choice in the matter, was drafted to the British West Indies Regiment'. The decision to place some 'men of colour' in the BWIR, and the failure to foresee any pension difficulties, on their own admission, put the government in an embarrassing situation. It seems that, once again, the way to deal with it, as in the commissioning of black officers, was to fall back upon the expedient of individual government officials taking decisions on the day – 'on the hoof' – with a possibly random outcome for the Black British plaintiff. This incident also showed that even in those bleak times there were still decent British governmental officials willing to plead the case of returning black soldiers.

Other Black British servicemen returned from the war to face difficulties caused by injuries sustained in battle. Florence Guy married Joseph Gibson, the Barbadian lodger of her parents Theophilus and Charlotte Guy in their Mill Street home in Liverpool. Joseph was in the Merchant Navy. When they were married in 1911, they moved to nearby Beaufort Street, a street that has cropped up more than once in this book as providing black army and naval recruits. In 1914 he enlisted in the Royal Army Medical Corps, serving as a stretcher bearer. It was in this role that he received a head wound from a German soldier he was trying to help. Joseph Gibson returned to the Merchant Navy after the war, dying in 1938 when a dizzy spell while working in Herculaneum dock in

12. Joseph Gibson is seated at the end of the first row in football strip. (Reproduced by permission of Anne Audley, representing the Guy/Gibson family descendants)

Liverpool caused him to fall. Whether this was a result of his wartime injury is difficult to say.

Other members of Florence's family were also suffering at the end of the war. Joseph's wife saw her two brothers go off to fight in the war. Her older brother, George, initially fought in the Dardanelles in Northern Turkey. He was wounded in Mesopotamia, losing both legs, and drowned in November 1918 in mysterious circumstances, only nine days before the Armistice. It appears that whilst being shipped home, depressed, he decided that he did not want to be a burden to his family. On the journey home, he disappeared from his berth, only an open porthole bearing an indication of what might have happened. His body was never found.

In 1914, Florence's younger brother, Jack, joined the Guards at the age of sixteen. Luckily, he survived the war unscathed and returned to his job in an oil mill,[52] unlike many black returnees who had worked in similar jobs, for some white employees refused to work with former black workmates.[53]

Horror on the Rhine

Black Tommies were not the only black soldiers to feel the effects of the pernicious rhetoric of the eugenics movement after the war. Black soldiers serving as combat troops in the French Army also came under the malevolent scrutiny of the press, not initiated by the French, in the first instance, but by a Briton. One of the most virulent attacks on black people after the war came from the secretary and part-founder of the Union of Democratic Control and editor of its journal *Foreign-Affairs*, E.D. Morel, a prominent left-winger. The son of a French father, his real name was Georges Edmond Pierre Achille Morel-de-Ville, and his beliefs appear to have taken an about-turn, for he had been the founder of the Congo Reform Association in 1904 and a prime mover in bringing about the end of King Leopold's infamously cruel regime in the Congo. Morel, a member of the Independent Labour Party and later a Labour MP, was described by a contemporary author as having suffered 'agonies of sympathy with his beloved black man'.[54]

Morel began his attack on France's African troops in Britain's leading left-wing newspaper the *Daily Herald*. The front-page banner headlines claimed: 'Black Scourge in Europe: Sexual Horror Let Loose by France on the Rhine'. The tone of his protest could not have been more vicious, drawing upon every prevailing negative stereotype and portraying black troops in occupied Germany as 'primitive African barbarians', 'spreaders of syphilis' and a 'terror and a horror unimaginable'. His claims that the corpses of young women had been found under manure heaps were accompanied by threats calculated to draw in the British working class, suggesting that they too had reason to fear the fate of their erstwhile foes in Germany. The *Daily Herald* warned that these African mercenaries might be used against white workers in the future as the British government had been complicit in the use of black troops against the German public.[55]

In a pamphlet called *The Horror on the Rhine*, Morel claimed that black troops 'must be satisfied upon the bodies of white women'. This pamphlet sold very well in Britain and when a free copy was given to delegates attending the 1920 Trades Union Congress it was said to have left them with 'a feeling of physical and spiritual revulsion'. What would now be called a 'media frenzy' ensued, with others calling the black French troops 'a horde of Senegalese savages' and referring to their 'horrible excesses'. There were some who would challenge Morel's campaign however. The young Jamaican poet, novelist and socialist Claude McKay was living in London at the time and is thought to be Britain's first black reporter and the first black socialist to write for a British periodical. Born in 1890, his experience in the United States had taught him 'how completely his race was being exploited', and his sonnet 'If We Must Die', written following the United States' own 1919 anti-black riots, won him instant fame. After a letter he wrote in response to Morel's claims in 1920 was rejected by the editor of the *Daily Herald*, George Lansbury, McKay succeeded in getting it published in the *Workers' Dreadnought*, a revolutionary socialist paper run by Sylvia Pankhurst, who had been the leader of the left wing of the women's suffrage movement before the war. In the letter, McKay questioned Morel's outburst about the sexual vitality of black men in the popular press, stating that black men were no more oversexed than white men, who had left mixed-race children throughout the West Indies.[56] In 1921, a disenchanted McKay left Britain, which had been a spiritual homeland, documenting his feelings in his autobiography, *A Long Way from Home*, published in 1937.[57]

REPATRIATION

In Glasgow, the Colonial Office referred black servicemen to the Board of Trade repatriation scheme, which had been offered by the marine department of the Board of Trade since February 1919 and was principally directed at black sailors who had come to Britain during wartime.[58] In Liverpool, black servicemen, mostly seamen unable to obtain employment in the city, were pressing for repatriation as many were being turned out of their lodgings onto the streets. In June 1919, a statement by a delegation headed by Mr D.T. Aleifasakure Toummanah of the Ethiopian Hall, Liverpool, protested:

> The coloured men have mostly served in the Forces, Navy and transport. They are largely British subjects, and are proud to have been able to have done what they have done for the Empire. The majority of negroes at present are discharged soldiers and sailors without employment; in fact, some of them are practically starving, work having been refused them on account of their colour [...]. Some of us have been wounded, and lost limbs and eyes fighting for the Empire to which we have the honour to belong [...]. We ask for British justice, to be treated as true and loyal sons of Great Britain.[59]

Dr Rufus Leicester Fennell, a West Indian medically trained in the United States, acted as the black community's spokesman in Cardiff. Fennel pleaded the case of those servicemen, particularly seamen, who wanted to be repatriated and succeeded in helping 600 black men to return home by mid-September 1919. Some black settlers were outraged at the very idea, as they were domiciled in Cardiff with families and felt themselves to be black Welshmen, despite the recent hostility shown towards them.[60] Other black victims of the violence in the ports knew of no other home than Britain.[61] Some 200 of those who did want to be repatriated were accompanied by Fennel to Plymouth on the train. Even the tiny gratuity that Fennell had fought for was never received despite the promises, as George Blackman (mentioned in Chapter Three) found upon his return to Barbados, although he was not one of those of Fennell's group of returning servicemen. The weekly paper *John Bull* fulminated that the black servicemen were penniless and given no food on the journey. When they boarded the ship, the staff were all off duty and the captain asleep. The paper reported that 'These coloured Britons had all done first-class war work, yet they were treated worse than repatriated enemy aliens'.[62]

These numbers increased, some 600 from Bristol in September, followed by a further 200 who sailed from Cardiff, and in 1921 *West Africa* magazine reported that a further 627 sailors had travelled in recent months.[63]

A fairly prominent figure of this time, there is some evidence that Dr Rufus Fennell was involved in his own right on the Western Front during the war in a support, if not a military, capacity. He is also described in an American publication as having survived 314 days of trench warfare and having been wounded three times while serving in Mesopotamia, where he attended thousands of British troops, which could imply service with an ambulance corps.[64]

Aliens Order 1920 and Special Restrictions (Coloured Alien Seamen) Order 1925

At the beginning of the war, security provisions had been made barring alien workers in favour of British labour. During the economic and civil crises during the 1920s and 1930s, these broad powers, granted by the Aliens Restrictions Order of 1914, originally applied to British subjects of German or 'alien' descent, were now applied by the establishment and union leaders to Black British subjects. Legitimising the exclusion of undesirables by manipulating nationality was given a patriotic face, and the 1914 Act was passed easily in the atmosphere of anti-German suspicion and wartime xenophobia. This severe wartime measure against Germans and Britons of German descent served as a precedent for discrimination against other categories of British subjects in peacetime, questioning an individual's loyalty and jeopardising his citizenship rights. Laura Tabili believes that wartime xenophobia, post-war isolationism and economic protectionism preserved and sustained anti-alien fervour after the war had ended, allowing measures to be implemented that would otherwise have seemed intolerable in peacetime.[65] Because of the frequent confusion over the categorisation of black people as 'aliens', black servicemen settling after the war were ready targets for the Aliens Restriction (Amendment) Act of 1919, and the stronger Aliens Order of 1920. In the case of seafarers, the Seamen's Union's anti-black agitation resulted in the 1920 Order, which was followed by the Special Restrictions (Coloured Alien Seamen) Order of 1925, which required British citizens of the Empire who might be classified as 'coloured', such as African, Asian and West Indian seamen, to register with the police as aliens. Under the terms of the 1920 Order, the police had the power to impose restrictions on 'aliens' who could not prove their British nationality as colonial subjects and were thus liable to arrest without warrant.[66] Many black ex-servicemen were forced to register as 'aliens' with the police, even if they were British and resident in the UK for some time, the most aggrieved being British-born Blacks in such old settlements as Liverpool, who could be harassed and threatened with 'repatriation' despite proof of British nationality.[67] The intended target was black seamen, but in practice all black men were under suspicion.[68] Clubs and restaurants frequented by black people were also closed down in the search for 'coloured aliens'. Some Sierra Leonean Kru were British subjects, but under the terms of the Act were classed as aliens and deported because they were not registered in their home country and many could not prove their status.[69] It was not unusual for threats of imprisonment or arrest to be used against those who had refused to be repatriated.[70] White British women married to so-called 'aliens' lost their own rights as citizens[71] and were not allowed to vote until 1948.

The Empire troops return home

Caribbean troops were also disappointed with the reward for their wartime efforts. They had held their own in battle situations and endured the injustices of not being allowed to carry out the duties they had visualised at the time of recruitment, but the final insult came at the end of the war. Transferred to a British Army base in Taranto, Italy, West Indian soldiers found themselves facing a situation that led them to the unthinkable – the possibility of a mutiny. There were several causes for this rebellion by what had been one of the most loyal sources of black colonial troops. Their days were long and tough, their routine labouring duties including cleaning clothes and latrines for white British soldiers.

The Taranto Mutiny

Among the causes of the Taranto Mutiny was the fact that at the time of recruitment, black West Indian troops were told by colonial officials that they would receive the same pay, training and equipment as their white British fellows, with the possibility of promotion.[72] This was clearly an untruth, as the War Office had made it plain in the *Manual of Military Law* of 1914 that black or mixed-race officers were officially forbidden to lead Europeans in the British Army,[73] though there were glitches in the system and the occasional anomaly, and black West Indians would have difficulty gaining promotion beyond the rank of sergeant to lead even black troops.

The question of promotion was only one of the enlisted men's problems. Relations with many of their fellow British soldiers could be equally difficult. A group of men disembarking in Egypt marched to a YMCA hut singing 'Rule Britannia', to the indignation of other British soldiers, who growled, 'Who gave you niggers authority to sing that? [...] Clear out of this building – only British troops admitted here'. In much the same vein, a contingent of the BWIR learned, apparently from official sources after repeated requests to meet the enemy in combat, that it was 'against British tradition to employ aboriginal troops against a European enemy'. This clearly told them that they were considered on a par with 'natives' in what had become the official British mindset.

The final indignity suffered by the West Indian troops was that pay increases during the last year of the war were granted to other Imperial troops, but denied to black troops. Army Order No. 1 of 1918 granted the British soldier one shilling and six pence a day, a gain of six pence. Once again, the West Indians did not receive the additional pay, the War Office ruled, because they were 'natives'. Some black soldiers wrote to the Governor of Barbados that this discriminatory policy was 'not only an insult to us who have volunteered to fight for the Empire, but also an insult to the whole West Indies'.[74]

An additional difficulty was the employment of battalions of the BWIR on tasks that should have been assigned to labour units.[75] The Taranto Mutiny began on 6 December 1918, with the BWIR's violent reaction to the War Office's racism, members of the 9th Battalion attacking their officers, including their unit commander. Some 180 sergeants petitioned the Secretary of State for the Colonies about the prevention of black West Indians from benefiting from Army Order No. 1 and requesting that they receive increased separation allowances like the other troops. The question of promotion in the army still loomed large. For several days, black troops refused to work and were generally insubordinate, during which time a shooting and a bombing occurred. It was decided to disband the 9th Battalion and distribute its members among other units, but feelings still ran high, causing the base commander to wire the War Office requesting the assistance of a battalion of white troops. A battalion of the Worcestershire Regiment, armed and 'in fighting order', and a machine gun company was sent to Taranto. All the battalions of the BWIR in Taranto were disarmed.

When demobilisation was raised as the best way to deal with the insurgent soldiers by the War and Colonial Offices, the Assistant Secretary of State for the Colonies, G.E.A. Grindle, pointed out that they could be punished by a further term of service as they were obviously 'cheap compared with white troops'. The War Office decided that repatriation was the easiest option, a move that would add fuel to the call for Caribbean independence from the British Empire. Some fifty to sixty sergeants of the BWIR formed the clandestine Caribbean League, an association promoting self-determination. At the League's second meeting, one sergeant demanded that the black man 'should have freedom and govern himself in the West Indies', 'and [...] force must be used, and if necessary bloodshed to obtain that object'. A general strike for higher wages after repatriation was decided upon, but the League was discovered by regimental officers and disbanded early in 1919. Most of the soldiers who had taken part were convicted of mutiny, receiving prison sentences of three to five years. Two men were dealt with more harshly: one received twenty years and the Worcestershire Regiment was called upon to serve as the firing squad to execute the other, who continued to lead a struggle against conditions.[76]

The veteran Eugent Clarke was among the thousands of BWIR troops held at the camp in Taranto for almost a year at the end of the war. The large barracks in which they were virtual prisoners still stands. Clarke and his fellow BWIR soldiers were assigned by their British Commanding Officer to hard labour and the inevitable demeaning tasks. Day passes and recreational time were refused.[77]

While the Taranto revolt was taking place, the 1st and 2nd Battalions of the BWIR had been engaged as front-line troops against the Turkish Army in Palestine, but when they, and another battalion that had not been stationed in Taranto at the time of the revolt, arrived in Taranto in 1919 to await demobilisation, they found that they had lost a number of privileges. Official documents referred to them as 'Coloured Natives', cinemas and YMCA huts were off-limits to West Indians and they were required to perform fatigue duties for other units. These were different conditions from what they had experienced under Colonel Chaytor in Palestine and would create new-found and lasting grievances.

It seems astonishing that it took a mutiny of Caribbean troops at Taranto for the Colonial Office to consider the issues of their treatment. Following this incident, which sent shock waves throughout the whole British Army, the Colonial Office now sought to secure the benefits of Army Order No. 1 for the BWIR. Though their links with the African continent and their fellows of African descent elsewhere in the African Diaspora were long-lost, in many ways this was the beginning of a feeling of black kinship that would drive moves for independence in the next few years. The War Office warned in a draft memorandum that 'in addition to racial riots in the near future we shall incur a sensible weakening of our hold on the West Indian Islands'. This recognition that continued discrimination in the question of pay would seriously affect the attachment of the 'Negro to the Empire'[78] led to the War Office's retroactive application of the full terms of Army Order No. 1 to the regiment in February of 1919.

The Colonial Office and the local authorities in Jamaica were apprehensive of the bitter resentment of soldiers of the BWIR on their return after the war. They were especially conscious of the fact that most of the men who had taken part in the Taranto Mutiny and led the Caribbean League were Jamaican. Efforts in the Jamaican Legislative

Council to allay the soldiers' resentment included passing a trade union law, an employers' liability law and an act in 1919 allowing each soldier to vote in the next election only.

The black soldiers' experience of unequal treatment, culminating in the Taranto Mutiny, increased desire for affirmative action against racial and class oppression in some colonies, whilst creating it in others. The worst fears of the Imperial authorities were confirmed in July of 1919, when a well-planned uprising broke out in Belize, the capital city of British Honduras. Demobilised BWIR soldiers systematically attacked businesses and the homes of the dominating class. The governor of the colony was convinced that the insurrection had been conceived at Taranto and during the homeward voyage. British Honduras was not the only colonial territory affected. In December of 1919, a militant strike in Port-of-Spain, Trinidad, was supported by former soldiers of the BWIR and, once again, official reports blamed Taranto, claiming that the mutinous spirit behind the strike there had reached the general population of Trinidad.[79]

There is little doubt that these rebellions were early demonstrations of black nationalism in the British West Indies, the leaders of the insurrection in Belize City stating that British Honduras should be 'the black man's country', mirroring the sentiments of their fellows in Port-of-Spain, who were 'imbued with the idea that there must be a black world controlled and governed by the black people of their own race'.[80] It is clear that the experiences of black soldiers during the First World War heightened existing nationalist sentiments in 1919 and the later West Indian political awakening of 1937–38 would owe a lot to these beginnings. The revolt at Taranto was thus the beginning of the national liberation struggle leading to the demise of colonial rule in most of the British Caribbean, and returning soldiers would play a large part in it. The British government realised that everything had changed too: 'Nothing we can do will alter the fact that the black man has begun to think and feel himself as good as the white'.[81] When George Blackman, the Barbadian veteran of the BWIR mentioned in Chapter Three, returned home from France, the Empire was changing. After the war, the newly

THE RETURN OF THE HEROES

politicised soldiers returning to the islands were encouraged to emigrate to Cuba, Colombia and Venezuela by the island governments, fearful that everything was now different. In 2002, George was partially blind and almost deaf, living in his niece Anita's house in northern Barbados. Still articulate and energetic, his comments about England, which he at one time considered his mother country, were still bitter, and had become increasingly so over the years. At the end of the war, West Indian troops were kept away from the victory parades and hurried back home under armed guard:

> When the war finish, there was nothing. [...] I had to eat and buy clothes. Who going to give me clothes? I didn't have a father or nobody. Now I said, 'The English are no good.' I went to Jamaica and I meet up some soldiers and I asked them, 'Here boy, what the government give you?' They said, 'The government give us nothing.' I said, 'We just the same.' 'I need help but the English government don't help me with nothing,' he says. 'It's she [Anita], she who give me this'.[82]

George Blackman took his cue from the government's encouragement and began travelling around South America, working first as a mechanic in Colombia, before finally retiring to Venezuela to live with his daughter. In 2002, the government of Barbados helped to bring him home at last. George was not entitled to a pension in Venezuela, though he had worked there for decades. In Barbados he still encountered difficulties, having been away for so long. At the time of his death, one dedicated civil servant was still processing his application for a pension in his home country. He received nothing from the British. George Blackman saw the situation in simple terms: 'England don't have anything to do with me now. England turned me over. Barbadians rule Barbados now'.[83]

African troops did not fare much better. The return home of the South African Native Labour Contingent (SANLC) was also disappointing. A year before the war ended, King George V addressed the SANLC in Abbeville on 17 July 1917 as 'part of my great Armies which are fighting for the liberty and freedom of my subjects of all races and creed[s] throughout the Empire'.[84] Having served on the Western Front, they were not issued medals or ribbons like their comrades of the High Commission Territories, who had originally served in the same units back home. Those who served in South-West Africa with the South African Artillery and the South African Mounted Rifles (SAMR) had also had their share of awards at the conclusion of hostilities. It seemed to the men of the SANLC that they were being penalised for serving overseas rather than rewarded. African troops returning to South Africa from the front were disbanded soon after arrival.[85]

The First World War had been traumatic for most of its participants, upsetting class structures in the United Kingdom and sparking movements for independence in her colonies. Despite the fact that black people had lived and worked in Britain for centuries, a negative vision of their presence assumed a new prominence after the First World War. The oft-heard mantra goes that the world would never be the same again, but this was indeed the beginning of change.

EPILOGUE

Though largely forgotten, soldiers of African descent have served in the British Army for centuries. It has been shown that there is even evidence that black soldiers had a role in recruiting others of their race into the armed forces during the late eighteenth and early nineteenth century. The fact that their story has all but disappeared from the public consciousness would seem to have had other additional causes than prejudice, such as the way they are recorded, each playing a part in their role being quietly forgotten. Countries such as the United States have long shown a heightened awareness of race in their census and other areas of public administration, which has prevented black servicemen becoming 'lost in the paperwork' over the course of their history to the same extent as British servicemen, although many African American historians would agree that prevalent racism has certainly kept the role of black US soldiers out of the spotlight. The history of slavery had shaped the treatment of America's black population and the documentation of a person's race or colour was still an issue at the time of the Passing Laws after the First World War. This heightened awareness of race meant that black soldiers were at least officially recorded in the United States, their names remaining visible in documents to be rediscovered by historians.

The racial prejudice shown towards black servicemen in the United

Kingdom of the early twentieth century was shaped by different circumstances, in spite of Britain's earlier role in the slave trade. The black population was proportionally much smaller and official documents in Britain were not adapted to record ethnicity, despite the British Empire having a huge black population in Africa and the Caribbean. Native Britons were assumed to be white, whilst black people were often assumed to be from the far-flung colonies of the Empire, resulting in Black British servicemen assuming an archival invisibility and confusion with soldiers from Africa and the Caribbean. The story of the Black Tommy would seem to have been something of a phased narrative, mingling in the public consciousness with that of other forces officially raised in the Empire from the Caribbean, Canada and Africa, all playing their own part in bringing alive the image of the Black Tommy as they passed through British ports of disembarkation, such as Liverpool, on their way to supplementing their comrades from the United Kingdom already serving on the Western Front.

The career of the Black Tommy developed from being a relatively small number of British-born Black and domiciled recruits, in some cases long-resident volunteers at the beginning of the war, added to by other volunteers mostly from the Caribbean and the African continent. All of these originally had at least some chance of fighting in regular units. Then something happened. If Black Tommies in the regular army have been forgotten through the racist imperial hubris of post-war historians and difficulties of identification, this had been added to by yet another factor in the course of the war: racist attitudes embedded in wartime governmental policies. With the arrival of the British West Indies Regiment (BWIR), the British-based Black Tommy appears to have been 'swallowed up' by the larger black force, in some cases losing certain privileges, such as pensions, and, if it has ever been a privilege, the right to take part in combat with the enemy.

The manner in which black soldiers in general served their countries of allegiance varied tremendously. In the British Army and the BWIR (not to mention the Canadian and French armies), the norm was for officers to be of wholly European descent, while black soldiers in the US Army could expect to be led by black officers, at least at a subordinate level. Colonial forces of all the European powers in Africa and the Caribbean comprised black soldiers led by white officers. We have seen that black soldiers could be found in regular units of the British Army and – confusingly – sometimes 'co-opted' into the BWIR, once it was based in the United Kingdom, as though Black British recruits were being reclassified with the arrival of Caribbean colonial troops on British soil.

Because of the irregularities and inconsistencies of recruitment, along with the fact that some had already been enlisted and not transferred into the BWIR, some Black Tommies, such as Albert James, appear to have continued in regular units until the end of the war. Those, like Private A. Francis, who had been placed in the BWIR when it arrived, appear to have had a long struggle after demobilisation to gain the rights of their fellows in regular units. The arrival of volunteers from the Caribbean and the African continent, 'big brother', in the form of officially raised, relatively large contingents from the countries of the ancestors of many Black British troops, may well have had the effect of causing the identity of 'home grown' Black Tommies to be lost amidst a general assumption of who they were. The effect of this has not only been an impact upon public awareness of the contribution of the home-based Black British presence in the First World War, but on any knowledge of a wider narrative of the Black British community ever existing at this time. This perhaps makes the role of Black Tommies even more important in helping to retrieve a wider sociological/community history in danger of becoming lost.

To a public still generally ignorant of the history of Britain's black community, with race now being dealt with only as a contemporary issue following the arrival of the *Empire Windrush* in 1948 and a more recent body of black immigrants, information about soldiers of African descent in the First World War comes as a surprise to most people, any discovery deemed newsworthy. The myth of Walter Tull being the first black officer in the British regular army has been shown to be as wrong as that of James Durham being the first black soldier in the British Army in 1905. This book began by questioning the story that the first shot of the Great War was fired by a bandsman of the 4th Royal Irish Dragoon Guards in August

EPILOGUE

1914, which it has shown to be unlikely and almost impossible to verify amongst other contenders. Similarly, using definitive terms such as 'first' has been shown to be a mistake, such claims often being made without even the most perfunctory of investigation.

One of the tasks of this study seemed to be to find examples of black officers, but it soon became clear in the course of this study that one soon became two, two became four, until it had become plain that more existed and simply quantifying them in a tabular way did not do them justice within the confines of this exploratory narrative. There is tremendous scope for further research into the world of the Black Tommy which will add significantly to the military history of the Great War. Though the King's Regulations forbade officers not of wholly European ancestry from holding a commission in the British Army, there were ways of contravening such strictures. It remains to be seen just how commonplace such appointments were, or at least the extent to which these 'concessions' were made. Besides medical officers, a number of black officers leading white troops have been identified in this book. In addition to these, Lieutenant J.A. Gordon Smyth of the BWIR led black troops, but should nevertheless have been precluded from being an officer, as even West Indian troops were led by white officers. Another, the Canadian Captain William A. White, one of many black leaders who had led the drive for a black unit, was given the honorary rank of captain. It is possible that these are not the sum total of black officers, and there is some wisdom in the words of the historian Jeffrey Green, who says of the First World War black officers he has chanced upon in his own research, 'There will be others: keep looking'.[1]

Although black people have lived in Britain for far longer than may be generally recognised by many of the British public, the First World War is commonly recognised as a period when large numbers of black working men arrived in Britain and Western Europe to cover wartime manpower shortages. In what many considered a white man's war, British military and colonising elites feared that black military assistance could have the effect of undermining imperial racial stratification. Communications between governmental bodies such as the War and the Colonial Offices often appeared almost frantic in their efforts to preserve existing colonial racial practices and power relationships, with new actors and imperatives arising within the unprecedented context of global, total war.[2]

The conflict and struggle amongst these historical entities appears to have become the determining factor of how Black Tommies were viewed and treated, rather than simply the casual racism prevalent in British society. This was often shown as having little consensus in the early twentieth century, as borne out by the experiences of black applicants seeking recruitment with varying results. Scrutiny of those episodes when blatant racism was shown towards black soldiers and ex-soldiers reveals the intervention of historical actors at an institutional level, bent on fomenting negative perceptions of black people, such as the actions of the Seamen's Union after the war and the appalling racism exhibited by the War and the Colonial Offices with their seemingly interminable bickering and intransigence at the slightest concession to colonial people of African descent fulfilling what they felt to be their patriotic duty. This is certainly not to deny the level of racism amongst the British public at this time, but in this study of soldiers of African descent it has been shown that the responses of racist individuals to black soldiers were likely to be *ad hoc* and perhaps lacking the seemingly determined efforts shown by certain government bodies to enforce negative policies.[3] Links with British labour struggles and imperial mechanisms are found to be added to issues of racial prejudice, readily identified in the experiences of Black Tommies both during and after the war, whether British-born, Caribbean or African. This conclusion points towards institutional racism and the experience of soldiers of African descent during the war certainly concurs with Laura Tabili's findings regarding civilian life after hostilities ended.[4]

It might not be too mischievous to ask who were the most patriotic, the prevaricating government officers, indulging their own private prejudices at a time when the country was in dire need of manpower from whatever source, or the British-based individuals, colonial West Indians and others, who fought for the right to raise forces from their own countries in order to serve the British Empire? Those British politicians mentioned at the beginning of this book who disagreed with prevalent governmental attitudes, such as the group including Winston Churchill which favoured the use of black colonial troops, would appear to have been merely assuming a purely pragmatic stance rather than entertaining any sympathy for black peoples' desire to participate, but at least they cannot be accused of being unpatriotic. In contrast, the attitude of the War Office and the Colonial Service would seem to have been driven by individuals giving free reign to their own negative impulses. The term 'Lions led by donkeys' has been widely used to blame the incompetent and indifferent generals who sent brave British infantry to their deaths during the First World War. Although some British historians have questioned this criticism of the military leadership of the period, it would seem that 'donkeys' could also be found in the Civil Service.

With the conclusion of hostilities, like comrades of other races, soldiers of African descent returning to their respective countries of origin brought home with them expectations of a 'brave new world' promised by politicians of all of the participating powers. Members of the British-born community, in some cases of several generations standing, had also answered the call of king and country. One contemporary author, born in a port city and familiar with Black British people, both born and domiciled, wrote:

> There were few Saturday night celebrations among Flukey Alley's Flukes [Polynesians, so called because their faces were thought to be flat], Sparling Street's Negroes and the Chinamen of Pitt Street. Even in these un-British sections tragedy and gloom had deepened for many half-caste boys had lost their lives in the war.[5]

The endurance and bravery shown by these soldiers and the patriotism towards the nation to which they chose to give their allegiance deserves to be remembered, as does the fact that their descendants continue to serve queen and country to the present day. Their absence from history books means that the whole story is not being told and other versions have been found to fill the lacunae, endangering the historical narrative of a people, reducing it to a secret history, sometimes oral, left in the metaphorical and literal shoe boxes of British history, to become weaker with each passing generation until it eventually disappears to be replaced by popular, even academic, assumptions. There is an old African belief, also found in ancient European folklore, that a person dies twice: first, when they 'shake off this mortal coil', and second, when they are forgotten and people stop saying their name and recalling their deeds. Finding the records of these soldiers was difficult after a century of neglect and it would not take very long for a final historical demise to occur. Another fifty years could mean the disappearance of these people from the records and even offering an incomplete history may serve to jog the collective memory at a critical point into seeking further information, thus helping to preserve that memory – one of the aims of this book.

As well as leaving a gap in British history, the consequences of not telling the story of black servicemen as members of a historically neglected group not only in the First, but in the Second World War, can sometimes be harsh and unpleasant, with particularly jarring effects on the lives of ordinary Black British people. June Burnett was a Liverpool-born black artist who staged national and international exhibitions in several European cities. She lived a colourful and sometimes sad life reflecting the prevalent racism of the times. In an interview with the author, she recalled her early childhood in Liverpool and the day she proudly asked her father, newly returned from army service, to come to her school:

> Although I had never thought of myself as different from other kids, I was to be pulled up short. With the war just over, soldiers who were really our brothers, uncles and dads dressed up, were coming back. I had asked my dad to meet me at four o'clock. Whilst I waited for him I played tick with my friends in the yard. Suddenly one of the boys stopped and, pointing to the school gate, shouted – 'Look, there's a nigger pretending to be in the army.' Everyone stopped playing and looked. 'He isn't a nigger; he's my dad.' I replied hotly. 'Anyway he is in the army!'[6]

This unfortunate incident requires little comment, other than to suggest that perhaps Sir Harry Hamilton Johnston's entreaty in a book written

EPILOGUE

during the First World War might still pertain today. Sir Harry Johnston was the archetypal British colonial imperialist, signing treaties and ruling colonial governments. Like many other British empire builders, he was influenced by the eugenics movement and believed in British and European superiority over 'lesser breeds', but nevertheless showed a tendency towards paternalistic governance. In spite of the fact that he was a man of his age and could hardly escape from prevalent influences, Johnston appears to have had a revelation ahead of his time when, even at such an early period, he felt moved to write in 1917:

> Every British boy and girl, every white, brown, and black child and student, above all those who are likely to rise to play a part, small or great in the affairs of State, should before all things be versed in a knowledge of the different races of man living at the present day. If this education were imparted in its simplest form to school-children as a subject of elementary tuition, if it were the incentive to scholarships, the cause of degrees at universities, the winner of many marks in Government examinations, we should not repeat the grievous mistakes recorded in our past colonial history and our foreign policy, our trade precepts and our warfare.[7] [...] Part of the blame, however, rests with our scholastic authorities; If nothing is taught in the schools, high or low, public, private or commercial, of the Ethnology of the British Empire, so we shall continue to blunt the sympathies of our coloured fellow-subjects by exposing them to the gibes and ill-treatment of white men too ignorant and narrow-minded to understand their responsibilities.[8]

This still seems to be a shameful omission in our present education system.

Amongst the outcomes of the war were economic considerations, Britain's new position on the world stage and issues of imperial unity. Not the least was the struggle for the redistribution of wealth and power by new players on the home front, such as the unions.[9] Claims that the war had stimulated support for colonial independence movements and encouraged a new-found racial pride are subject to debate, as beliefs that the European 'masters' had now been shown to be vulnerable and untrustworthy did not result in the sort of armed insurrection by black veterans feared by some white colonisers. Another view is that the war, if anything, strengthened loyal troop's bond with the monarchy, but in the West Indies this led rather perversely to a feeling of entitlement following the loyalty shown, subversive in its own right of the imperial order in spite of the initial feeling of unity with the Mother Country. This meant that following the war, movements for independence in the West Indies were inevitable.[10]

Military service away from their own homeland had given many soldiers of the African Diaspora experience of political units larger than their own neighbourhoods and hometowns, and recognition of the existence of a much larger territorial entity. This would play its part in promoting a sense of racial identity as well as their place in the nations they served. And this would not only apply to Black British soldiers, but to other soldiers of the African Diaspora. The first African Americans to arrive at the Western Front had been in for a surprise, not least a company of African Americans specially recruited for stevedore service:

> The negroes had been outfitted with old cavalry overcoats of a period shortly after the Civil War. They wore blue coats with gold buttons and the lining was a tasteful but hardly somber shade of crimson. Nor were the negroes without picturesque qualities even when they had shed their coats and gone to work. Their working shirts of white were inked all over with pious sentences calculated to last through the submarine zone, but piety was mixed. One big negro, for instance, had written upon his shirt: 'The Lord is my shepherd', but underneath he had drawn a large starfish for luck. A few daring ones had ornamented themselves with skulls and crossbones. To the negroes fell the bitterest disappointment of the American landing in France. Two Savannah stevedores caught sight of a black soldier in the French uniform and rushed up to exchange greetings. The Senegalese shrugged his shoulders and turned away from the flood of English.
>
> 'That,' said one of the American darkies, 'is the most ignorantest and stuck up nigger I ever did see.' They were not yet ready to believe that the negro race had let itself in for the amazing complications of a foreign language.[11]

The African Americans in question were using the term of abuse in a way that is surprisingly similar to modern 'street' usage, which turns it around and makes of it a term of self-affirmation and group membership, however maligned that group may be and however others might choose to use it. The commentator saw this as a humorous incident, but even those who see it as offensive may be missing its significance. Something was happening that was far more important. In those days of comparatively poor communication between black people of the Diaspora, here we have two groups of people of African descent meeting for the first time after centuries of separation, taking the first steps, probing each other in a way that would lead to the development of a worldwide relationship between people of the Caribbean, Canada, the United States, the African continent and British-born Blacks, speaking many different languages. These connections would range from Marcus Garvey, Martin Luther King Jr and the American Black Freedom movement to Nelson Mandela and the concept of a Black Diaspora.

At the time of the 1919 riots, an elite group of professionals and students found common cause in their concern for the plight of returning servicemen. When the Guyanese lawyer Edward Nelson of Manchester defended black men in Liverpool, the London-based African Progress Union paid part of his legal fees. The attacks on people of African descent did not go unnoticed in many parts of the British Empire. Open violence had broken out in Trinidad in December 1919 and in Sierra Leone, where there were also problems with the rice crop and anti-Syrian agitation. Repatriated black sailors were familiar with the racial disturbances in Liverpool and Cardiff, carrying with them at least the danger of the possibility of reprisals against white residents. The Universal Negro Improvement Association (UNIA) led by Marcus Garvey, who published papers in New York such as the weekly *Negro World*, and other American black-led political movements of the time were blamed for the growing unrest in the British colonies, but the suffering experienced by the black and other communities considered 'coloured' after the First World War was long-lasting and negative attitudes continued after the outbreak of violence in 1919.[12] Black-led political groups such as the Pan-African movement and African American initiatives were important for the Black Diaspora, fuelling demands for local representation and, in some cases, self-government. The impact of Garvey's UNIA was not lost upon Black British servicemen and led the way in revealing deficiencies and negative thinking behind the Imperial system. Not only those who had experienced violent attacks in the riots of 1919, but men from black fighting units who had encountered a general prejudice and insensitivity from the military authorities felt anger at the British authorities.[13]

Although the war should have bound together the disparate parts of the Empire, early home front propaganda, along with jingoism and nationalism, may only have forestalled the dissolution of domestic order at home and in the colonies. This was witnessed at the outbreak of the war in the protestations of loyalty for the duration of the war by both the South African Native National Congress and Marcus Garvey's Universal Negro Improvement Association and African Communities (Imperial) League, mentioned earlier. It would seem that, if anything, the war intensified and accelerated challenges to the distribution of power and wealth in both Britain and the Empire.[14]

Soldiers of African descent were not the only colonial subjects to find their confidence in British honour and fair play eroded by official bungling and colonial racial practices. Close proximity and first-hand experience of Europeans also affected the view of the both the colonial rulers and the self-perception of the Indian troops and the Chinese labour corps. Before the war ended, there was already a sense of 'a compact betrayed' between colonial subjects and the Mother Country,[15] not to mention an opportunity lost. Following the war, on the home front the British authorities were prompted to not only maintain, but strengthen race, class and gender structures to support the prevalent system of wealth and power. The decline of British merchant shipping also played its part in reinforcing the racial, geographic and economic barriers between black and white workers in Britain and black working people in the colonies. At the beginning of the First World War, the notion of a gradualist colonial policy which promised eventual power and equality to Britain's colonies had already been losing traction. The view that political autonomy, if not independence, required a lengthy period of European tutelage was now to be weakened by middle-class educated colonial elites, already shown to be active at the outset of the war and continuing to make demands between the wars.[16]

The Tomb of The Unknown Warrior holds an unidentified British soldier killed on a European battlefield during the First World War. He was buried 'amongst the kings' with due ceremony in Westminster Abbey to represent the many hundreds of thousands of Empire dead of all races. Yet many people in modern Britain are not aware of the presence of soldiers of African descent on the battlefields of France and elsewhere during the First World War. Besides the technical reasons already described, they are frequently often only 'invisible' because we do not expect to see them or have shut them out for another reason, such as not rating them in the past because of prevalent attitudes towards their colour, much as servants were often ignored in the houses of the wealthy. Some British soldiers who served alongside them, reliant on their support at an individual level in the heat of battle, did not forget Black British soldiers. To many white British Tommies, black soldiers were 'our' men and were often known personally, respected and remembered; those who lost their lives continued to live on in their memories long after the greatest war ever known was over. Around the main inscription on the tombstone at Westminster Abbey are four short separate texts, one of which serves particularly well as an epitaph for the many 'invisible' soldiers of African descent from continental Africa, the Caribbean and those Black Tommies born on British soil who took part in the Great War:

> UNKNOWN AND YET WELL KNOWN,
> DYING AND BEHOLD WE LIVE.

NOTES AND REFERENCES

INTRODUCTION

1 Martin Gilbert, *The First World War: A Complete History* (London: Phoenix, 2008), 55. See also Max Hastings, *Catastrophe: Europe Goes to War* (London: William Collins, 2013), 203–04.
2 'The Gold Coast Mobilized, A Proud Record: The Case of Sergeant Grunshi', *The Times*, London, Monday, 25 March 1940, Issue 48,572, 7, col. G.
3 J. Lee Thompson, *Forgotten Patriot: A Life of Alfred, Viscount Milner of St. James's and Cape Town, 1854–1925* (Madison, NJ: Fairleigh Dickinson University Press, 2007), 311.
4 *The Times*, 25 March 1940, Issue 48,572, 7, col. G.
5 John Keegan, *The First World War* (London: Hutchinson, 1998), 8. See also Klaus J. Bade, *Migration in European History: The Making of Europe*, trans. Allison Brown (Oxford: Blackwell, 2003), 167–68. See also H. Willmott, *World War I* (New York, NY: Dorling Kindersley, 2003), 307.
6 David, Killingray, *The Conquest of Togo: Companion to World War I*, ed. John Horne (London: Blackwell, 2012), 115–16.
7 Keegan, *The First World War*, 224.
8 David Killingray, 'Repercussions of World War I in the Gold Coast', *Journal of African History*, 19.1 (1978), 39.

NOTES AND REFERENCES

9 Killingray, 'Repercussions of World War I', 39, note 4.
10 E.H. Gorges, *The Great War in West Africa* (Uckfield: Naval & Military Press, 2004), 19.
11 Gorges, *The Great War in West Africa*, 33–35.
12 L. Gann and Duignan, *The Rulers of German Africa 1884–1914* (Redwood City, CA: Stanford University Press, 1977), 217.
13 Keegan, *The First World War*, 228.
14 Keegan, *The First World War*, 228–29.
15 Bruce Baker, *Escape from Domination in Africa: Political Disengagement and its Consequences in Sub-Saharan Africa* (Oxford: James Currey, 2000), 83.
16 Keegan, *The First World War*, 230.
17 Keegan, *The First World War*, 230.
18 Harry Hamilton Johnston, *The Black Man's Part in the War: An Account of the Dark-Skinned Population of the British Empire* (London: Simpkin, Marshall, Hamilton, Kent & Co. Ltd, 1917), 66–67.
19 Keegan, *The First World War*, 230.
20 TNA WO 25/454. WO 25. 69 Foot 1826–1830.
21 Ray Costello, *Black Liverpool: The Early History of Britain's Oldest Black Community 1730–1918* (Liverpool: Picton Press, 2001), 43–44. See also Laura Tabili, *We Ask for British Justice: Workers and Racial Difference in Late Imperial Britain* (Ithaca, NY: Cornell University Press, 1994), 16.
22 E.J. Scott, *The American Negro in the World War* (Chicago: Homewood Press, 1919), 9. This book is held in the Schomburg Center for Research in Black Culture, a research unit of the New York Public Library.
23 Scott, *The American Negro in the World War*, 443.
24 Scott, *The American Negro in the World War*, 16.
25 Scott, *The American Negro in the World War*, 231.
26 'History: Range and content', *Teaching and Learning, The School Curriculum*, Secondary National Curriculum until 2014, Department of Education, 5 http://webarchive.nationalarchives.gov.uk/20130123124929/http://www.education.gov.uk/schools/teachingandlearning/curriculum/secondary/b00199545/history/programme/range (accessed 3 September 2015).

CHAPTER ONE: WHOSE WAR?

1 Peter Warwick, 'Myth of the White Man's War', *Black People and the South African War, 1899–1902* (Cambridge: Cambridge University Press, 1989), 6–28.

2 Richard Smith, *Jamaican Volunteers in the First World War: Race, Masculinity and the Development of National Consciousness (Politics, Culture & Society in)* (Manchester: Manchester University Press, 2010), 63.
3 D. Killingray, 'The Idea of a British Imperial African Army', *Journal of African History*, 20 (1979), 421–36.
4 Howe, *Race War and Nationalism*, 29–30.
5 Christian Koller, 'The Recruitment of Colonial Troops in Africa and Asia and their Deployment in Europe during the First World War', *Immigrants & Minorities*, 26.1–2 (March–July 2008), 113–14.
6 'Coloured Men (British Forces)', (Hansard, 30 July 1918) HC Deb 30 July 1918 vol. 109 cc 229-30 229), 29.
7 Koller, 'The Recruitment of Colonial Troops in Africa and Asia', 114.
8 'Coloured Men (British Forces)', (Hansard (30 July 1918) HC Deb 30 July 1918 vol. 109 cc229-30 229), 29.
9 Harold E. Raugh, *The Victorians at War, 1815–1914: An Encyclopedia of British Military History* (Santa Barbara, CA: ABC-CLIO Ltd, 2004), 120.
10 Rudyard Kipling, *Collected Poems of Rudyard Kipling*, intr. R.T. Jones (Ware: Wordsworth Editions, 1994), 413.
11 Koller, 'The Recruitment of Colonial Troops in Africa and Asia', 121.
12 Koller, 'The Recruitment of Colonial Troops in Africa and Asia', 114.
13 Graham A. Smith, 'Jim Crow on the Home Front (1942–1945)', *New Community*, 8.3 (Winter 1980), 318.
14 Howe, *Race War and Nationalism*, 34.
15 Howe, *Race War and Nationalism*, 35–36.
16 Frank Cundall, *Jamaica's Part in the Great War 1914–1918* (London: The Institute of Jamaica by the West India Committee, 1925), 27. See also Howe, *Race War and Nationalism*, 37.
17 Howe, *Race War and Nationalism*, 39–40.
18 Timothy C. Winegard, *Indigenous Peoples of the British Dominions and the First World War* (Cambridge: Cambridge University Press, 2011), 143; also TNA 363–64.
19 Smith, *Jamaican Volunteers in the First World War*.
20 A.B. Ellis, *The History of the First West India Regiment* (London: Chapman and Hall, 1885; also Project Gutenberg EBook (EBook #29984)), 26; see also Brian Dyde, *The Empty Sleeve: The Story of the West India Regiments of the British Army* (St John's, Antigua: Hansib, 1997), 22.
21 Dyde, *The Empty Sleeve*, 253.
22 Dyde, *The Empty Sleeve*, 254.

23 Dyde, *The Empty Sleeve*, 260–61.
24 Guy Grannum (ed.), *Tracing your Caribbean Ancestors: A National Archives Guide* (London: A. & C. Black Publishers Ltd., 2012), 75.
25 Fryer, *Staying Power: The History of Black People in Britain* (London: Pluto Press, 1985), 315.
26 TNA CO 318/333/50043, 'West Indian Contingent'. Min. by Grindle, 21 December 1914.
27 Graham Maddocks, *Liverpool Pals: 17th, 18th, 19th, 20th (Service) Battalions, The King's (Liverpool Regiment)* (Barnsley: Pen and Sword Military, 2008), 25–29, 231–80.
28 In my earlier book *Black Salt: Seafarers of African Descent on British Ships* (Liverpool: Liverpool University Press, 2012), young black maritime recruits are shown to have made the same sort of joint decision (see page 176).
29 'Enlistment', Ch. X, 28, *Manual of Military Law 1907* (London: Printed for His Majesty's Stationery Office by Harrison and Sons, St Martin's Lane, 1907), 190.
30 'Special provisions as to Persons to be Enlisted. Enlistment 95', ARMY ACT, *Manual of Military Law 1907*, 358.
31 'Special provisions as to Persons to be Enlisted. Enlistment 95', 358.
32 G. Milne, 'Sailortown: Representing the Maritime-Urban Frontier' (unpublished conference paper, School of History, University of Liverpool), 15.
33 Tabili, *We Ask for British Justice*, 4.
34 Smith, *Jamaican Volunteers in the First World War*, 64–65.
35 Killingray, 'All the King's Men?', 167–69.
36 Killingray, 'All the King's Men?', 169.
37 Gary Mead, *The Good Soldier: The Biography of Douglas Haig* (London: Atlantic Books, 2007), 91.
38 Mead, *The Good Soldier*, 98.
39 Mead, *The Good Soldier*, 195–96.
40 Mead, *The Good Soldier*, 472, note 8.
41 Smith, *Jamaican Volunteers in the First World War*, 67.
42 TNA WO32/4765 General White. New York to WO (copy of Secret telegram), 19 February 1918.
43 Tabili, *We Ask for British Justice*, 22.
44 Howe, *Race War and Nationalism*, 132.
45 Sir Etienne Dupuch, *A Salute to Friend and Foe* (Nassau, Bahamas: Tribune, 1982), 57. See also Howe, *Race War and Nationalism*, 132.

NOTES AND REFERENCES

46 Howe, *Race War and Nationalism*, 32.
47 Fryer, *Staying Power*, 159–81.
48 TNA WO363, 0426, Albert James.
49 Fryer, *Staying Power*, 165–80. See also Elof Axel Carlson, *The Unfit: A History of a Bad Idea* (Cold Spring Harbor, NY: Cold Spring Harbor Laboratory Press, 2001), passim.
50 R. Soloway, 'Counting the Desperates: Race Deterioration in Edwardian England', *Journal of Contemporary History*, 17.1 (1982), 137–64.
51 Stephen McGreal, *Cheshire Bantams: 15th 16th & 17th Battalions of the Cheshire Regiment* (Barnsley: Pen and Sword Ltd., 2006), 20–37.
52 Smith, *Jamaican Volunteers in the First World War*, 104.
53 Winston Spencer Churchill, *The River War* (London: Four Square Books, 1960), 92.
54 Stan Hugill, *Sailortown* (London: Routledge and Kegan Paul, 1967), l.
55 Ann Clayton, 'Chavasse, Noel Godfrey (1884–1917)', *Oxford Dictionary of National Biography* (Oxford: Oxford University Press, 2004).
56 *Third Annual Report of the Harrington Free School for the Education of Poor Children in Toxteth Park* (5 May 1818) (From the author's private collection, acting as official keeper of the document).
57 Norman Manley, 'The Autobiography of Norman Washington Manley', *Jamaica Journal*, 7.1 (March–June 1973), 6–7.
58 Miller et al., *As Good As Any Man*, 93–94.
59 Manley, 'The Autobiography of Norman Washington Manley', 8.
60 Agnes Brew, née James, sister of Albert James, in an interview in July 1970.
61 Peter Hart, *1918, A Very British Victory* (London: Weidenfeld and Nicolson, 2008), 356.

CHAPTER TWO: THE INVISIBLE ARMY – THE SEARCH

1 John Lichfield, 'Images Rescued from Dump Reveal Black British "Tommy" at the Somme', *The Independent*, Saturday 23 May 2009.
2 *Untold stories: Black Families in the First World War* (Exhibition, Museum of Liverpool, 2013–14).
3 Robert Porter, Henry Gannett and William Hunt, 'Progress of the Nation', *Report on Population of the United States at the Eleventh Census: 1890, Part 1* (Washington, D.C.: Government Printing Office, 1895), xviii–xxxiv.

NOTES AND REFERENCES

4 Costello, *Black Salt*, 60.
5 Jeffrey Green, *Black Edwardians: Black People in Britain 1901–1914* (London: Cass, 1998), 68–70.
6 Costello, *Black Liverpool*, 8.
7 E. Marke, *In Troubled Waters* (London: Karia Press, 1986), 24–25. There is now some doubt that the poster referred to existed during the war and that it only became popular after the war ended. It is possible that Ernest Marke did see a similar poster with the same image however. At the time of writing, James Taylor, a researcher of the history of recruitment posters, is writing a book which shows how the Kitchener image inspired similar posters, including a cover by Alfred Leete, 5 September 1914 on the *London Opinion* magazine, with the word BRITONS, above the same picture of the Field Marshal pointing, with the words 'wants YOU – Join Your Country's Army!' beneath, and the words 'God Save The King' printed along the bottom (See James Taylor, *Your Country Needs You: The Secret History of the Propaganda Poster* (Glasgow: Saraband, 2013), 9.
8 Morag Miller, Roy Laycock, John Sadler and Rosie Serdville, *As Good As Any Man* (Stroud: The History Press, 2014), 9–10.
9 Miller, et al., *As Good As Any Man*, 21.
10 Miller, et al., *As Good As Any Man*, 18–19.
11 Miller, et al., *As Good As Any Man*, 27.
12 Miller, et al., *As Good As Any Man*, 45.
13 Miller, et al., *As Good As Any Man*, 120.
14 Miller, et al., *As Good As Any Man*, 77.
15 Miller, et al., *As Good As Any Man*, 149.
16 Miller, et al., *As Good As Any Man*, 136.
17 Miller, et al., *As Good As Any Man*, 174–75.
18 Phil Vasili, *Colouring over the White Line: The History of Black Footballers in Britain* (Edinburgh: Mainstream Publishing Company, 2000), 51.
19 Tabili, *We Ask for British Justice*, 141. See also Sydney Collins, *Coloured Minorities in Britain: Studies in British Race Relations based on African, West Indian and Asiatic Immigrants* (London: Lutterworth Press, 1957), 36.
20 Stephen Bourne, *Black Poppies: Britain's Black Community and the Great War* (Stroud: The History Press, 2014), 48–49.
21 David Killingray, 'All the King's Men? Blacks in the British Army in the First World War, 1914–1918', in Rainer Lotz and Ian Pegg (eds), *Under the Imperial Carpet: Essays in Black History 1780–1950* (Crawley: Rabbit Press, 1986), 176.

22 RDP, Birth Certificate for Harold Brown, Application Number 4491681-1.
23 IWM Documents 5579 Private Papers. Poplar 1C 647. I am indebted to the historian Stephen Bourne, who very kindly alerted me to the presence of this soldier.
24 CWGC, France Area, 5–7 rue Angèle Richard, BP 109, 62217 Beaurains, France; interview with Barbara Tasker and Suzanne Morris, cousins of Walter Colebourne.
25 J. Green, 'George William Christian: A Liverpool "Black" in Africa', *Transactions of the Historical Society of Lancashire and Cheshire*, 134 (1986), 141–46.
26 Walter Richards, *His Majesty's Territorial Army* (London: Virtue, 1910), 137.
27 Everard Wyrall, *The History of the King's Regiment (Liverpool) 1914–19* (Uckfield: Naval and Military Press, 2002), 72.
28 J.O. Coop, *Story of the 55th (West Lancashire) Division* (Uckfield: Naval and Military Press, 2001), 26.
29 Gary Sheffield, *The Somme* (London: Cassell, 2003), 68.
30 Keegan, *The First World War*, 396–97.
31 Private Walter Colebourne, Pier and Face 1 D 8 B and 8 C Thiepval Memorial, CWGC.
32 Anthony Bruce, *The Last Crusade: The Palestine Campaign in the First World War* (London: Thistle Publishing, 2013), 47.
33 Bruce, *The Last Crusade*, 53–56.
34 LRBDM, Birth Certificate of Albert's second child, Edith, 24 December 1914, Cert. No. 3.
35 Costello, *Black Liverpool*, 52.
36 Costello, *Black Liverpool*, 44–46.
37 As told by Agnes Brew, née James, sister of Albert James, in a personal interview in July 1970.
38 TNA WO363, 0426, Albert James, War Office: Soldiers' Documents, First World War 'Burnt Documents' (Microfilm Copies); National Archives Microfilm Publication.
39 As told by Agnes Brew, née James, sister of Albert James, in a personal interview in July 1970.
40 TNA WO363, 0428, Albert James.
41 TNA WO363, 0426, Albert James.
42 TNA WO363, 0429, Albert James.
43 TNA WO363, 0444, Albert James.

44 TNA WO363, 0433, Albert James.
45 TNA WO363, 0467, Albert James.
46 As told by Agnes Brew, née James, sister of Albert James, in an interview in July 1970.
47 TNA WO363, 0453, Letter to Albert James from his wife, Ethel.
48 TNA WO363, 0459, Albert James.
49 As told by Agnes Brew, née James, sister of Albert James, in a personal interview in July 1970.
50 C. Guy Powles and A. Wilkie, *The New Zealanders in Sinai and Palestine: Official History New Zealand's Effort in the Great War. Volume III* (Auckland: Whitcombe & Tombs, 1922), 231–35.
51 'Anzac Mounted Division General Staff War Diary', *First World War Diaries* AWM4, 1 60-31, Canberra, Australian War Memorial, September 1918, Part 2, Appendix, 38, 2-3. See also 'New Zealand Mounted Rifles Brigade War Diary', *First World War Diaries* AWM4, 35-1-41, Canberra, Australian War Memorial, September 1918.
52 '503 Lance Corporal R. Turpin, 1 Battalion British West Indies Regiment (La Brea, Trinidad)', Supplement to the *London Gazette*, 25 February 1920, 2296–97.
53 '6357 Private H. Scott, 1 Battalion British West Indies Regiment (St. Anns, Jamaica)' Supplement to the *London Gazette*, 25 February 1920, 2293.
54 'Anzac Mounted Division General Staff War Diary', *First World War Diaries* AWM4, 1-60-31, Canberra, Australian War Memorial, September 1918, Part 2, Appendix 38, 2–3.
55 '1454 Sjt. W.E. Julien, 1 Battalion British West Indies Regiment (St. Georges, Grenada)' Supplement to the *London Gazette*, 25 February 1920, 2288.
56 TNA WO364 2674, Frank Nelson. Soldiers' records (1914–1920), Pension Records.
57 *Liverpool Echo*, 29 June 1915, 7, col. 3.
58 TNA WO364 2674.
59 Costello, *Black Salt*, 109–10.
60 Charles Kay, 'McDavid, Sir Herbert Gladstone (1898–1966)', *Oxford Dictionary of National Biography* (Oxford: Oxford University Press, 2012). See also Captain S.W. Roskill, *A Merchant Fleet in War: Alfred Holt & Co. 1939–1945* (London: Collins, 1962).
61 John Ramsland, *Remembering Aboriginal Heroes* (Melbourne: Brolga Publishing, 2006), 2–15.
62 Manley, 'The Autobiography of Norman Washington Manley', 12.

63 Killingray, 'All the King's Men?', 176.
64 Howe, *Race War and Nationalism*, 23.

CHAPTER THREE: BLACK VOLUNTEERS – THE EMPIRE AND BEYOND

1 Howe, *Race War and Nationalism*, 30–31.
2 TNA CO 318/333/50043 'West Indian Contingent', Minute of Grindle, 21 December 1914, cited in Howe, *Race War and Nationalism*, 32.
3 Howe, *Race War and Nationalism*, 31–32.
4 Howe, *Race War and Nationalism*, 33.
5 Tony Martin, *Marcus Garvey, Hero: A First Biography* (Dover, MA: Majority Press, 1983), 15–38.
6 Fryer, *Staying Power*, 287–88.
7 Martin, *Marcus Garvey, Hero*, 15–38.
8 TNA T 1/12482.
9 Smith, *Jamaican Volunteers in the First World War*, 63.
10 Green, *Black Edwardians*, 266.
11 Smith, *Jamaican Volunteers in the First World War*, 65.
12 Killingray, 'All the King's Men?', 171–72.
13 Smith, *Jamaican Volunteers in the First World War*, 104.
14 TNA WO364/4505, Egbert Watson. Soldiers' records (1914–1920), Pension Records.
15 'Effects of the European War on Colour Prejudice: James Slim of Jamaica, B.W.I., Enrolls in Coldstream Guards' *Indianapolis Recorder*, 24 April 1915, 1, col. 4 (Digital Collection, Indianapolis Recorder Newspaper Collection, IUPUI University Library).
16 Smith, *Jamaican Volunteers in the First World War*, 63.
17 Smith, *Jamaican Volunteers in the First World War*, 94.
18 John Joseph, Pershing, *My Experiences in the World War*, Military Classics Series Vol. 2 (Blue Ridge Summit, PA: Tab Books, 1989), 64.
19 Smith, *Jamaican Volunteers in the First World War*, 94.
20 Smith, *Jamaican Volunteers in the First World War*, 84–85; also Julian Putkowski and Piet Chielens, *Unquiet Graves/Rusteloze Graven: Execution Sites of the First World War in Flanders* (London: Francis Boutle Publishers, 2000), 41.
21 TNA WO71/594; see also Private Herbert Morris, 'Shot at Dawn', *Webmatters*, http://www.webmatters.net/txtpat/?q=auto&s=Search&sort=name&cat=sad (accessed 11 December 2012).

NOTES AND REFERENCES

22 Simon Rogers, 'Soldiers of the Empire: There Were no Parades for Us', *Guardian*, G2 Section, Wednesday 6 November 2002, 2.
23 Rebecca Tortello, 'Old Soldiers Never Die, They only Fade Away', A Special Gleaner Feature on Pieces of the Past, Jamaica and the Great War – The First 500 Years, *The Gleaner*, http://old.jamaica-gleaner.com/pages/history/story0014.html, 12 November 2001 (accessed 26 August 2015).
24 This information was very kindly passed on to me by the historian Jeffrey Green, who interviewed the veteran Frederick Chandler, a relative, in the 1980s (8 July 2013).
25 Rogers, 'Soldiers of the Empire', 2.
26 Pietermaritzburg Archives, Colenso papers, A204 Box 11, C. Calvert to HC, dd. East Finchley, London N, 24 July 1922, University of Loughborough Archives, dd. Christmas 1922.
27 Forces War Records, Record Details for Charles Alexander F Calvert (Machine Gun Corps) https://www.forces-war-records.co.uk/ViewRecord/924626?reference=arrowLinks (accessed 30 July 2013).
28 University of Loughborough Archives, dd. Christmas 1922.
29 TNA WO372/18, Melrose Goda Sishuba, First World War medal index cards.
30 *California Eagle*, 37, 2 November 1923, Los Angeles, 8, col. 1.
31 James T. Campbell, *Songs of Zion: African Methodist Episcopal Church in the United States and South Africa* (Chapel Hill, NC: The University of North Carolina Press, 1998), 256, 274.
32 Killingray, 'All the King's Men?', 176–77.
33 Vasili, *Colouring over the White Line*, 51.
34 Trefor Jones, *The Watford Football Club Illustrated Who's Who: All the Players and Managers since 1881* (Twickenham: T.G. Jones, 1996).
35 'Special provisions as to Persons to be Enlisted. Enlistment 95', ARMY ACT, *Manual of Military Law 1907*, 358.
36 David Killingray and Willie Henderson, 'Bata Kindai Amgoza ibn LoBagola and the Making of an African Savage's own Story', in Bernth Lindfors (ed.), *Africans on Stage: Studies in Ethnological Show Business* (Bloomington and Indianapolis, IN: Indiana University Press, 1999), 228–65.
37 Killingray and Henderson, 'Bata Kindai Amgoza ibn LoBagola', 244–45.
38 Peter Betts, the son of Gunner George Betts, in a communication on 28 July 2014.
39 'Blighty Wounds', *Spartacus Educational*, www.spartacuseducational.com (accessed 21 April 2013).

NOTES AND REFERENCES

40 George Coppard, *With a Machine Gun to Cambrai* (London: Cassell Military Paperbacks, 1999), 103.
41 Colonel G.H. Addison, C.M.G., D.S.O., M.A., M.I.Mech.E., *The Work of the Royal Engineers in the European War, 1914–1918 (Miscellaneous)* (Chatham: The Institution of Royal Engineers, 1926), passim. The Royal Engineers Coloured Section may have been the British-raised 'coloured unit' unit heard of by Laura Tabili, mentioned in *We Ask for British Justice*, 16.
42 TNA CO 323/786, 256.
43 TNA CO 123/287.
44 TNA CO 127/16.
45 TNA CO 123/283.
46 TNA CO 123/285.
47 TNA CO 318/333, Stamfordham to Harcourt, 17 April 1915.
48 TNA CO 123/285.
49 Costello, *Black Liverpool*, 43–44.
50 Killingray, 'All the King's Men?', 177–78.

Chapter Four: Black Officers, White Soldiers

1 Vasili, *Colouring over the White Line*, 40.
2 Vasili, *Colouring over the White Line*, 50.
3 Vasili, *Colouring over the White Line*, 42.
4 Vasili, *Colouring over the White Line*, 49.
5 Vasili, *Colouring over the White Line*, 52–54.
6 Constitution of the Forces, *Manual of Military Law 1914* (London: HM Stationery Office, 1914), 198.
7 Vasili, *Colouring over the White Line*, 55.
8 Vasili, *Colouring over the White Line*, 39.
9 Neil Oliver, *Not Forgotten* (London: Hodder & Stoughton, Ltd., 2005), 233–34.
10 Aaron Gullickson, 'The Significance of Color Declines: A Re-Analysis of Skin Tone Differentials in Post-Civil Rights America', *Social Forces*, 84.1 (September 2005), 157–80.
11 J. Douglas Smith, 'The Campaign for Racial Purity and the Erosion of Paternalism in Virginia, 1922–1930: Nominally White, Biologically Mixed, and Legally Negro', *Journal of Southern History*, 68.1 (2002), 67. See also C. Vann Woodward and William S. McFeely, *The Strange*

NOTES AND REFERENCES

Career of Jim Crow (New York, NY: Oxford University Press, 2001), passim.

12 Paul Brown, *The Unofficial Football World Championships: An Alternative Soccer History* (North Shields: Tonto Press, 2006), 123.
13 Smith, *Jamaican Volunteers in the First World War*, 65.
14 Killingray, 'All the King's Men?', 174.
15 TNA CO 318/336/57697. Mins. of 17 December 1915; Killingray, 'All the King's Men?', 175.
16 Madison Grant, *The Passing of the Great Race* (New York, NY: Charles Scribner's Sons, 1936), 18.
17 Conrad Phillip Kottak, 'Chapter 11: Ethnicity and Race', *Mirror for Humanity: A Concise Introduction to Cultural Anthropology* (New York, NY, McGraw-Hill, 2009), 238.
18 Peggy Pascoe, *What Comes Naturally: Miscegenation Law and the Making of Race in America* (Oxford: Oxford University Press, 2010), 185.
19 JeffriAnne Wilder, 'Revisiting "Color Names and Color Notions": A Contemporary Examination of the Language and Attitudes of Skin Color among Young Black Women', *Journal of Black Studies*, 41.1 (September 2010), 184–206, esp. 191–92.
20 Aaron Gullickson, 'The Significance of Color Declines', 157–80. The belief in the decline of shadism in the education and labour market after 1940 is contested by Arthur H. Goldsmith, Darrick Hamilton and William Darity Jr. in 'Shades of Discrimination: Skin and Wages', *The American Economic Review*, 96.2 (2006), 242–45.
21 NARA, Washington, D.C.; *Crew Lists of Vessels Arriving at Boston, Massachusetts, 1917–1943*; T938; Roll: 116 (Micropublication T843. RG085). Although I have not necessarily followed his sources, I was inspired to research Second Lieutenant Bemand by a private study by the military historian Simon Jervis.
22 Birth Certificate of George Edward Kingley Bemand, No. 8636, Registrar General's Department, Twickenham Park, Spanish Town, Saint Catherine, Jamaica.
23 '7455 George Edward Kingley Bemand', *Dulwich College Register*, 1619–1926, 467.
24 TNA WO 339/30835, Register No. 53600, M.T. 392.
25 TNA WO 339/30835, Register No. 53600, M.T. 392.
26 Marika Sherwood, 'Blacks in the Royal Navy', *Black and Asian Newsletter*, 23 (January 1999), 15.
27 TNA WO 339/30835, Telegram no. 848 OHMS, 30 December 1916.

NOTES AND REFERENCES

28 TNA WO 339/30835, letter Ref. 8/21127.
29 Harold Leslie Bemand, Commonwealth War Dead, Grave/Memorial Reference: Enclosure No. 2 I. F. 15, Bedford House Cemetery, Jamaica.
30 TNA WO339/69930.
31 Crockford's Clerical Directory. Minutes Board of Guardians of the Lewisham Union, 14 May 1906, 36, and 23 July 1906, 144–45; Obituary *Kentish Mercury*, 7 May 1937, 12.
32 TNA WO372/18.
33 Supplement to the *London Gazette*, no. 29905, 17 January 1917, 678.
34 I am indebted to the historian David Killingray for this information on Smyth. He gives the source of the comment on John F. Smyth as Nemata Blyden's *West Indians in West Africa, 1808–1880: The African Diaspora in Reverse* (Rochester, NY: University of Rochester Press, 2000).
35 TNA WO 339/62717, 11 September 1916, Reginald Emanuel Collins.
36 TNA WO 339/62717, 11 September 1916, Reginald Emanuel Collins.
37 Jean Besson, *Martha Brae's Two Histories: European Expansion and Caribbean Culture-Building in Jamaica* (Chapel Hill, NC: The University of North Carolina Press, 2001), 66.
38 Charles Owen Mountague, *The Sewels of the Isle of Wight* (Manchester: Manchester Courier Ltd., 1906), 80.
39 John Venn and Archibald Venn (eds), *Alumni Cantabrigenses* Part 2 Vol. 5 (Cambridge: Cambridge University Press, 1922–54), 486.
40 Western Front Association, *Land War, Generals Nicknames*, http://www.westernfrontassociation.com/great-war-on-land/71-gen-ls/209-generals-o-s.html (accessed 10 February 2013).
41 Venn and Venn, 486.
42 Venn and Venn, 486.
43 Cundall, *Jamaica's Part in the Great War*, 116.
44 Supplement to the *London Gazette*, no. 10904, 4 November 1915, Pembroke (Castlemartin) David Louis Clemetson to be Second Lieutenant. Dated 27 October 1915.
45 Cundall, *Jamaica's Part in the Great War*, 116.
46 A photograph of the First Trinity and Fifth Boat (also known as the 'Rugger Boat') team that rowed in the Lent Bumps in February 1914. Clemetson is shown in the back row, centre (Add.PG.65).
47 Note, Sub-section (2). *Natives of India*, 'THE ARMY ACT', *Manual of Military Law*, 428.
48 Green, *Black Edwardians*, 68.

NOTES AND REFERENCES

49 'The Story of Jimmy Durham the First Black African to Join the British Army as a Fully Enlisted Soldier', *Tyne Roots: Black History Month, BBC*, October 2004.
50 Killingray, 'All the King's Men?', 172–73.
51 Killingray, 'All the King's Men?', 172–73.
52 MMM, D/B/176A/B/3-4, The Sandbach Tinne and Cobham Papers from the Bryson Collection, *Report on Plantation Operations from William Russell to Mr. Cowie*.
53 Jeffrey Green, 'Russell, James Samuel Risien (1863–1939), Neurologist', *Oxford Dictionary of National Biography* (September 2010), 96832.
54 Gordon Holmes, *Queen Square and the National Hospital 1860–1960* (London: Edward Arnold, 1960), 100–01.
55 M. Critchley, *The Ventricle of Memory* (New York, NY: Raven Press, 1990), 175.
56 Green, 'Russell, James Samuel Risien', 96832.
57 Howe, *Race War and Nationalism*, 114–15.
58 Howe, *Race War and Nationalism*, 115.
59 Calvin W. Ruck, *The Black Battalion 1916–1920: Canada's Best Kept Military Secret* (Halifax, Canada: Nimbus Publishing Company, 1987), 20.
60 Ruck, *The Black Battalion*, 46.
61 Killingray, 'All the King's Men?', 175.
62 TNA CO 28/294/56561. Min. by Fiddian, 18 December 1918. See also Killingray, 'All the King's Men?', 174.

CHAPTER FIVE: THE BLACK EMPIRE ARRIVES – CONSCRIPTION

1 Winston James, *Holding aloft the Banner of Ethiopia: Caribbean Radicalism in Early Twentieth-Century America* (London and New York, NY: Verso, 1998), 62.
2 Jennifer M. Ingham, *Defence, Not Defiance: A History of the Bermuda Volunteer Rifle Corps* (Pembroke, Bermuda: The Island Press Ltd., 1992), 3.
3 TNA WO 95/397 C697074, War Diary of Bermuda Contingent, Royal Garrison Artillery.
4 Johnston, *The Black Man's Part in the War*, 76, note 1.
5 James K. Matthews, 'Reluctant Allies: Nigerian Responses to Military Recruitment 1914–18', in Melvin Page (ed.), *Africa and the First World War* (New York, NY, St. Martins, 1987), 97.

6 Johnston, *The Black Man's Part in the War*, 80–81.
7 Donald A. Low, *The Mind of Buganda: Documents of the Modern History of an African Kingdom* (London: Heinemann Educational Publishers, 1971), 80.
8 Toyin Falola, 'The First World War', in Dickson Eyoh and Paul Tiyambe Zeleza (eds), *Encyclopedia of Twentieth-Century African History* (Oxford: Routledge, 2003), 104.
9 A. Adu Boahen (ed.), *General History of Africa VII: Africa under Colonial Domination 1880–1935* (Paris: UNESCO; Berkeley, CA: University of California Press; London: Heinemann, 1985), 295.
10 Charles Miller, *Battle for the Bundu: The First World War in East Africa* (New York, NY: MacMillan, 1974), 218.
11 Matthews, 'Reluctant Allies', 96.
12 S.B. Spies, 'South Africa and the First World War', in S.B. Spies and B.J. Liebenberg (eds), *South Africa in the 20th Century* (Pretoria: J.L. van Schaik Publishers, 1993), 94.
13 C. Saunders (ed. and consultant), *Reader's Digest Illustrated History of South Africa: The Real Story* (Cape Town: The Readers Digest Association of South Africa, 1992), 303.
14 S. Horwitz, 'The Non-European War Record in South Africa', in E. Hellman (ed.), *Handbook on Race Relations in South Africa* (New York, NY: Octagon Books, 1975), 537–38, 778.
15 A. Grundlingh, *Fighting their own War: South African Blacks and the First World War* (Johannesburg: Ravan Press, 1987), 106–07.
16 Johnston, *The Black Man's Part in the War*, 79, note 1.
17 Johnston, *The Black Man's Part in the War*, 79–80.
18 Johnston, *The Black Man's Part in the War*, 80.
19 N. Clothier, *Black Valour: The South African Native Labour Contingent, 1916–1918 and the Sinking of the Mendi* (Pietermaritzburg: University of Natal Press, 1987), 96–98. See also I. Uys, *Survivors of Africa's Oceans* (Minneapolis, MN: Fortress Publishers, 1993), 38–48.
20 S.B. Spies, 'The Outbreak of the First World War and the Botha Government', *South African Historical Journal*, 1 (November 1969), 47–57.
21 S. Horwitz, 'The Non-European War Record in South Africa', in E. Hellman (ed.), *Handbook on Race Relations in South Africa* (New York, NY: Octagon Books, 1975), 537–38.
22 G. Swinney 'The Sinking of the SS Mendi, 21 February 1917' (incorporating Museum Review), *Military History Journal*, 10.1 (June

1995), http://samilitaryhistory.org/vol101gs.html (accessed 26 August 2015).
23 Ruck, *The Black Battalion*, 16.
24 Ruck, *The Black Battalion*, 9–10.
25 Ruck, *The Black Battalion*, 10.
26 Ruck, *The Black Battalion*, 15.
27 Ruck, *The Black Battalion*, 15–16.
28 Ruck, *The Black Battalion*, 20.
29 Ruck, *The Black Battalion*, 16.
30 Ruck, *The Black Battalion*, 23.
31 Simon Schama, *Rough Crossings* (London: BBC Books, 2006), 463–65.
32 Ruck, *The Black Battalion*, 23.
33 TNA NATS 1/1040. Anglo-American Military Service Law, 1918. See also Killingray, 'All the King's Men?', 178.
34 TNA WO 32/4765, 'Enlistment of Coloured British subjects in USA'. Gen. White to WO, 5 September 1917. See also Killingray, 'All the King's Men?', 178.
35 TNA WO 32/4765, Reading to Lord Derby, Min. of Nat. Service, 10 March 1918. See also Killingray, 'All the King's Men?', 178.
36 TNA WO 32/4765, B.B. Cubitt, WO, to Sec, Min. of Nat. Service, 13 June 1918. See also Killingray, 'All the King's Men?', 178.
37 TNA CO 318/347/25696. Algernon E. Aspinall to Fiddian, CO, 5 June 1918. See also Killingray, 'All the King's Men?', 178.
38 Ruck, *The Black Battalion*, 29–31.
39 Cundall, *Jamaica's Part in the Great War*, 25–26.
40 Cundall, *Jamaica's Part in the Great War*, 25–26.
41 Howe, *Race War and Nationalism*, 74.
42 Howe, *Race War and Nationalism*, 82.
43 TNA CO 123/285.
44 TNA CO 123/283.
45 TNA CO 318/333, Stamfordham to Harcourt, 17 April 1915.
46 Fenner Brockway, *Bermondsey Story* (London: Allen and Unwin, 1949), 67–68. The chronology of Hall's story has been questioned by 'Gabriel', an anonymous contributor to the *The World is My Country* website, which highlights people and movements that opposed the First World War. Gabriel points out that although the NCF knew of his case in October 1916, Hansard shows that he was not released until early 1918. See 'What the Hell Have we Got to Do with the War?' posted 27 November 2014 by 'Gabriel', http://theworldismycountry.

info/what-the-hell-have-we-got-to-do-with-the-war/ (accessed 14 April 2015). See also http://hansard.millbanksystems.com/commons/1918/jan/17/conscientious-objectors

47 John S.D. Eisenhower (foreword), Spencer C. Tucker (ed.), Priscilla Mary Roberts (ed.), 'No-Conscription Fellowship', in *World War I: A Student Encyclopedia, Vol. I* (Santa Barbara, CA: ABC-CLIO Ltd, 2005), 1339–40.
48 Brockway, *Bermondsey Story*, 67–68.
49 'Why He Will Not Fight: A Negro's Argument', *Tribunal*, 19 October 1916.
50 Killingray, 'All the King's Men?', 177–78.
51 Gary Mead, *The Good Soldier*, 321.
52 Killingray, 'All the King's Men?', 179.

Chapter Six: The Return of the Heroes

1 Walt Whitman, *The Walt Whitman Megapack* (Rockville, MD: Wildside Press, 2014), 532.
2 Johnston, *The Black Man's Part in the War*, 42–43, note 1.
3 Johnston, *The Black Man's Part in the War*, 66–67.
4 Arthur Bishop, 'Of Rebellion and Rescue', *Legion Magazine: Canada and the Victoria Cross* (March–April 2004), 1.
5 'War Office, January 4, 1867' (Private Samuel Hodge), *London Gazette*, 23205, 4 January 1867, 84.
6 Dyde, *The Empty Sleeve*, 253.
7 Dyde, *The Empty Sleeve*, 260–61.
8 Killingray, 'All the King's Men?', 176.
9 BL, c12343-01 'The Man Whom White Soldiers Call "The Black V.C.;" Though Undecorated', *African Telegraph*, March 1919, 146.
10 TNA 30/30/8, Progress of demobilisation, December 1918.
11 Rudyard Kipling, *Selected Poems*, 18–19.
12 F.O. Shyllon, 'The Black Presence and Experience in Britain', paper presented to the International Conference on the History of Blacks in Britain, London, 28–30 September 1981, 8.
13 'The Belmont Hospital Affair', *African Telegraph*, 1/8, December 1918, 94–95.
14 'The Belmont Hospital Affair', 94–95.
15 M. Rowe, 'Sex, "Race" and Riot in Liverpool, 1919', *Immigrants and*

Minorities: Historical Studies in Ethnicity, Migration and Diaspora, 19.2 (2000), 66.
16 *African Telegraph*, May–June 1919, 231; see also Killingray, 'All the King's Men?', 180.
17 Killingray, 'All the King's Men?', 181.
18 Killingray, 'All the King's Men?', 181.
19 Fryer, *Staying Power*, 299.
20 Jacqueline Jenkinson, 'The 1919 Race Riots in Britain: A Survey', in Rainer Lotz and Ian Pegg (eds), *Under the Imperial Carpet: Essays in Black History 1780–1950* (Crawley: Rabbit Press, 1986), 184.
21 Jacqueline Jenkinson, *Black 1919: Riots, Racism and Resistance in Imperial Britain*, (Liverpool: Liverpool University Press, 2009), 27.
22 Jenkinson, 'The 1919 Race Riots in Britain', 186.
23 Jenkinson, 'The 1919 Race Riots in Britain', 189.
24 *The African Telegraph*, May–June 1919, 209, as cited in Jenkinson, 'The 1919 Race Riots in Britain', 189–90.
25 Fryer, *Staying Power*, 299.
26 Fryer, *Staying Power*, 301.
27 *Evening Express Liverpool*, Monday 9 June 1919, 3, col. 5.
28 Killingray, 'All the King's Men?', 180.
29 Jenkinson, 'The 1919 Race Riots in Britain', 189–91.
30 Fryer, *Staying Power*, 165–80; see also Carlson, *The Unfit*, passim.
31 R.W. July, *The Origins of Modern African Thought* (London: Faber and Faber, 1968), 461–62.
32 *Eugenics Review*, 12 (1920–21), 76–77.
33 *Eugenics Review*, 12 (1920–21), 76–77.
34 *Eugenics Review*, 12 (1920–21), 69.
35 *The Times*, 14 June 1919, 126, col. 8. For a general discussion on race, gender, class structures and the notion of 'Imperial manhood', see also Tabili, *We Ask for British Justice*, 10.
36 Tabili, *We Ask for British Justice*, 23.
37 *Derby Daily Telegraph*, Saturday 14 June 1919, 3.
38 Jenkinson, 'The 1919 Race Riots in Britain', 201.
39 *Evening Express* (Liverpool), 10 June 1919, 3, col. 5.
40 *Evening Express* (Liverpool), 11 June 1919, 5, col. 3.
41 Marke, *In Troubled Waters*, 30–31.
42 Costello, *Black Liverpool*, 88.
43 *Western Mail*, no. 15,618, 14 June 1919, 8.
44 Fryer, *Staying Power*, 304–09.

45 *Daily Record*, 20 June, 1919, 8.
46 *Daily Record*, 25 June, 1919, 8.
47 'A West African Soldier "Walking Out" In London', *African Telegraph*, 1919, BL, c12343-02.
48 TNA T1/12482, Letter from the Ministry of Pensions to the Treasury 9 February 1920.
49 T1/12482, Letter 9 February 1920.
50 TNA T1/12482, Letter from the Ministry of Pensions to the Treasury 10 March 1920.
51 TNA T1/12482, Letter from the Ministry of Pensions to the Treasury 25 March 1920 *and* TNA T1/12482, Letter from the Ministry of Pensions to the Treasury 7 June 1920.
52 Anne Audley, representing the Guy/Gibson family descendants in a communication on 29 October 2014.
53 Fryer, *Staying Power*, 299.
54 H.M. Swanwick, *Builders of Peace: Being Ten Years' History of the Union of Democratic Control* (London: Swarthmore Press Ltd., 1924), 187.
55 *Daily Herald*, no. 1,313, 10 April 1920, 4, col. 1.
56 'A Black Man Replies', *Workers' Dreadnought*, VII/5, 2 (24 April 1920), 72.
57 Claude McKay, *A Long Way from Home* (New York, NY: Arno Press and the New York Times, 1969).
58 TNA MT 4/761, Marine Department, Board of Trade letter to all Mercantile Marine offices, 7 February 1919.
59 Tabili, *We Ask for British Justice*, 136; see also *Evening Express Liverpool*, Tuesday 10 June 1919, 1, col. 1.
60 Fryer, *Staying Power*, 309.
61 Jenkinson, 'The 1919 Race Riots in Britain', 198.
62 Fryer, *Staying Power*, 309.
63 Jenkinson, 'The 1919 Race Riots in Britain', 198–99.
64 Killingray, 'All the King's Men?', 180.
65 Tabili, *We Ask for British Justice*, 33.
66 I. Law and J. Henfrey, *A History of Race and Racism in Liverpool, 1660–1950* (Liverpool: Merseyside Community Relations Council, 1981), 31.
67 George Quarless, an elder of the Liverpool British-born Black community, in an interview recorded in August 2000.
68 Tabili, *We Ask for British Justice*, 119.
69 Diane Frost, *Work and Community among West African Migrant Workers since the Nineteenth Century* (Liverpool: Liverpool University Press, 1999), 74.
70 Law and Henfrey, *A History of Race and Racism*, 31.

71 TNA HO 45/11897/332087, Immigration Officers Report, 1921.
72 W.F. Elkins, 'A Source of Black Nationalism in the Caribbean: The Revolt of the British West Indies Regiment at Taranto, Italy', *Science & Society, S & S Quarterly*, 34.1 (Spring 1970), 99.
73 Constitution of the Forces, Ch. XI., 15 (b), *Manual of Military Law 1914*, 198.
74 Elkins, 'A Source of Black Nationalism in the Caribbean', 99–100.
75 Elkins, 'A Source of Black Nationalism in the Caribbean', 100–01.
76 Elkins, 'A Source of Black Nationalism in the Caribbean', 101–02.
77 Tortello, 'Old Soldiers Never Die', 14.
78 Elkins, 'A Source of Black Nationalism in the Caribbean', 102.
79 Elkins, 'A Source of Black Nationalism in the Caribbean', 102–03.
80 Elkins, 'A Source of Black Nationalism in the Caribbean', 103.
81 Rogers, 'Soldiers of the Empire', 2.
82 Rogers, 'Soldiers of the Empire', 2.
83 Rogers, 'Soldiers of the Empire', 2.
84 Horwitz, 'The Non-European War Record', 538.
85 K.W. Grundy, *Soldiers without Politics: Blacks in the South African Armed Forces* (Berkeley, CA: University of California Press, 1983), 56.

Epilogue

1 Jeffrey Green, *Post Card*, http://www.jeffreygreen.co.uk/066-lieutenant-reginald-collins-of-jamaica (accessed 27 April 2013).
2 Tabili, *We Ask for British Justice*, 16.
3 Tabili, *We Ask for British Justice*, 2.
4 Tabili, *We Ask for British Justice*, 14.
5 P. O'Mara, *The Autobiography of a Liverpool Irish Slummy* (Liverpool: Bluecoat Press, 2009), 201. Fluke is a flatfish of that name, enjoyed by sailors. This order of fish includes flounders, soles, turbots and halibut.
6 Ray Costello, *Liverpool Black Pioneers* (Liverpool: Bluecoat Press, 2007), 45.
7 Johnston, *The Black Man's Part in the War*, 10–11.
8 Johnston, *The Black Man's Part in the War*, 100–01.
9 Tabili, *We Ask for British Justice*, 30.
10 Tabili, *We Ask for British Justice*, 18.
11 Heywood Broun, *The A.E.F. with General Pershing and the American Forces* (New York, NY; London: D. Appleton and Company, 1918), 19–20.

12 Jenkinson, 'The 1919 Race Riots in Britain', 206–07.
13 Jenkinson, 'The 1919 Race Riots in Britain', 184.
14 Tabili, *We Ask for British Justice*, 31.
15 Tabili, *We Ask for British Justice*, 20.
16 Tabili, *We Ask for British Justice*, 30–31.

BIBLIOGRAPHY

PRIMARY SOURCES

THE NATIONAL ARCHIVES

Catalogue Reference: 30/30/8, Speech by Lord Milner, Progress of Demobilisation, December 1918

Colonial Office

CO 28/294/56561	Min. by Fiddian, 18 December 1918
CO 123/283	Despatches from Wilfred Collet, Governor of British Honduras, 1914–17
CO 123/285	Despatches from Wilfred Collet, Governor of British Honduras, 1914–17
CO 123/287	Despatches from Wilfred Collet, Governor of British Honduras, 1914–17
CO 127/16-18	British Honduras, later Belize, Government Gazettes, 1914–19
CO 318/333	Stamfordham to Harcourt, 17 April 1915
CO 318/333/50043	'West Indian Contingent'. Min. by Grindle, 21 December 1914
CO 318/336/57697	Mins. of 17 December 1915
CO 323/786	Royal Engineers Coloured Section, 13th Division, Marquil Depot to CO, 29 January 1918

BIBLIOGRAPHY

Home Office
HO 45/11897/332087 Immigration Officers Report, 1921

Ministry of War Transport
MT 4/761 Marine Department, Board of Trade letter to all Mercantile Marine offices, 7 February 1919

Ministry of National Service Records
NATS 1/1040 Anglo-American Military Service Law, 1918

Treasury Papers
T1/12482 Letter from the Ministry of Pensions to the Treasury 9 February 1920
T1/12482 Letter from the Ministry of Pensions to the Treasury 10 March 1920
T1/12482 Letter from the Ministry of Pensions to the Treasury 25 March 1920
T1/12482 Letter from the Ministry of Pensions to the Treasury 7 June 1920

War Office
WO 25/454, WO 25 69 Foot 1826–1830
WO 32/4765 'Enlistment of Coloured British subjects in USA'. Gen. White to WO, 5 September. 1917
WO 32/4765 General White. New York to WO (copy of Secret telegram) 19 February 1918
WO 32/4765 Reading to Lord Derby, Min. of Nat. Service, 10 March 1918
WO 32/4765 B.B. Cubitt, WO, to Sec, Min. of Nat. Service, 13 June 1918
WO 71/594 Private Herbert Morris
WO 95/397C697074 War Diary of Bermuda Contingent, Royal Garrison Artillery
WO 339/30835 letter Ref. 8/21127
WO 339/30835 Register No. 53600, M.T. 392
WO 339/30835 Telegram no. 848 OHMS, 30.12.16
WO 339/62717 11 September 1916

BIBLIOGRAPHY

WO 339/69930	John Albert Gordon Smyth
WO 363 0426	Albert James, War Office: Soldiers' Documents, Soldiers' records (1914–1920), Service Records. First World War 'Burnt Documents' (Microfilm Copies); National Archives Microfilm Publication.
WO 363 0428	Albert James
WO 363 0429	Albert James
WO 363 0433	Albert James
WO 363 0444	Albert James
WO 363 0453	Albert James
WO 363 0459	Albert James
WO 363 0467	Albert James
WO 364 2674	Frank Nelson. Soldiers' records (1914–1920), Pension Records.
WO 364/4505	Egbert Watson. Soldiers' records (1914–1920), Pension Records.
WO 372/18	Melrose Goda Sishuba, First World War medal index cards.

Overseas Archives

AWM 'Anzac Mounted Division General Staff War Diary', *First World War Diaries* AWM4, 160–31, Part 2, Appendix 38. Canberra, September 1918

AWM 'New Zealand Mounted Rifles Brigade War Diary', *First World War Diaries,* AWM4, 35-1-41, Canberra, September 1918

Commonwealth War Dead, Bemand, Harold Leslie, Grave/Memorial Reference: Enclosure No. 2I. F. 15, Bedford House Cemetery, Jamaica

NARA, Washington, D.C., *Crew Lists of Vessels Arriving at Boston, Massachusetts, 1917–1943*; *T938*; Roll: *116*, Micropublication T843. RG085

Pietermaritzburg Archives. Colenso papers, A204 Box 11, C. Calvert to HC, dd. East Finchley, London N, 24 July 1922, University of Loughborough archives, dd. Christmas 1922

Registrar General's Department, Birth Certificate of George Edward Kingley Bemand, No. 8636, Twickenham Park, Spanish Town, Saint Catherine, Jamaica

BIBLIOGRAPHY

Commonwealth War Graves Commission

CWGC, France Area, 5–7 Rue Angèle Richard, BP 109, 62217 Beaurains, France
CWGC, Private Walter Colebourne, Pier and Face 1 D 8 B and 8 C Thiepval Memorial

Other Archives and Libraries

Crockford's Clerical Directory, *Minutes Board of Guardians of the Lewisham Union*, 14 May 1906
Dulwich College Register, '7455 George Edward Kingley Bemand', 1619–1926
IWM Documents 5579 Private Papers. Poplar 1C 647
LRBDM, Birth Certificate of Albert's second child, Edith, 24 December 1914, Cert. No. 3. Liverpool Register Office
MMM, D/B/176A/B/3-4, The Sandbach Tinne and Cobham Papers from the Bryson Collection, *Report on plantation operations from William Russell to Mr. Cowie*
RDP, Birth Certificate for Harold Brown, Application Number 4491681-1
Third Annual Report of the Harrington Free School for the Education of Poor Children in Toxteth Park (5 May 1818) (From the author's private collection acting as official keeper of the document)
Trinity College, Cambridge, A photograph of the First Trinity and Fifth Boat (also known as the "Rugger Boat") team that rowed in the Lent Bumps, February 1914 (Add.PG.65) (The Master and Fellows of Trinity College, Cambridge)

Parliamentary Reports and other Governmental Journals

Hansard, 'Coloured Men (British Forces)', (HC Deb 30 July 1918 vol. 109 cc 229-30 229), 30 July 1918
London Gazette, War Office, 23205, Private Samuel Hodge, 4 January 1867
London Gazette (Supplement) 10904, David Louis Clemetson, 4 November 1915
London Gazette (Supplement) 29905, 678, John Albert Gordon Smyth, 17 January 1917

London Gazette (*Supplement*) 2288, 1454 Sjt. W.E. Julien, 1 Battalion British West Indies Regiment (St Georges, Grenada) 25 February 1920

London Gazette (*Supplement*) 2293, 6357, Private H. Scott, 1 Battalion British West Indies Regiment (St. Anns, Jamaica) 25 February 1920

London Gazette (*Supplement*) 2296-7, 503 Lance Corporal R. Turpin, 1 Battalion British West Indies Regiment (La Brea, Trinidad) 25 February 1920

Manual of Military Law 1907, 'Enlistment', Ch. X, 28 (London: Printed for His Majesty's Stationery Office, by Harrison and Sons, 1907)

Manual of Military Law 1907, 'Special provisions as to Persons to be Enlisted. Enlistment 95', Army Act (London: Printed for His Majesty's Stationery Office, by Harrison and Sons, 1907)

Manual of Military Law, 428 Army Act, Note 2 'Sub-section (2). Natives of India' (London: Printed for His Majesty's Stationery Office, by Harrison and Sons, 1914)

Manual of Military Law 1914, Constitution of the Forces, Ch. XI., 15 (b) (London: Printed for His Majesty's Stationery Office, by Harrison and Sons, 1914)

Report on Population of the United States at the Eleventh Census: 1890, Part 1, Porter, Robert; Gannett, Henry; Hunt, William (Washington, D.C., Government Printing Office, 1895)

INTERVIEWS

Brew, Agnes, née James, sister of Albert James, 10 July 1970
Betts, Peter, the son of Gunner George Betts, 28 July 2014
Quarless, George, 9 August 2000
Tasker, Barbara and Suzanne Morris, cousins of Walter Colebourne, 23 October 2014

NEWSPAPERS AND PERIODICALS

African Telegraph, 'The Man Whom White Soldiers Call "The Black V.C.;" Though Undecorated', March 1919
California Eagle, 37, Los Angeles, California, 2 November 1923
Evening Express Liverpool, Monday 9 June 1919
Evening Express Liverpool, Tuesday 10 June 1919
Eugenics Review, 12, 1920–21

Daily Herald, 1,313, 10 April 1920

Daily Record, 20 June 1919

Derby Daily Telegraph, Saturday 14 June 1919

The Gleaner, Tortello, Rebecca, 'Old Soldiers Never Die, They only Fade Away', A Special Gleaner Feature on Pieces of the Past, Jamaica and the Great War – The First 500 Years, *The Gleaner*, http://old.jamaica-gleaner.com/pages/history/story0014.html, 12 November 2001

Guardian, Simon Rogers, 'Soldiers of the Empire: There were no Parades for us', Wednesday 6 November 2002

Independent, John Lichfield 'Images Rescued from Dump Reveal Black British "Tommy" at the Somme', Saturday 23 May 2009

Indianapolis Recorder, 'Effects of the European War on Colour Prejudice: James Slim of Jamaica, B.W.I., Enrolls in Coldstream Guards' Digital Collection, Indianapolis Recorder Newspaper Collection, IUPUI University Library, 24 April 1915

Kentish Mercury, 23 July 1906, Obituary, 7 May 1937

Liverpool Echo, 29 June 1915

The Times, 14 June 1919

The Times, 'The Gold Coast Mobilized, A Proud Record: The Case of Sergeant Grunshi', 48572, Monday 25 March 1940

Tribunal, 'Why He Will Not Fight: A Negro's Argument', 19 October 1916

Western Mail, no. 15,618, 14 June 1919

Workers' Dreadnought, 'A Black Man Replies', VII/5, cf. Cooper and Reinders, 24 April 1920

SECONDARY SOURCES

Books and articles

Addison, Colonel G.H., C.M.G, D.S.O., M.A., M.I.Mech.E., *The Work of the Royal Engineers in the European War, 1914–1918 (Miscellaneous)* (Chatham: The Institution of Royal Engineers, 1926)

Bade, Klaus J *Migration in European History: The Making of Europe*, trans. Allison Brown (Oxford: Blackwell, 2003)

Baker, Bruce, *Escape from Domination in Africa: Political Disengagement and Its Consequences in Sub-Saharan Africa* Paperback (Martlesham: James Currey, 2000)

Besson, Jean, *Martha Brae's Two Histories: European Expansion and Caribbean Culture-Building in Jamaica* (Chapel Hill, NC: University of North Carolina Press, 2001)

Bishop, Arthur, 'Of Rebellion and Rescue', *Legion Magazine: Canada and the Victoria Cross* Part 2 of 18 (March–April 2004)

Blyden, Nemata, *West Indians in West Africa, 1808–1880: The African Diaspora in Reverse* (New York, NY: University of Rochester Press, 2000)

Boahen, A. Adu (ed.), *General History of Africa VII: Africa under Colonial Domination 1880–1935* (Paris: UNESCO; Berkeley, CA: University of California Press; London: Heinemann, 1985)

Bourne, Stephen, *Black Poppies: Britain's Black Community and the Great War* (Stroud: The History Press, 2014)

Brockway, Fenner, *Bermondsey Story* (London: Allen and Unwin, 1949)

Broun, Heywood, *The A.E.F. with General Pershing and the American Forces* (New York, NY; London: D. Appleton and Company, 1918). This unique book is held in Cornell University Library.

Brown, Paul, *The Unofficial Football World Championships* (North Shields: Tonto Press, 2014)

Bruce, Anthony, *The Last Crusade: The Palestine Campaign in the First World War* (London: Thistle Publishing, 2013)

Campbell, James T., *Songs of Zion: African Methodist Episcopal Church in the United States and South Africa* (Chapel Hill, NC: University of North Carolina Press, 1998)

Carlson, Elof Axel, *The Unfit: A History of a Bad Idea* (Cold Spring Harbor, NY: Cold Spring Harbor Laboratory Press, 2001)

Churchill, Winston Spencer, *The River War* (London: Four Square Books, 1960)

Clayton, Ann, 'Chavasse, Noel Godfrey (1884–1917)', *Oxford Dictionary of National Biography* (Oxford: Oxford University Press, 2004)

Clothier, N., *Black Valour: The South African Native Labour Contingent, 1916–1918 and the Sinking of the Mendi* (Pietermaritzburg: University of Natal Press, 1987)

Collins, Sydney, *Coloured minorities in Britain: Studies in British Race Relations based on African, West Indian and Asiatic Immigrants* (London: Lutterworth Press, 1957)

Coop, J.O., *Story of the 55th (West Lancashire) Division* (Uckfield: Naval and Military Press, 2001)

Coppard, George, *With a Machine Gun to Cambrai* (London: Cassell Military Paperbacks, 1999)

Costello, Ray, *Black Liverpool: The Early History of Britain's Oldest Black Community 1730–1918* (Liverpool: Picton Press, 2001)
Costello, Ray, *Liverpool Black Pioneers* (Liverpool: Bluecoat Press, 2007)
Costello, Ray, *Black Salt: Seafarers of African Descent on British Ships* (Liverpool: Liverpool University Press, 2012)
Critchley, M., *The Ventricle of Memory* (New York, NY: Raven Press, 1990)
Cundall, Frank, 'Obituary Notices of Commissioned Officers', *Jamaica's Part in the Great War 1914–1918* (London: The Institute of Jamaica by the West India Committee, 1925)
Dupuch, Sir Etienne, *A Salute to Friend and Foe* (Nassau, Bahamas: Tribune, 1982)
Dyde, Brian, *The Empty Sleeve: The Story of the West India Regiments of the British Army* (St John's, Antigua: Hansib, 1997)
Eisenhower, John S.D. (foreword), Spencer C. Tucker (ed.) and Priscilla Mary Roberts (ed.), 'No-Conscription Fellowship', *World War I: A Student Encyclopedia, Vol. I* (Santa Barbara, CA: ABC-CLIO, 2005)
Ellen, Hellmann (ed.), *Handbook on Race Relations in South Africa* (New York, NY: Octagon Books, 1975)
Elkins, W.F., 'A Source of Black Nationalism in the Caribbean: The Revolt of the British West Indies Regiment at Taranto, Italy', *Science & Society, S & S Quarterly*, 34.1 (Spring 1970), 99–103
Ellis, A.B., *The History of the First West India Regiment* (London: Chapman and Hall, 1885)
Falola, Toyin, 'The First World War', in Dickson Eyoh and Paul Tiyambe Zeleza (eds), *Encyclopedia of Twentieth-Century African History* (London: Routledge, 2003)
Frost, Diane, *Work and Community among West African Migrant Workers since the Nineteenth Century* (Liverpool: Liverpool University Press, 1999)
Fryer, P., *Staying Power: The History of Black People in Britain* (London: Pluto Press, 1985)
Gann, L. and P. Duignan, *The Rulers of German Africa 1884–1914* (Stanford, CA: Stanford University Press, 1985)
Gilbert, Martin, *The First World War: A Complete History* (London, Phoenix, 2008)
Goldsmith, Arthur H., Darrick Hamilton and William Darity Jr., 'Shades of Discrimination: Skin and Wages', *The American Economic Review* 96.2 (2006)
Gorges, E.H., *The Great War in West Africa* (Uckfield: Naval & Military Press, 2004)

Grannum, Guy (ed.), *Tracing your Caribbean Ancestors: A National Archives Guide* (London: A. & C. Black Publishers Ltd., 2012)

Grant, Madison, *The Passing of the Great Race* (Fourth Revised Edition, New York, Charles Scribner's Sons, 1916 [1936])

Green, J.P, 'George William Christian: A Liverpool "Black" in Africa', *Transactions of the Historical Society of Lancashire and Cheshire*, 134 (1986)

Green, Jeffrey, *Black Edwardians: Black People in Britain 1901–1914* (London: Cass, 1998)

Green, Jeffrey, 'Russell, James Samuel Risien (1863–1939), Neurologist', *Oxford Dictionary of National Biography* (Oxford: Oxford University Press, 2010)

Grundlingh, A., *Fighting their own War: South African Blacks and the First World War* (Johannesburg: Ravan Press, 1987)

Grundy, K.W., *Soldiers without Politics: Blacks in the South African Armed Forces* (Berkeley, CA: University of California Press, 1983)

Gullickson, Aaron, 'The Significance of Color Declines: A Re-Analysis of Skin Tone Differentials in Post-Civil Rights America', *Social Forces*, 84.1 (September 2005), 158–80

Hart, Peter, *1918, A Very British Victory* (London: Weidenfeld and Nicolson, 2008)

Hastings, Max, *Catastrophe: Europe Goes to War* (London: William Collins, 2013)

Holmes, Gordon, *Queen Square and the National Hospital 1860–1960* (London: Edward Arnold, 1960)

Horwitz, S., 'The Non-European War Record in South Africa', in E. Hellman (ed.), *Handbook on Race Relations in South Africa* (New York, NY: Octagon Books, 1975)

Howe, Glenford Deroy, *Race War and Nationalism: A Social History of West Indians in the First World War* (Oxford: James Curry, 2002)

Hugill, Stan, *Sailortown* (London: Routledge and Kegan Paul, 1967)

Ingham, Jennifer M., *Defence, Not Defiance: A History of the Bermuda Volunteer Rifle Corps*, (Pembroke, Bermuda: The Island Press Ltd., 1992)

James, Winston, *Holding aloft the Banner of Ethiopia: Caribbean Radicalism in Early Twentieth-Century America* (London; New York, NY: Verso, 1998)

Jenkinson, Jacqueline, 'The 1919 Race Riots in Britain: A Survey', in Rainer Lotz and Ian Pegg (eds.), *Under the Imperial Carpet: Essays in Black History 1780–1950* (Crawley: Rabbit Press, 1986)

Jenkinson, Jacqueline, *Black 1919: Riots, Racism and Resistance in Imperial Britain* (Liverpool: Liverpool University Press, 2009)

Johnston, Harry Hamilton, *The Black Man's Part in the War: An Account of the Dark-Skinned Population of the British Empire* (London: Simpkin, Marshall, Hamilton, Kent & Co. Ltd., 1917)

Jones, Trefor, *The Watford Football Club Illustrated Who's Who: All the Players and Managers since 1881* (Twickenham: T.G. Jones, 1996)

July, R.W., *The Origins of Modern African Thought* (London: Faber and Faber, 1968)

Kay, Charles, 'McDavid, Sir Herbert Gladstone (1898–1966)', *Oxford Dictionary of National Biography* (Oxford: Oxford University Press, 2012)

Keegan, John, *The First World War* (London: Hutchinson, 1998)

Killingray, David, 'Repercussions of World War I in the Gold Coast', *Journal of African History*, 19.1 (1978), 39–59

Killingray, D., 'The Idea of a British Imperial African Army', *Journal of African History*, 20 (1979), 421–36

Killingray, David, 'All the King's Men? Blacks in the British Army in the First World War, 1914–1918', in Rainer Lotz and Ian Pegg (eds.), *Under the Imperial Carpet: Essays in Black History 1780–1950* (Crawley: Rabbit Press, 1986), 164–81

Killingray, David, *The Conquest of Togo. Companion to World War I*, ed. John Horne (London: Blackwell, 2012)

Killingray, David and Willie Henderson, 'Bata Kindai Amgoza ibn LoBagola and the Making of an African Savage's own Story', in Bernth Lindfors (ed.), *Africans on Stage: Studies in Ethnological Show Business* (Bloomington and Indianapolis, IN: Indiana University Press, 1999), 228–65

Kipling, Rudyard, *Collected Poems of Rudyard Kipling*, intr. R.T, Jones (Ware: Wordsworth Editions, 1994)

Koller, Christian, 'The Recruitment of Colonial Troops in Africa and Asia and their Deployment in Europe during the First World War', *Immigrants & Minorities*, 26.1–2 (March–July 2008), 111–33

Kottak, Conrad Phillip, *Mirror for Humanity: A Concise Introduction to Cultural Anthropology* (New York, NY: McGraw-Hill, 2009)

Law, I. and J. Henfrey, *A History of Race and Racism in Liverpool, 1660–1950* (Liverpool: Merseyside Community Relations Council, 1981)

Low, Donald A., *The Mind of Buganda: Documents of the Modern History of an African Kingdom* (London: Heinemann Educational Publishers, 1971)

McKay, Claude, *A Long Way from Home* (New York, NY: Arno Press and the New York Times, 1969)

McGreal, Stephen, *Cheshire Bantams: 15th 16th & 17th Battalions of the Cheshire Regiment* (Barnsley: Pen and Sword Military, 2006)

Maddocks, Graham, *Liverpool Pals: 17th, 18th, 19th, 20th (Service) Battalions, The King's (Liverpool Regiment)* (Barnsley: Pen and Sword Military, 2008)

Manley, Norman, 'The Autobiography of Norman Washington Manley', *Jamaica Journal*, 7.1 (March–June 1973), 2–20

Marke, E., *In Troubled Waters* (London: Karia Press, 1986)

Martin, Tony, *Marcus Garvey, Hero: A First Biography* (Dover, MA: Majority Press, 1983)

Matthews, James K., 'Reluctant Allies: Nigerian Responses to Military Recruitment 1914–18', in Melvin Page (ed.), *Africa and the First World War* (New York, NY: St. Martins, 1987), 95–114

Mead, Gary, *The Good Soldier: The Biography of Douglas Haig* (London: Atlantic Books, 2007)

Miller, Charles, *Battle for the Bundu: The First World War in East Africa* (New York, NY: MacMillan, 1974)

Miller, Morag, Roy Laycock, John Sadler and Rosie Serdville, *As Good as any Man* (Stroud: The History Press, 2014)

Oliver, Neil, *Not Forgotten* (London: Hodder & Stoughton, 2005)

O'Mara, P., *The Autobiography of a Liverpool Irish Slummy* (Liverpool: Bluecoat Press, 2009)

Owen, Mountague Charles, *The Sewels of the Isle of Wight* (Manchester: Manchester Courier, 1906)

Pascoe, Peggy, *What Comes Naturally: Miscegenation Law and the Making of Race in America* (Oxford: Oxford University Press, 2010)

Pershing, John Joseph, *My Experiences in the World War*, Military Classics Series Vol. 2 (Blue Ridge Summit, PA: Tab Books, 1989)

Powles, C. Guy and A. Wilkie, *The New Zealanders in Sinai and Palestine, Official History New Zealand's Effort in the Great War. Volume III* (Auckland: Whitcombe & Tombs, 1922)

Putkowski, Julian and Piet Chielens, *Unquiet Graves/Rusteloze Graven: Execution Sites of the First World War in Flanders* (London: Francis Boutle Publishers, 2000)

Ramsland, John, *Remembering Aboriginal Heroes* (Melbourne: Brolga Publishing, 2006)

Raugh, Harold E., *The Victorians at War, 1815–1914: An Encyclopedia of British Military History* (Santa Barbara, CA: ABC-CLIO, 2004)

Richards, Walter, *His Majesty's Territorial Army* (London: Virtue, 1910)

Roskill, Captain S.W., *A Merchant Fleet in War: Alfred Holt & Co. 1939–1945* (London: Collins, 1962)

Ruck, Calvin W., *The Black Battalion 1916–1920: Canada's Best Kept Military Secret* (Halifax: Nimbus Publishing Company, 1987)
Rowe, M., 'Sex, "Race" and Riot in Liverpool, 1919', *Immigrants and Minorities: Historical Studies in Ethnicity, Migration and Diaspora*, 19.2 (2000), 53–70
Saunders, C. (ed. and consultant), *Reader's Digest Illustrated History of South Africa: The Real Story* (Cape Town: The Readers Digest Association of South Africa, 1992)
Schama, Simon, *Rough Crossings* (London: BBC Books, BBC Worldwide Ltd., 2006)
Scott, E.J., *The American Negro in the World War* (Chicago: Homewood Press, 1919) This unique book is held in the Schomburg Center for Research in Black Culture, a research unit of The New York Public Library
Sheffield, Gary, *The Somme* (London: Cassell, 2003)
Sherwood, Marika, 'Blacks in the Royal Navy', *Black and Asian Newsletter* (January 1999), 13–16
Smith, Graham A., 'Jim Crow on the Home Front (1942–1945)', *New Community*, 8.3 (Winter 1980), 317–28
Smith, J. Douglas, 'The Campaign for Racial Purity and the Erosion of Paternalism in Virginia, 1922–1930: Nominally White, Biologically Mixed, and Legally Negro', *Journal of Southern History*, 68.1 (2002), 65–106
Smith, Richard, *Jamaican Volunteers in the First World War: Race, Masculinity and the Development of National Consciousness (Politics, Culture & Society in)* (Manchester: Manchester University Press, 2010)
Soloway, R., 'Counting the Desperates: Race Deterioration in Edwardian England', *Journal of Contemporary History*, 17.1 (1982), 137–64
Spies, S.B., 'South Africa and the First World War' in Spies and B.J. Liebenberg (eds), *South Africa in the 20th Century* (Pretoria: J.L. van Schaik Publishers, 1993)
Swanwick, H.M., *Builders of Peace: Being Ten Years' History of the Union of Democratic Control* (London: Swarthmore Press Ltd., 1924)
Swinney, G., 'The Sinking of the SS Mendi, 21 February 1917', *Military History Journal*, 10.1, (June 1995), http://samilitaryhistory.org/vol101gs.html
Tabili, Laura, *We Ask for British Justice: Workers and Racial Difference in Late Imperial Britain* (Ithaca, NY: Cornell University Press, 1994)
Taylor, James, *Your Country Needs You: The Secret History of the Propaganda Poster* (Glasgow: Saraband, 2013)
Thompson, J. Lee, *Forgotten Patriot: A Life of Alfred, Viscount Milner of St. James's*

and Cape Town, 1854–1925 (Madison, NJ: Fairleigh Dickinson University Press, 2007)

Uys, I., *Survivors of Africa's Oceans* (Minneapolis, MN, Fortress Publishers, 1993)

Vasili, Phil, *Colouring over the White Line: The History of Black Footballers in Britain* (Edinburgh: Mainstream Publishing Company, 2000)

Venn, John and Archibald Venn (eds), *Alumni Cantabrigenses*, 10 Volumes (Cambridge, Cambridge University Press, 1922–54)

Warwick, Peter, 'Myth of the White Man's War', in Warwick, *Black People and the South African War, 1899–1902* (Cambridge: Cambridge University Press, 1989)

Wilder, JeffriAnne, 'Revisiting "Color Names and Color Notions": A Contemporary Examination of the Language and Attitudes of Skin Color among Young Black Women', *Journal of Black Studies*, 41.1 (September 2010), 184–206

Willmott, H.P., *World War I* (New York: Dorling Kindersley, 2003)

Winegard, Timothy C., *Indigenous Peoples of the British Dominions and the First World War* (Cambridge: Cambridge University Press, 2011)

Woodward, C. Vann and William S. McFeely, *The Strange Career of Jim Crow* (New York, NY: Oxford University Press, 2001)

Wyrall, Everard, *The History of the King's Regiment (Liverpool) 1914–19* (Uckfield: Naval and Military Press, 2002)

UNPUBLISHED MATERIAL AND EXHIBITIONS

Milne, G., 'Sailortown: Representing the Maritime-Urban Frontier', unpublished conference paper, School of History, University of Liverpool, 2011

Shyllon, F.O., 'The Black Presence and Experience in Britain', paper presented to the International Conference on the History of Blacks in Britain, London, 28–30 September 1981

Untold Stories: Black families in the First World War, exhibition, Museum of Liverpool, 2013–14

BIBLIOGRAPHY

ELECTRONIC RETRIEVAL

Forces War Records, Record Details for Charles Alexander F Calvert (Machine Gun Corps) https://www.forces-war-records.co.uk/ViewRecord/924626?reference=arrowLinks (accessed 30 July 2013)

Green, Jeffrey, *Post Card*, http://www.jeffreygreen.co.uk/066-lieutenant-reginald-collins-of-jamaica (accessed 27 April 2013)

'History: Range and Content', *Teaching and Learning, The School Curriculum*, Secondary National Curriculum until 2014, *Department of Education*, http://www.education.gov.uk/schools/teachingandlearning/curriculum/secondary/b00199545/history/programme/range (accessed 14 December 2012)

'Shot at Dawn', *Webmatters*, http://www.webmatters.net/txtpat/?q=auto&s=Search&sort=name&cat=sad (accessed 11 December 2012)

Spartacus Educational, 'Blighty Wounds', www.spartacuseducational.com (accessed 21 April 2013)

Western Front Association, *Land War, Generals Nicknames*, http://www.westernfrontassociation.com/great-war-on-land/71-gen-ls/209-generals-o-s.html (accessed 10 February 2013)

TELEVISION PROGRAMMES

'The Story of Jimmy Durham the First Black African to Join the British Army as a Fully Enlisted Soldier', Tyne Roots: Black History Month, *BBC*, October 2004

INDEX

1919 Race Riots 49

Aborigines 64, 65, 83
African Communities League 71
African National Congress (ANC), 119
Ali, Dusé Mohamed 71
Aliens Order 1920 15, 155
Allenby, General Sir Edmund H. H. 59
Allwood, Dr S. J. 106, 107
Anchoy, Louis 52
Archer, John 146
Army Order No. 1 of 1918 157, 158, 159
Army Service Corps 72, 75
Asquith, Herbert 131
Australia 64, 65, 144

Bahamas 24
Bakr Ridge 60
'Bantam' Battalion 37
Barbados 24, 29, 91, 154, 157, 161
Basuto State 117

Bechuanaland 4, 117
Belmont Road Military Auxiliary Hospital 139
Bemand, George Edward Kingsley 98
Bemand, Harold Leslie 100
Bermuda 79, 113, 114, 115, 129
Bermuda Contingents of the Royal Garrison Artillery 114
Bermudian troops 43, 114
Betts, George 83
Bigland, Alfred 37
Billingham, Private T. 93
'Black Battalion' 13, 43, 111, 124, 125, 127
Black Freedom movement 70, 172
Blackman, George 78, 80, 154, 160, 161
Black prisoners of war 62
Bonar Law, Andrew 23
Bouzincourt 115
British Egyptian Expeditionary Force (EEF) 56

INDEX

British Expeditionary Force (BEF) 32, 54, 104
British Guiana 24, 73, 95
British Honduras 7, 24, 85, 87, 129, 160
British nationality 29, 141, 156
British Nyasaland forces 7
British Recruiting Mission 33
British War Medal 55, 81
British West Indies Regiment (BWIR) 22, 24, 30, 34, 67
Brown, Eugene 82
Brown, Harold 53
Brown, John 82
Buganda 117

Calvert, Charles Alexander F. 80
Cambrai, Battle of 104, 136, 140
Cameroon 2, 3, 4, 54
Canada 18, 20, 67, 111, 114, 123, 124, 125, 127, 128, 135, 144, 149, 164, 172
Canadian Expeditionary Force (CEF) 124, 125
Canadian troops 34, 123, 124
Cardiff 10, 26, 86, 140, 142, 143, 144, 146, 154, 172
Caribbean League 158, 159
Cetywayo – the former King of Zululand 120
Challenor G. 35
Chaytor, Major General Edward W.C. 59, 61
Cheshire Regiment 37
Chinese labourers 34
Churchill, Winston 18, 19, 21, 38, 168
Clarke, Eugent 79, 158
Clarke, W. 89

Clarke, Flight Sergeant W. 'Robbie' 73
Clemetson, David Louis 104
Coldstream Guards 74, 75
Cole, R. 89
Colebourne, Private Walter 39, 54, 56, 58, 62
Coles, Obadiah 131
Collier, Bob 66
Collins, Reginald Emanuel 102
Colonial Office 18, 22, 23, 67, 68, 70, 71, 85, 96, 106, 110, 127, 132, 153, 159
conscription 72, 113, 114, 116, 118, 127, 128, 129, 130, 131

Damieh Bridgehead 61
Demerara 95, 107
Demerette, John 139
Derby, Earl of 26, 72
Derby Scheme 72, 147, 149
Dernancourt 115
Distinguished Conduct Medal 134, 135, 136
Dorset Regiment, 142
Dove, Fred W. 140
Dundonald, Earl of 22
Durham, James Francis 47

Egerton Shyngle J. 65
Elder Dempster shipping line 142
Empire Windrush 165
Ethiopian Hall, Liverpool 153
Eugenics Movement 6, 36, 64, 142, 152, 170

Facey, Edwin Ebenezer 89
Favreuil 93
Fennell, Dr Rufus Leicester 154

INDEX

Fenner Brockway, Archibald, Baron Brockway 130
Fijians 83
Fletcher, William 8
Francis, Private A. 29, 72, 88, 147, 165
Freeman, Patrick 66

Garvey, Marcus 70, 71, 172, 173
German East Africa 2, 3, 4, 5, 119, 136
German prisoners 80, 120
Gibson, Joseph 150, 151
Glasgow 50, 51, 52, 83, 92, 95, 140, 141, 153
Gold Coast Regiment, 1, 2, 3
Grant, Douglas 64, 65
Grenada 24, 60, 128, 129
Grindle, Gilbert, Principal Clerk at the Colonial Office 26, 69
Grubb, Harold 89
Grunshi, Alhaji 1
Guy, George 151
Guy, Jack 151

Harcourt, Secretary of State for the Colonies, Lewis 70
Haig, Douglas, the Commander in Chief 31
Hall, Isaac 130
Hall, William 135
Harcourt, Lewis, Secretary of State for the Colonies 23
Harlem Hellfighters 14
Harman, Private 74
Hodge, Samuel 135, 136
Horner, Alfred 77
'Horror on the Rhine' 152

Intermarriage 142

Jackson Brown, Dr James 106, 107
Jalu, Sergeant Major Ebrima 134
Jamaica 23, 24, 71, 75, 78, 98, 102, 103, 104, 112, 130
James, Albert 36, 40, 42, 53, 56, 58, 59, 99, 145, 165
Johnston, Sir Harry 18, 134, 170
Jordon, L. 136
Julian, Serjeant W.E. 60

Kenya 5, 6, 7, 25
King George 22, 23, 53, 78, 161
King's Own Scottish Borderers (KOSB) 50
King's African Rifles (KAR) 5
King's (Liverpool Regiment) 39, 62
King's Regulations 12, 102, 110, 166
Kitchener, Lord Herbert 23, 37, 50, 78
Kru 156

La Neuville 115
Légion d'honneur 79, 103, 104
Lettow-Vorbeck, Colonel Paul Emil von 5
Liverpool Black Community 64, 146
Liverpool Hereditary Society 143
Liverpool Local War Pensions Committee 58
Liverpool 26, 37, 39, 46, 54, 56, 72, 86, 89, 139, 142, 145, 149, 151, 153, 172
Lloyd George, David 132, 138

INDEX

Lobagola, Bata Kindai Amgoza Ibn 82
London 8, 10, 25, 29, 30, 37, 49, 53, 63, 64, 74, 82, 91, 95, 98, 101, 102, 104, 107, 108, 112, 117, 130, 142, 147, 149, 153, 172

Machine Gun Corps 81, 82, 101, 102
Macauley, Tommy 50
McDavid, Herbert Gladstone 39, 62, 63, 64, 65, 112
McDowall, Dr. J. 109
McIntosh, Sergeant L. 73
McKay, Claude 153
Mangin, General Charles Emmanuel Marie 19
Manley, Norman 40, 41, 65, 74, 112
Manley, Roy 73
Manual of Military Law 27, 28, 82, 92, 105, 157
Maoris 83
Marke, Ernest 50, 145
Medical Officers 106
Meldrum, Brigadier General William (Bill) 61
Mendi, SS 21, 121, 122
Middlesex Regiment 92, 93
Military Services Convention Act 1917 126
Milner, War Secretary Lord Alfred 138
Ministry of Reconstruction 138
Moore, W.A. 69
Morel, E. D. 152
Morris, Herbert 76, 78
Mumford, Private, 8

Nathan, Alonzo 75, 76
Naturalization Act 1870, 27
Nelson, Frank 61, 62
Neuve Chapelle, Battle of 75
Newcastle, 26, 52, 120
Njilima, Frederick 82
No-Conscription Fellowship (NCF), 130
Northern Nigeria Regiment 3
Northern Rhodesia 117, 134
Nova Scotia 79, 111, 121, 124, 127

Officer Training Corps 97, 105
'one-drop rule' 97

Palestine 25, 55, 56, 59, 87, 103, 159
Pan-African movement 173
Passchendaele, Battle of 51
'passing' 94, 95, 100
'passing' laws 94, 97
Pershing 14, 18
Personal/close relationships 40
Phills, Isaac 128
Pilckem Ridge, Battle of 41, 51
Poperinghe 77, 78, 116
Pseudo-scientific racism 35, 36
Public Morals Committee of Cardiff 143

Queen's (Royal West Surrey) Regiment 53

Raincheval 115
Rathbone, Basil 39
Reubens, Robert 131
Risien Russell, Dr James Samuel 106, 107

Roberts, Private Arthur William David 41 50
Romani, Battle of 56
Royal Army Medical Corps 106, 108, 150
Royal Engineers Coloured Section 26, 27, 67, 84, 85, 88
Royal Field Artillery 56, 73, 83, 98, 99, 100
Royal Fusiliers 59, 83, 101, 102, 103, 104
Royal Scots Fusiliers 50
Rushdie-Gray, G. O. 96

'sailortown' 12, 38, 49
Salonika 85, 104
Schutztruppe 5
Scott, Private H. 60
Scramble for Africa 20
Seaford Camp 24, 37, 89
Sewell, The Hon. Brigadier-General Horace Somerville 103
shadism 73, 97, 98
Shirley, Ivan 112
Sierra Leone 3, 24, 50, 65, 101, 106, 125, 136, 172
Sierra Leone Battalion 3
Sierra Leonean seamen 141
Simons, Leo 10
Sishuba, Melrose Goda 81
Slim, James 74
Smuts, General Jan Christiaan 4
Smyth, John Albert Gordon 101, 102, 166
social class 12, 38, 74, 80, 94, 95, 103, 135, 138
Social Darwinism 36
Soldiers' and Sailors' Families Association 40, 58

Solomon, Henry 53
Somme, Battle of the 45, 54, 55, 92, 93
South Africa 4, 6, 23, 39, 80, 81, 94, 117, 119, 120, 139, 144, 162
South African Artillery 162
South African Labour Corps 118, 119
South African Mounted Rifles 162
South African Native Labour Contingent 13, 65, 113, 119, 161
South African Native National Congress (SANNC) 119, 173
South Shields 52, 141
South West Africa 4, 6, 119, 162
Southern Nigeria Regiment 3
South-West Africa 2
'Spanish Flu' 59
Special Restriction (Coloured Seamen) Order of 1925 15, 155
St. Lucia 24
St. Vincent 24, 109
Stowe, Br. 116
Sudanese troops 31

Taranto Mutiny 157
Thiepval Memorial 55
Thomas, Corporal Edward 1
Tirailleurs Senegalais 3
Togoland 1, 2, 3, 4
Torres Strait Islanders 64
Toummanah, D. T. Aleifasakure 153
Tregaskis, Sergeant 116

Trinidad 24, 69, 101, 129, 160, 172
Tull, Second Lieutenant Walter 13,
    52, 91, 92, 94, 98, 101, 103,
    104, 106, 111, 165
Turpin, Dick 73
Turpin, Lance Corporal R. 60
Turpin, Lionel Fitzherbert 73
Turpin, Randolph 52, 73
Tyneside area 52, 141

Uganda Protectorate 118
United States 2, 10, 13, 18, 20, 46,
    70, 71, 75, 81, 82, 94, 95, 98,
    100, 111, 114, 123, 125, 127,
    153, 154, 163, 172
Universal Negro Improvement
    Association and African
    Communities (Imperial)
    League (UNIA) 71, 173

Veterinary Department of the War
    Office 96
Victoria Cross 39, 135
Victory Medal 55, 81

War Office 18, 19, 22, 23, 24, 30,
    31, 33, 47, 66, 67, 68, 70, 75,
    96, 100, 106, 107, 109, 110,
    112, 120, 125, 126, 132, 157,
    158, 159, 168

Watson, Egbert 74
Weatherhead, Lieutenant E.K.G.
    35
West African Frontier Force
    (WAFF) 3
West African Rifles 3
West Indian Contingent Committee
    23, 110
West India Regiment (WIR) 24,
    136
White, Brigadier General Wilfred
    A. 33
White, Reverend Captain William
    A. 111, 166
'White Man's War' 13, 14, 17
Willcocks, Brigadier-General Sir
    James 18
Williams, Charles Augustus 52
Williams, George 66
Williams, Henry Sylvester 101
Williams, John 136, 138
Wolseley, Field Marshal Lord
    Garnet Joseph Lord 30
Wotten, Charles 144

Xhosa 119, 122

Ypres, Third Battle of 41

Zulu 22, 119